A Separate Country

A Separate Country

Postcoloniality and American Indian Nations

Elizabeth Cook-Lynn

Texas Tech University Press

This book is typeset in Adobe Garamond. The paper used in this book meets the minimum requirements of ANSI/NISO Z39.48-1992 (R1997). ∞

Library of Congress Cataloging-in-Publication Data
Cook-Lynn, Elizabeth.
    A separate country : postcoloniality and American Indian nations / Elizabeth Cook-Lynn.
      p. cm.
    Includes bibliographical references and index.
    Summary: "Essays questioning the academic notion that "postcoloniality" is the current condition of American Indian communities. Argues that American Indians remain among the most colonized people in the modern world; revises the popular view of the American West and explores the forgotten history of Indigenousness in America"—Provided by publisher.
    ISBN 978-0-89672-734-2 (hardcover : alk. paper) — ISBN 978-0-89672-725-0 (pbk. : alk. paper) 1. Indians of North America—West (U.S.)—Historiography. 2. Indians of North America—Colonization—West (U.S.) 3. Indians, Treatment of—West (U.S.)—History. 4. Postcolonialism—West (U.S.)—History. 5. West (U.S.)—History. 6. West (U.S.)—Race relations. I. Title.
    E78.W5C575 2012
    978.004'97—dc23

                                    2011024877

Printed in the United States of America
12 13 14 15 16 17 18 19 20 / 9 8 7 6 5 4 3 2 1

Texas Tech University Press
Box 41037 | Lubbock, Texas 79409-1037 USA
800.832.4042 | ttup@ttu.edu | www.ttupress.org

Contents

Preface

The essays and reviews in the following pages reveal the private expressions of the tail end of a long career in teaching Native studies literature. In selecting them I have sought to bring about a new historical consciousness to the familiar drama of colonial tribal nation narrative. Some of these essays are quite new, others seem out of the past, but all of them, I'm hoping, may be useful to those seeking careers in teaching.

It never occurred to me as I was growing up along the Crow Creek that I would really become a teacher or a writer or a critic; indeed I had little perspective on what I would become. But after I had taught for twenty-five years as the result of "affirmative action" protections and after I knew of the Supreme Court ruling in 2003 that the use of "race" (or what I like to call indigenous origin) was permissible for the purpose of achieving equality in academia, I began to see the study of coloniality for what it was. At that moment I began to understand what was at stake. I finally knew for certain that the national tragedy of white privilege in the United States, which had worked against Native intellectualism since the beginning, would be a "given" for the foreseeable future in spite of the lip service given to its denial. The passage of time often assists in the development of the courage of one's convictions, which assists me now to say: Alas, it will be a long time before colonization (defined as the policy by which a nation maintains or extends its control over foreign dependencies) is considered a crime in this new land of the settler/émigré called America. Native peoples continue to be the most colonized and poorest people in the land; it is time, then, to give rise to new, relevant Native narratives expressing a more complex and less marginalizing history.

Despite what I believe to be true, some in the intellectual world have been and are hopeful. Writing for the Supreme Court in 2003, Sandra Day O'Connor said that in twenty-five years *we would not need "affirmative action"* in order to achieve the fundamental equal protection principle so long sought. In 2008, when a black man was elected to the highest political office in the country, many thought O'Connor's aspiration had come true. Yet the reality is that omission of indigenous intellectualism continues to be the case, just as it was when I started my career more than four decades ago. In 2009 a longtime Chicano legislator from Colorado was chosen to head the U.S. Department of the Interior, giving the impression that the population of treaty tribal nations in the West is synonymous with Chicano/a (immigrant) populations north of the border. Members of treaty tribal nations in this country are not immigrants; they are not "minorities" in the politically correct sense. They are indigenous peoples who have lived on this continent for thousands of years.

Yet indigenous origins, accepting indigeneity as it is understood by the treaty tribes in the West, are still misunderstood, keeping coloniality, assimilation, and immigration, not indigeneity, the focal concepts of origin in this country, as they have been characterized in much of the scholarship. For the indigenes, decolonization, then, or resistance to coloniality, is not merely a process of opposition to dominance. It is clearly a matter of preventing the disappearance altogether of their indigenous presence in the modern world. Some believe this prediction that U.S. immigration and assimilation will lead to the disappearance of the indigenous presence is not warranted, that it presents an illogical gap based in fear. Perhaps that is so; the colonial conditions in other parts of the globe certainly speak to more widespread disappearances, and this collection briefly addresses them. A crucial question in defining indigeneity, however, must include the theories of origin that connect subjects to specific geography and, frankly, immigration and assimilation as we know it in the United States are the enemies of that possibility. The indigenous condition should not be overwhelmed by or reduced to describing indigenous peoples simply within the conflict in the imperial process, but should be expressed in indigeneity's own theories.

There is little collective political understanding of indigeneity and its history in this country. There is little understanding of the great body of Indian law and treaty activity that influences Native nationhood. What we are now calling "postcoloniality" does not mean "equal rights," because the historical experience of an entire population for several centuries is either misunderstood or absent from the narrative. Nor does this recent activity on the national scene give us hope that indigeneity as a category of analysis in American history and government will be taken seriously by governors or scholars, because indigenousness is overwhelmed by the interest in diversity and assimilation.

In 2009 Godfrey Hodgson, a British journalist and an associate fellow at the Rothermere American Institute, published *The Myth of American Exceptionalism*,[1] which suggests that scholars have shaped American historiography and politics to describe the United States as a nation of unrivaled virtue, a chosen land with a special destiny and a duty to spread democracy throughout the globe. (He says little about the spreading of a special brand of aggressive Christianity, i.e., religious fervor.) This special destiny probably accounts for more deaths and wars than any other phenomenon. Because of this notion of "exceptionalism," the discourse concerning colonialism as it applies to Native peoples in this country has always been embedded in a global theory of the imperialistic intentions of the United States. Scholars such as Henry Louis Gates, Jr., Edward Said, and Homi Bhabha are major critics in the field of postcoloniality, collections like this one on indigenous populations in the United States are much indebted to their works.[2]

Hodgson begins his treatise with the understanding that American historians like Frederick Jackson Turner are congratulatory narrators and ends by saying that American hubris backed by a lack of critical analysis by historians can no longer be tolerated as a global influence.[3] This small collection of essays on postcoloniality agrees with much of Hodgson's point of view and tries to make the connections between what some say is his better-late-than-never assessment and the historiography of indigenous peoples in the United States. With the motive to change our academic dialogue and explorations, these essays, too, suggest that without being truthful about the history of the American Native population, U.S. imperialism, already a cautionary tale amid two contemporary colonial wars and dominance throughout the economies of world institutions, will undoubtedly become even more dangerous to the idea of indigeneity in the coming decades.

One way to begin this inquiry into historiography is to look seriously at the war period of the nineteenth century, and even later, when shapers of Euro-history and Ameri-history were at their zenith in terms of the law, and when the frontier answer to indigenous-settler conflict was the extermination of Natives. Some sought what they deemed a more humane resolution in those early years; thus peace treaties and reservations became the solution, which we now perceive as colonization of Native nations, denying Native peoples self-rule. For the policymakers who did not demand the killing of Indians and the brutal handling of Native peoples throughout the land, colonization seemed tolerable. As it turns out, nineteenth-century colonization of Native nations as a tool for the American imperialists of the immediate past has resulted in a continuing struggle for primacy and survival among the tribes in the twenty-first century, to say nothing of disenfranchisement, displacement, poverty, death, and racism.

Daniel Jonah Goldhagen, a former political science professor at Harvard University, introduced what he calls the phenomenon of "eliminationism" in his investigation into genocide throughout the world.[4] He defines eliminationism as a political ideology that employs five forms: transformation, repression, expulsion, prevention of reproduction, and extermination. He does not specifically reference American Indians, nor is there any other study of eliminationism that concerns Indians; though some would point to Ward Churchill's *A Little Matter of Genocide* and perhaps some of Jerry Mander's work, I have not found them useful to Indian studies scholarship. Goldhagen's global examples suggest that such a phenomenon is related to fierce colonialism, and those who study the American experience, continuing into modernity, can find common energies and perceptions. This is the kind of thinking that needs to be expressed so that governments and ordinary people can understand the destructive and even criminal nature of colonialism for the purpose of finding solutions. The critique of *Little House on the Prairie* on p. 135 of this collection, which describes the literary elimination of Indians on the prairie, may be useful for this understanding. The case study on p. 147 also employs Goldhagen's forms for the exploration of genocidal events.

Though I am not a scholar in the strictest disciplinary sense, I have been blessed by the company of many thinkers and editors, from Mario Gonzalez to James Riding In to Elizabeth Dulany to an editor in Colorado who says he is a fan of my work and tells me that I am not a socialist, nor am I a feminist, nor a capitalist, nor am I just a malcontent. I am, rather, he says, a radical who, quite simply, "has a passion for intellectual honesty." Those who have had a keen interest in my writing and teaching often argue in my defense that our responsibility as radicals is to each other, to others, and to ourselves as we investigate the role of scholarship in searching for answers to hard questions. One thing is clear to all of us: material progress since the mid-1970s continues in our education and in Indian studies, and in Indian reservation casinos all over the country. Yet, we know that material progress alone will not cure our ills.

Colonial powers have always deprived indigenous peoples of their riches and their very lives because Natives often inhabit a world too plentiful and desirable to be resisted by aggressive, needy dominators.

Introduction

Words to "Dazzle the Mind"

For an indigenous scholar to be sympathetic to postcolonial studies is to be relentlessly optimistic or unaccountably interested in expanding one's conceptual vocabulary. As a person always fascinated by words and how they are used, I may be both. Or, perhaps, to be sympathetic is just to be massively confused about how to account for the practices of the past four centuries toward indigenous populations in the United States and the propaganda that supports the continuing changes we face.

Many scholars believe that at some point there will be an end to the sprawling aggression of colonialism and the resistance to it—not an end to colonialism, mind you, as a crime against humanity, as slavery in the United States was eventually described, but an end that leaves no one a "subaltern" and everyone a "post-"reconstructionist. That's why we talk of postcoloniality in the twentieth and twenty-first centuries. Others have claimed that postcoloniality is whatever comes after colonization has been achieved. Yet others, such as Russell Jacoby in a 1995 essay titled "Marginal Returns: The Trouble with Post-colonial Theory," called the term "postcoloniality" "the latest catchall term to dazzle the academic mind."[1] Thus the term is fraught with ambiguity. Jacoby's brilliant prophecy, however, suggests that such dazzlement, resulting in a vain hope for an end to colonial aggression, is at the very least misguided, at the worst dangerous.

Take, for instance, the 1950s. It was in that decade that disgraceful laws were passed to remove indigenous tribal peoples, particularly the Sioux

(Lakota/Dakota/Nakota) of the Northern Plains of the United States, from their treaty lands, ostensibly to "allow" them to join the American mainstream. So began the decade of "termination" and "relocation," an urbanization scheme now recognized as a failure, which resulted in the loss of thousands of acres of treaty lands from tribal title and in endemic poverty for Native peoples in cities and elsewhere. How the deed was plotted and how it was achieved has been written about by Native scholars in recent years, during the rise of the discipline of Indian studies at western universities.[2]

It is useful to study particular cases. As current academics ruminate about the success or failure of colonial schemes, the 1950s cases of indigenous people other than American Natives come to mind. The case of the island peoples of Diego Garcia, the largest island in the Indian Ocean's Chagos archipelago, is just one of dozens of examples from the mid-twentieth century that suggest historians and social scientists can be wrong no matter how persistent their ideas may be. One does not have to return to 1830 and President Andrew Jackson's removal of the Cherokees from Georgia to understand how it is that stubborn colonial behavior is pursued relentlessly by the greatest democracy of our age, the United States of America. While classical historians bemoan the Cherokee case of 1830 and 1840, and Native scholars endlessly tell the saga to their students, the story of Diego Garcia remains unpublicized and forgotten by the mainstream dialogues of this country, though such stories are commonplace in the histories Indians tell. While indigenous peoples all over the world struggle for survival, it becomes more and more apparent to some scholars that manipulations of such peoples are symptoms of the bankruptcy of democratic ideals and the inflation of imperialistic rule. Perhaps this is the way of democratic rule, for, as one reads history, one recognizes the fact that democracies and republics like ours don't last long. They often become something else. Germany in the 1930s is a prime example. It seems important, then, to recall these events from time to time, and especially now, when persistent mainstream scholars in the academy are reluctant to say that postcoloniality is mere fantasy, a dazzlement. Scholars really ought to continue to resist self-delusion and find ways to orchestrate a historiography of Indian nationalism without elitism and prejudice.

How to move a people off their lands and control vast territories and oceans (which is one definition of colonization) has been a focus of U.S. imperialism almost from the beginning, making it impossible to discuss postcoloniality as anything but words to dazzle the mind. Diego Garcia, in the middle of the Indian Ocean, was ruled early on by the United Kingdom but was home to indigenous Africans and East Indians when it was decided in the 1950s that placing military bases on the lands of other nations would be useful to the domination of the region and, ultimately, the Persian Gulf. This would be called "the strategic island concept." The island's inhabitants would have to be moved out. The United States and Great Britain, the most persistent of the uncontested colonists in the West, would be co-conspirators in the deed to overtake this place.

Diego Garcia was emptied of its indigenous people as early as 1968; it would become one of the "black holes" so much in the news in 2009, when we learned that "extraordinary renditions" (i.e., torture) had taken place during the Bush administrations. It was the base of some of the U.S. planes used to bomb Afghanistan and Iraq, and for anyone with a conscience about unchecked political power, it is an ongoing silent outrage.

Such modern-day colonization would be shocking if contemporary societies believed that black and brown populations were anything but expendable. Because they do not, public silence is the norm. The anthropologist David Vine has recently chronicled this shocking tragedy in his book *Island of Shame*.[3] This text may be one of the most accessible books of our time on this subject. Vine tells us that even as nations in the region have said no to U.S. military occupation, thousands of cases such as Diego Garcia show that unless there is an international movement to protect indigenous peoples, decolonization will continue to be talk, talk, talk, and no action.

It reminds one of a time in 1940 when the Lakota Sioux objected to their removal from their treaty lands on the Oglala Sioux Indian Reservation. They were given two weeks to get out. The U.S. Military wanted their thousands of acres of treaty lands in what is now South Dakota for a bombing range.[4] After all, the United States was engaged in the Great War, and everyone had to sacrifice. The Lakota had no place to turn for help, as usual. No court. No politician. No humanities scholar. No church folk. This is always the case for indigenous peoples in North America, the most colonized folk on the planet, who possess lands and resources desired by their powerful "trustee," the U.S. government. There is no place to turn for help, which means that such outrages persist. The treaty lands were actively occupied by the U.S. Air Force for the duration, were never fully returned to the tribal nation nor compensated for, nor were the contamination sites of ordnance cleaned up sufficiently for people to live there safely.

Such a modern-day act of genocide as the Diego Garcia matter is called "displacement," and it is not unlike, for example, the removal of the Cherokees in 1830, and even the "termination and relocation" laws that affected all of the U.S. tribal peoples in the 1950s and 1960s. Like the Dakota and Lakota peoples of the Northern Plains, the Chagossians have refused to disappear; instead they have endured decades of poverty in places like Port Louis in Mauritius, where unemployment and alcohol and drug abuse are rampant and the World Health Organization has found numerous lethal health concerns. These indigenous peoples are waiting to be reinstated by a government that claims compassion for them. Does this sound familiar? To anyone who has visited the survival centers called American Indian First Nations Reserved Lands, of course it does.

While emptying tribal lands held by treaty in the United States was an investment in resources and geography eventually "given" to early settlers for three cents an acre, the removal of the Chagossians was, in some ways, a far more essentialist, sinister crime, something like the use of Bikini Atoll to develop the atomic bomb, which eventually killed millions of innocents in Japan. The atoll of Diego Garcia in the middle of the Indian Ocean has been used during the early twenty-first century as a "black site" to hold suspected terrorists and support unlawful interrogations, while the lands of the Sioux remain almost uninhabitable and fear reigns in their communities. These are the awful crimes of the newest century, rendering the U.S. journey into its own form of cannibalism more than mere theory. There are dozens of such places, we are told by investigators, and they have become models for the colonized world we have come to loathe.

To suggest, then, that the North American continent, and particularly its relationship with its indigenous peoples, can be called postcolonial is an outrageous fraud perpetrated by scholars, thinkers, politicians, and historians. When one looks at the Americanization of the continent (and the globe), such imperial colonization is not just some general process from which dominated peoples and lands can recover in the modern age through ordinary means. Colonization may be one of the most powerful and persistent impulses of humankind, and now that we know the consequences of such impulses, mechanisms must be put in place to resist such takeovers, for, in the end, there are no winners except those who pursue riches and power at the expense of others. Indeed there is little history of decolonization without violent revolution anywhere in the world.

Anticipating such an inevitable conflagration, key areas of debate must be designated in Indian studies. Further analyses of the phenomenon take on urgency, and the questions of whether or not Native America can fulfill its destiny to live in harmony on this earth cannot be articulated without serious debate in the academy.

The development of Indian studies as an academic discipline is a start in the right direction, but it is clear that the state of the discipline is one in which there is considerable debate, opposition, and fraud. The present need is to combine clarity of terms, intent, and persuasion.

One of the thoughts that dominates this book is that colonists who laid down the principles of history in the beginning have continued to write the history of our country as lonely narcissists rather than co-inhabitants. They told of the populations of America's first source in dismissive terms. Yet they were wrong to think that colonized peoples would be content to occupy a philosophical, apologetic subcategory throughout history. They were wrong to believe that a unified paradigm of landless beggars could be formed into a coherent concept of convenient marketplace worldview and democratic ideal.

First, then, the essays in part I of this text situate the colonial climate endured for nearly five hundred years by the Indians of North America, which has resulted in an unconscionable Indian-white paradigm of continuing conflict. In these essays, I examine postcoloniality as an elaborate and indefensible scholarly endeavor, both in academia (in Indian studies) and in political life, either for the purpose of obfuscation, denial, and discrimination; or as a deliberate strategy to take away the nationalistic or tribal autonomy from millions of people; or, finally, to find solutions. The United States needs to take seriously the twentieth-century struggles for self-determination and national independence on the part of Indian nations. A new treaty-based defense against dispossession of resources and lands is a place to start.

Part II contains a series of separate but connected explorations I call "imponderables." These commentaries are based on the notion that even if the power of indigeneity can offer a responsive chord at the academic level, there are some issues beyond academia that defy rationality. The implication is that the practical as well as the intellectual aspects of community and culture require us to say that the finality of the colonialist's vision throughout Indian Country and the world cannot and should not be sustained. The essays in parts III and IV offer discussions of historiography, migrations, and movements directed toward the present.

Part I

The Indian Postmodern

Situating Colonial and Postcolonial Studies

Rather than trying to master the language of postcoloniality, settler-ism, assimilation, and the quest for dominance, scholars in Indian studies are now beginning to think more appropriately in terms of indigenous theory. They define indigeneity as *a condition of indigenousness to be used as a category of analysis: an intellectual and cultural recognition of the indigenes as class rather than margin, as expanding rather than vanishing or diminishing, as a presence that is innate, not introduced, occurring and living naturally in a given geography; as a presence of intrinsic geographically based origins in the North American continent; promoted and expressed in scholarship to be used as a category of analysis of findings and methods of proof in history and culture at modernity's end.*

Such a definition must, of necessity, transcend the values of a society made up of settlers and immigrants. Such a definition implies a doctrine, that is, a principle or a creed of principles to be taught. It can challenge the Doctrine of Discovery which has been the mainstay of colonial thought and scholarship.

Little can be done about the reality of historical events that have been based on a quest for power through colonization, except to reengage and throw into question white superiority and privilege, which has been the basis of the period and the geography of the westward movement. Scholarly tradition in the United States, which this definition engages, has become a provider and promoter of the colonizer's status toward indigenous peoples instead of providing recognition of indigeneity as a category of analysis.

It has created a body of scholarship unwilling to sacrifice its central place in imperialistic power over the indigene. Instead of eliciting rebuke of its past and discipline for its future, American scholarship generally offers further glorification of expansionism and aggression by a settler-immigrant population. This must be challenged vigorously by scholars throughout academia, and especially Indian studies academics.

Indian reservations in the United States have become the measures by which some scholars of history now evaluate colonialism, if they think about colonialism at all; yet, oddly, the unfortunate history of these reserved and colonized lands has not impacted the broader foreign policy of the United States, a nation that continues to fight colonial wars throughout the globe. It's as though the failure that is before their very eyes is mere gloss. Whatever the questions posed in this reality, and whatever the answers, the fact that the colonial relationship between the United States and indigenous nations has failed to matter in global relationships may mean that postcoloniality and indigeneity, words that have already been shown to be ambiguous, are meaningless to a large number of people in the real world.

Given the extent of human suffering brought about as the function of aggressive colonialism, it seems necessary to examine the pervading behaviors that reflect that reality. Indian peoples all over the United States have moved further into colonial-based entities since the 1800s, driven into deeper poverty and unrest. Still being defined as "wards of the government," Indian nations have struggled to set up governing systems on the colonial model, have had their lands held "in trust" by the federal government, and are rarely in charge of their own economic success or failure. Indians are colonial subjects who not only mouth such terms as "sovereignty" and "home rule" as though those words have actual power, but who since the beginning have fiercely tried to defend themselves against colonial law. How these enclaves are to move within sovereign contexts in keeping with the treaties and accords they have signed with more powerful governments is a discourse that is ongoing and, often, is played out in a maze of conflict and compromise.

If the words most salient in today's academic dialogue concerning the present condition of the Native nations of the United States are not necessarily the key words directing domestic or foreign policy, it is possible that this paradox has no saliency in describing what is really going on in Indian Country. If it means that postcoloniality and indigeneity as concepts are disregarded in mainstream political narratives, we are forced to ask: What is the future for Native enclaves as they move into the twenty-first century? Continued isolation? Further disintegration? What is the future of the United States if it continues to create a fantasy about its history for a deluded public? Further thuggery toward others and a disastrous decline of legal principles of democratic rule, as witnessed in current Middle Eastern foreign policy of the past decade?

The wars for colonial power are waged, as they have always been waged, for land, resources, political power, and the strengthening of colonial institutions. The unfortunate histories of Indian reservations have not been evidence enough, so far, to convince the political powers of the United States to disavow their own fallen institutions; thus colonial wars, like the present ones in Iraq and Afghanistan, continue.

Few ask about the morality of such wars. Does the United States have the right to invade other sovereign countries who have not attacked us? Occupy the lands of "others"? Kill millions of innocent bystanders? Obliterate cities thousands of years old? Decimate indigenous societies? Does the United States have those rights? Obligations? These are the questions that give meaning to historical indigeneity and postcolonial experiences in this country. They should be the questions of the larger global discussion.

As we move within the stunning narratives of cultural self-representation that have characterized much of the scholarship of Indian studies of the past thirty years, what is the meaning of those works in terms of making Indian lives better and reducing conflict? As the new work stemming from all manner of colonial and Native subjects in the United States catalogues disagreements, not only about the morality of the past behavior of so-called imperial nations of the globe but about how colonialism and postcolonialism have been narrated in global histories, the United States maintains its claimed and exclusive plenary power over Indians.

What is the meaning for the future that these ideas possess? When Professor Vine Deloria, Jr. began the Indian studies discussion using the term "nations-within-a nation" to describe indigenousness on U.S. soil, he was using his own powerful interpretive insight as a Dakota Indian scholar, which made his work required reading in the discipline. His work brought the promise that our search for self-rule would prevail.

In opposition to coloniality, *indigeneity* has recently become the category of historical criticism used by Native scholars in the United States for analysis of the politics of colonialism in the twenty-first century. *Indigene-*

ity, a reference to the intellectual defense of Native existence as standard in a specific geography, is now being given some fragile agency in revisionist U.S. discourse. Thus there may be hope for the future of democratic ideals and the validity of historic treaty making between nations.

Gerald Vizenor, a major figure in humanities studies, has introduced the term "post-Indian" as an example of the new vocabulary for the inter-rogation of postcoloniality. The function of this new language is to clarify for postmodern scholars the concern that for Native nations in the United States there has been little or no evidence that "postcolonial" is a useful or even an accurate term. It suggests that "indigeneity" as a category of analy-sis and definition may be more appropriate. "Post-Indian," Vizenor tells us, embodies the hope that a change can occur in Indian-white relations in the United States. The term "Indian," after all, says Vizenor, is a misnomer used in error since Columbus thought he had reached India instead of the New World. The word, then, in no way describes the indigenous popula-tion of this continent. "Post-Indian" implies that we must move on from that historical error into self recognition and self-definition.

Most Native scholars agree that if the term "postcolonial" is simply taken to refer to whatever follows the chaos in the vital and active colonial decades, it is meaningless if what is expected is massive change. The term relies on the status quo or empirical history rather than substantive change in the relationship between colonists and indigenes. As for the actual abuse by colonists toward indigenous populations, Vizenor says, "survivance," another term he has introduced in this dialogue, is more than survival, more than endurance or mere response. The stories of survivance, he says, are an active presence: "The live stories of survivance are successive and natural estates; survivance is an active repudiation of dominance, tragedy, and victimry."[1]

Because of this survival of indigenous peoples, the introduction of the terms "indigenization" and "indigeneity" as root language seeks to reclaim whatever came before colonization and occupation. Such scholars as Linda Tuhiwai Smith, Taiaiake Alfred, and Angela Cavender Wilson, as well as the Native Nations Institute at the University of Arizona and the Harvard Project on American Indian Economic Development at Harvard Univer-sity have been providing the epistemological basis for what is now being called "nation building" on Native enclaves throughout the country.[2] This is being done in the hope of educating a new generation in preserving indigenous presences and throwing off the influence of centuries of colonization.

These efforts reflect the survivance Vizenor speaks of and include a series of tactics used to work within a colonial system to make the system more humane. Unfortunately, few language tactics offer a real long-term strategy to rid governance and land issues of the heavy hand of the plenary power of the U.S. Congress, which is the seat of colonization. It is not suggested here that a renewal of congressional intent is not a necessary tool in fighting off other interests of the state. Neither is it suggested that the trust apparatus may not be vital to the survival of Native nationhood and early treaty promises in the context of thousands of other power grids of a wildly visible democracy based in profit, land, and resources. What is suggested here is that the concept of the plenary power of Congress vis-à-vis Native nations is implacably opportunistic, out of control, and due for revision.

A critique of postcolonial reason based in these terms, however impotent it seems at the academic level, may eventually do what David Wilkins, a Lumbee scholar and a professor of political science at the University of Minnesota, insists must be done. The United States and its courts and political institutions, he says, must "disavow the use of *plenary* (read: virtually absolute) power, and repudiate the despised, outmoded, and always inaccurate doctrine of discovery."[3] This, he says, is the path to real postcoloniality and indigenous power.

Global enclaves are at work, trying to put in place the postcolonial strategies for recovery of formerly colonized peoples. The report by the United Nations Committee on the Elimination of Racial Discrimination, submitted to the UN in 2008, for example, contributes to this struggle when it states that the committee will "put in place a framework for identifying indicators for monitoring compliance with international human rights instruments."[4] That means that most of the work being done by well-meaning academics at universities concerning the decolonization efforts of tribal nations needs constant monitoring, since it amounts to the "masking of justice" accusation leveled against the justice system by Wilkins and other scholars in political science and Native studies enclaves.

A Separate Country, which has as its aim the examination of the question *What about the meaning of postcoloniality?*, is a collection of essays that agree with the notion of disavowing the plenary power claimed by the U.S. Congress vis-à-vis Indian nations and that agree with Vizenor that survivance, that is, the idea that the so-called postcolonial rationale of mainstream academic scholarship as it applies to Native enclaves in the United States is largely a fantasy. I posit that indigeneity (defined as the presence of geographically based origins in the North American continent) as a category of criticism of colonial realms is not only useful for clarification of the condition of colonization, but necessary to the future of tribal nationhood.

The current theory about colonial and postcolonial discourse is that colonialism or imperialism can safely be placed in the past simply by declaring that it is a done deal, and scholars can assume that postcolonial is whatever comes after the colonial period of and earlier than 1800 and early 1900, following the direct and violent colonization of the first years of occupation. This theory seems to suggest that the struggle for autonomy in indigenous nations and the third world is just a matter of economics. It emphasizes economic territories rather than actual estate territories in which industrial and postindustrial capitalism is the determinant for the benign passage of the colonial world into modernity. It is a theory suggesting that colonial empires are firmly in place, and the illegal and rigged histories of how they got there can be ignored. A quick look around the globe and a focus on the present Middle East war initiated by the greatest colonizer of them all, the United States, tries to assure even thoughtful readers that such a fantastic deconstruction into economic terms can be tolerated. It tries to assure readers that whatever is happening in indigenous lands that counters a Pollyanna worldview of the success of colonization and occupation has fragile legitimacy.

It is true that for the indigenous nations of the United States, as is evidenced in contemporary life, colonial structures are still in place on tribal enclaves and are probably as powerful as they've ever been, or perhaps are even more powerful than ever. These structures are based in two corrupt U.S. theories that have always been at odds with democracy and consistent with imperialism: the doctrine of discovery and the subsequent U.S. congressional claim of plenary power, as Wilkins describes it. These are enormously powerful historical theories. Some fear they cannot be disclaimed without further stripping Native enclaves of the lands and estates that have miraculously survived them.

The doctrine of discovery is a rationale for colonization now deeply entrenched in U.S. laws regarding Indians.[5] At first, *terra nullius* (empty lands) was the rationale expressed for taking over the continent, but the discovery concept, which gained agency during the first settler contact years, was eventually expressed more forcefully and specifically in Chief Justice Marshall's decision in *Johnson v. McIntosh*: "The tribes had lost title to the land (could not alienate it) but retained the rights of use and occupancy which could be extinguished by purchase or conquest." European law theory, made up as settlement was ongoing, justified the doctrine of discovery by saying that the "character and religion of [the inhabitants of *terra nullius*] afforded an apology for considering them as a people over whom the superior genius of Europe might claim an ascendancy."[6]

The U.S. Congress claimed extensive plenary power as the legislative mechanism that feeds into that history, and the courts have built precedents that have defended that power. For the United States to disclaim this power that the U.S. Constitution has never recognized but which the courts have wrongfully nurtured will take more political courage and skill than any human rights organization has heretofore accomplished. This history cannot be defended as ethical legal thinking, but the inevitable political defense of it and the subsequent and obvious discrimination against indigenous populations that results from it demonstrate the urgent need for further ethical scrutiny.

Some pessimists believe there is little hope for change. Kim Tallbear, a former faculty member in Indian studies at Arizona State University, Tempe, an enrolled member of the Sisseton Wahpeton Oyate, and presently an assistant professor of science, technology, and environmental policy at the University of California, Berkeley, is one of the young Native scholars who is dubious about that kind of change in Indian law. She argues that the long-held faith in the old-school idea that the federal tribal trust doctrine can be made acceptable is bleak and probably makes real reform unlikely.[7] The major reason for her pessimism stems from what she sees as the continuing dominance of the ideology of "exceptionalism," expressed by the British scholar Godfrey Hodgson in the introduction to this text. Tallbear agrees that scholars have bought into the notion of exceptionalism and says that this ideology informs all of the political, scientific, and historical power of the United States. She fears it is too deeply entrenched to be disavowed. She says that both liberals and conservatives preach exceptionalism alongside a mantra of democracy and inclusiveness, ignoring a U.S. history of vicious colonialism, implacable imperialism in federal Indian policy, and land thefts of and genocidal tactics toward the indigenes. Sustaining this ideology gives credibility, Tallbear suggests, that the inevitability of the voice of America's reluctant slaveholders (who still regret the fall of the southern aristocracy) will continue to dominate the dialogue and the economic furthering of the ideas of the expansionist founders. This implacable ideology, Tallbear says, will give agency to the continued betrayal of treaty violations toward Indian nations, which very likely will never be addressed in any official forum; thus we can resist, she says, but we don't need to hope for substantive change in the pattern of colonial domination. She speaks for many ancestral communities who have witnessed generations of failed efforts by tribal leaders to be heard. Her pessimism, before it becomes a fait accompli on the part of aggressors, must be used to demonstrate the crucial need for the revival and reinvention of the treaty process between whites and Indians. This implies returning stolen lands to tribal title, among other things, as the only postcolonial solution to be effective toward indigenous survival and growth.

Because the doctrine of discovery (theoretically, at least) helped put in place many U.S. economic structures, many of which had to be disclaimed eventually, pessimism may be useful to the discussion. Though the history of institutionalized slavery in the United States, for example, is far removed from indigenous issues about land and indigenous rights, it may be an example that massive and shocking change can indeed occur in spite of years and years of pessimistic outlook. Slavery, the obscene buying and selling of African human beings for profit, an economic structure and theory of great significance for over a hundred years, was not easily given up by powerful interests. Indeed it took a civil war to end it. Thus history suggests that other corrupt concepts can also be scrutinized and ended, and so it is possible that the corrupt concept of the plenary power of Congress can be abandoned, as Indian populations have wished. Using a civil war to do so seems a highly skeptical way to manage such a change in today's United States. But the time seems right to open the debate as a first step.

It may be that colonization, when it is understood as a corrupt concept that embodies the devastation of entire peoples and lands through the use of plenary power, may follow in these historic footsteps. The passage of time sometimes behaves as a grand moral evaluator. The inchoate United States became more mature as a nation and could not allow slavery to thrive in the midst of a democracy. Slavery was recognized as an abusive morality, that white Americans owning African persons for profit could not be sustained. Finally, the institution of slavery was declared unconstitutional and illegal. Yet, as Tallbear knows, and as all Natives born and raised in the current colonization world know, bringing an end to U.S. colonization of indigenous enclaves would require the total deconstruction of historical precedence. Global scholarship, which some believe has now taken upon itself the will to addresses this controversy in other parts of the world, may be the beginning of the end of the colonizing power of the Western nations.

It may be that the controversy that surrounds the war in Iraq, the modern colonial version of occupation and exploitation, can offer a salient example of such corrupt foreign policy and its consequences. If U.S. "righteousness" and "exceptionality" can be seen as nonfundamental to the U.S. story of hope for the world, to be examined in the cold light of contradictory experiences, colonial behavior can then be acknowledged as the seat of atrocities never before accepted as such in the narrative. The United States may have to examine its past more honestly than it has before.

If the United States can see itself as no better, yet no worse, than any other colonizing nation, renegotiation can occur. Renegotiation, then, is the key concept for future Indian-white relations. The reconciliation talk so prominent in the Midwest can be silenced as mere babble unconnected to justice and self-examination, and the pessimistic throwing up of the hands in despair can give way to hope. Renegotiation must become the tool for further action and policy.

It may be that the question of whether or not the United States will eventually have to declare colonization unconstitutional and illegal, as it did slavery, cannot be answered in ordinary ways. Some may argue that the major cause for the conflict in reasoning brought to this topic is that the colonization of indigenous peoples is a doctrine centered in land, in territorial estate rather than personhood. They may say that doing away with colonization is not just a question of lessening the bonds of federal control over human beings. It may not be just a question of learning from the mistakes of history and rectifying them. It may not be a question of individual freedom or management of cultural differences.

It may be, instead, a question of the United States being forced by some conflagration into turning over huge tracts of indigenous lands to their legitimate owners, estates taken through the illegal and unconstitutional means called colonization. At the moment, this is an unthinkable deconstruction of American history, democracy, and economics, yet such a deconstruction might end the everlasting debates about poverty and genocide, offering a new conception of the ordering of the so-called third world toward equality. It is an idea that should not be abandoned.

Claiming title to lands as the result of conquest and the principle of *terra nullius*, or discovery, and initiating colonial structures in these estates under the guise of law and morality constitute the American historical view that must be challenged. There is no doubt that a major upheaval would be required to overturn the concept of the deeply rooted and re-vered colonization of the United States. That is why many Native activists have turned to the United Nations and third-worldists around the globe for support.

In this radical discussion, which is offensive to those in power, the defense of colonization and the hope for postcoloniality on unreasonable terms is in danger of becoming a scholarship of excuses and accusations, alibis for domination and exploitation, while the abandonment of coloni-zation as an ongoing practice is too risky a concept to contemplate. The American Indian, some say, must remain unmistakably American simply because of the charge of political history, and yet must remain distinctly indigenous because of the charge of origin history and colonization. These are the oppositions facing Native Americans in scholarship as well and politics and law.

Others are still hoping for complete assimilation, which was always the goal of the colonization of indigenous peoples on this continent. The re-sult has been constant indigenous-colonial friction as well as some version of nation-within-a-nation sovereignty and limited political autonomy. Meanwhile the title to vast Native lands as economic loot remains in the hands of the colonizer, and the indigene remains in poverty. The economic instability of the indigene is the price that is paid. Who was it who said "The poor will always be with us"? God, apparently (Matthew 26:11). This is the mantra that follows this colonial concept of historical precedence, and it is a mere rationale for the continuation of aggressive capitalism, suggesting that the poverty of the colonized is tolerable. Obstacles too insurmountable to be contemplated, such as renegotiation of treaties and restoration of land as economic renewal for the large land-based treaty tribes in the West, can be ignored.

In the meantime, small and historically devastated tribal nations hav-ing only two hundred members and sparse enclaves of fifty acres of trust land will be encouraged to negotiate with their state government predators for gambling rights, which means that they get to dominate the political dialogue in Washington. This has meant that gambling enclaves, just a small percentage of the people, thrive, while the plunder of the real and primordial assets of water and land resources of large treaty tribes goes unnoticed. Hundreds of thousands of acres of land and uncounted resources are squandered and stolen by state interests and mainstream looters, while thousands of tribal citizens live in dire poverty. The tribes whose future lies in the land find that their voices are not heard.

If postcoloniality continues in academia and government circles to be defined sloppily as whatever it is that comes after the period of a powerful nation's active claim to the land, the occupation of a weaker state will go unchallenged. Indigeneity, survivance, and post-Indianism will have a difficult time becoming significant and authoritative categories for the critical analysis of and destruction of the concept of colonization. In view of the alarming and depressing realities of reservation life, there should be no more important conversation than the one that might force policymakers to stop the fragmentation and pauperization of Indians through the colonizing of assets on their own homelands.

Indigeneity as a Category of Analysis

When Indian studies as an academic discipline was born in the 1970s, some of the scholars who became the most prominent champions of that movement, such as Vine Deloria, Jr., understood the political implications of that framing and began thinking about what it was that defined the modern tribal nation. They did not write about a doctrine of indigenousness to counteract the doctrine of discovery, but they did not succumb to the prevailing discourse of Western theory. Instead Deloria's seminal works, such as *We Talk, You Listen,*[1] demonstrated that an Indian nationalism had to begin with the denunciation of the colonist legacy.

Indians, Deloria said in various ways, are not just some sociological phenomenon to be studied until they vanished. They are nations of people who have learned over thousands of years to live in a tribal manner, in a specific and particular geography. This was how he, as a lawyer, theologian, and political science scholar, defined a new doctrine of sovereignty that would guide Indian studies as an academic discipline. He suggested that U.S. education should reflect that reality. However, since then indigeneity as a category of analysis in the discussion of the colonizing of Native populations has been troubled by disparaging and sometimes irrelevant discourses throughout the academy.

Many Native and non-Native scholars have thought of Indian studies only as an educational concept that can assist modern Indians in becoming participants in the academic and economic world, an assimilationist model becoming the alternative consciousness. Others thought of the coming change in history and literature and education as simply telling the story differently, believing that there are two sides to every story. This has meant that indigeneity (defined as not introduced, innate, occurring or living naturally *in a given, specific geography*) has been neglected as a category of analysis for the development of Indian studies as well as Indian law and as a category of criticism in other fields of scholarly inquiry. Unfortunately, the idea that indigeneity is not just a political category, though it is certainly that, gets lost within the dominant society discourse and is often omitted throughout the academic world.

Indigeneity it not just a political system based in economics and the hope for a fair playing field. Nor is it a belief system like religion. It is, rather, a category of being and origin and geography, useful for refuting other theories of being and origin, such as what Christianity offers, as well as science's theory of the migration of people across the Bering Strait, among others. Today indigeneity may be thought of as the strongest focus for resistance to imperial control in colonial societies and as critical to a disciplinary approach to Native studies. There is no question that disciplines within the academy, such as literary studies and sociology and the law, have all failed to expose what happens in the real world when the ideal of indigenous presence is diminished and scholarship proceeds toward its own meanings.

An example of interventionary divergences from indigenous thinking was the publication by Dee Brown, a librarian at the University of Illinois, of *Bury My Heart at Wounded Knee,* in which he talked of broken promises and oppression and the systematic plunder taking place in the 1800s, but said nothing of indigenous life.[2] In telling the story his way, he inadvertently brought up the subject of the role of historians and the function of educational enclaves, even though he was a librarian, not a historian. This may have been his contribution to early Indian studies, but the flaws inherent in Brown's position soon became obvious. His work was colonial in origin, rather than indigenous. The term "indigeneity" was still a long way from finding its place in the academic vocabulary of folks who wrote about Indian affairs and Indian history, and, certainly the term "colonization" was almost an unmentionable.

Brown's work fed into charges and countercharges when he said that the "Indian Cause" was a good one, but then said little about what must be done to rectify a bad history and a badly told history. He charged that books about Indians were biased toward a history of savagery, not realizing that his own book was biased toward pathos and suffocating sympathy. He helped Middle America do its bleeding heart breast beating of regret, which may have had a calming effect on public interest in a time of emerging modern militancy (the coming American Indian Movement of the 1970s was still in its infancy), but it had little effect on the U.S. Congress and Indian policy.

Most readers thought his was a history that would not stand the test of time, but they were wrong. It is still the history that is on every library shelf, regardless of its flaws as a white colonial perspective. One of the reasons it continues to seem to be an acceptable text is that it works, perhaps unintentionally, to invite American Indians to look at themselves from the perspective of a rather sympathetic white man's world. It shows Indian readers the white man's need to promote a universal "We are all humans" context, saying that, after all, change is always violent, alas, and, yes, the white man has demonstrated human shortcomings. But in order to deflect U.S. criminality against Natives, Brown's effective and useful historicism made one human history to unite all humanity. With no solutions, this text cannot be called an indigenous work, in that it does not look at precontact origins nor at geography as origin, nor does it cast a problem-solving discussion as a focal point. Brown's book, nonetheless, is useful for the beginning of a much needed dialogue.

Bury My Heart at Wounded Knee is probably not a history in the classical sense. Nor is it a tragedy in the classical sense, though it is often described in those terms. Empirical history about American Indians requires that it follow a line of thought in which no one is to blame, that it all is just a function of the passage of time. This work does not do that; it has no interest in examining the gangsterism taking place in the 1980s or the failings of democracy of the period by racist legislation, nor in calling a spade a spade. As for the use of the term "tragedy" to describe this history, this is obfuscating language. In order for a work to be a classical endeavor, scholars of literary criticism will tell you, three traits must be evident: first, there must be a protagonist with a serious character flaw (one could, perhaps, make the case that the Indian's "flaw" is that he is not a Christian); second, the protagonist must fall from a high position (the Shakespearean model); and third, and most important of all, the protagonist's fall must be the result of his "destiny." Fate, a great concern of the Greeks, is still, even today, an answer to failed systems. The classical illustration of the fateful events of tragedy requires the intervention of the gods because events are out of the control of mere humans.

No one knows more than Indians how wrong that supposition has proven to be, because it was not destiny nor fate nor the hand of the gods that brought about oppressive law and genocidal practice. It was practical American politicians, greedy capitalistic developers, the everyday settlers making up the Anglo foundation of the United States in terms of economics and Christianity that masterminded and interpreted these events. This complex structure validated the European claimed right to rule over inferior peoples, or "manifest destiny," which, ironically, will be heard in all the writings to come. Tragedy, then, the term often used to describe this history, is not only ineffectual and inaccurate; it is a monstrous excuse used by scholars and thinkers to rationalize colonial crimes.

On one level, Brown's text was a story of atrocity and genocide, though neither word was given much agency as the vocabulary of his work. On another level it might have been called the history of the growth of anti-Indianism in law and politics, though few writers examine that possibility with much critical enthusiasm. On the most important level of effect, the book allowed white people in America to mourn *their* loss, the loss of the ideal of fair democracy and compassionate Christianity, both having shamefully failed to bring justice and peace between peoples. If not a justification of that awful history, the book was at least a rationale for it, and it helped spread the notion that little can be done about the American history faced by indigenous peoples. Upon reading Brown's work, one regretfully comes to the conclusion that even as we oppose hegemonic power, it is up to Indians to sacrifice themselves for the next stage of colonial burdens. No retribution. No return of stolen lands. No identification of crimes that can be litigated. White readers mourned their own loss and felt sympathy for their own victimhood and betrayal. And that may have been a good thing for the American public, because it gave them the idea that there was a lot of reconstruction needed in the future.

But the most dangerous effect of the book, and other books like it that followed, is that it helped to weaken Indian resolve. Native militancy in the period when the book was on the bestseller list was seen to be a bad thing, even by a lot of Indians. The days of significant political movements like the American Indian Movement, probably the most important protest movement of the twentieth century, were numbered. Even today there is an insidious and unflattering AIM critique that is ongoing and that has been helped along by the continuing effect of simpatico offered in Brown's work.

Even a postmodern text such as *Like a Hurricane,* though it does not claim to be a classical history, but a "testimony," says in its epilogue that AIM leaders were outmaneuvered at their own game by White House aides. Victory was uncertain at best, and Indians failed to win their dreams.[3] In the context of Deloria's notion of "nationalism" as a way of thought, here nationalism operates as a general force of resistance, but its perception by Euro-American-influenced narratives reflects its failure.

Scholars like Timothy Brennan and Homi Bhabha retheorize nationalism as one of the most importantly debated topics of contemporary theory, but in the scholarship by non-Native historians like Brown, it is given little agency. This theoretical view of the importance of nationalism may be gaining agency among third world peoples throughout the world, but not in the United States as it continues to look uncritically and with little useful analysis at its own national origins.[4]

As for scholarship and actual courses to be offered in the discipline of Native studies, ambiguity has continued. In 1998 Duane Champagne of the Department of Sociology at UCLA and editor of the influential *American Indian Culture and Research Journal* published at that institution wrote, "Indian students should take undergraduate degrees in mainstream disciplines such as business and education. . . . We believe that it is better for Indian students to receive training and scholarly preparation in the mainstream majors rather than work on an Indian Studies degree."[5] This was probably not the point of view of the "nationalists" and did little to disarm them in their own problematic occupation with effecting justice.

Many other scholars felt and continue to feel that nationalism in Indian studies is simply another "political" movement. They have a tendency to dismiss it along with its excesses. At the same time, perhaps to assuage the backlash that came from more conservative quarters, Champagne wrote, "Indian Studies is for everyone," which suggests that Indian Studies was still looking for an audience.[6] This sentiment reflected the reality that scholars who wrote about so-called postcolonial topics were becoming increasingly wary of nationalism in Indian studies and considered it a dangerous move.

This idea gained agency at a conference in 2009, reported in an article in the *Chronicle of Higher Education,* "New Association Takes 'Big Tent' Approach to Studying Native Peoples." A fledgling organization, the Native American and Indigenous Studies Association, was apparently established as "the brainchild" of Robert A. Warrior, the newly appointed director of the Department of American Indian Studies and Native American House at the University of Illinois, who stressed, "We want to have a big-tent view."[7] Held at the University of Minnesota, Twin Cities, this conference had connections to the University of Oklahoma and the University of Georgia, where Warrior and a colleague in literary studies, Jace Weaver, taught courses for several years and tried to help move the discussion from the theoretical milieus of humanities and English departments, where it had been nurtured for at least a decade, into political science and law.

This "big tent" approach has been the flavor of the week of the past decade in the field of Indian studies; it is a safe trajectory not only for students but also for faculty and Native enclaves of all types. Until recently such thinking directly influenced curricular offerings in the field toward literary studies rather than political science. Such framing often, by deliberate design, omits the essential political implications of future growth and development of indigenous nations and enclaves. These nations have not disappeared into the vast historical and academic wilderness, but have instead continued reluctantly in a colonial mode: weak, poor, and unmotivated. Today this curricular trend suggests that by putting forth the economic, diversity, and cross-cultural doctrines demanded by the "big tent" approach, nationalistic tendencies can be disarmed. More nationalistic third world scholars worry about the long-term efficacy of that approach for Indian nationhood and sovereignty, and those concerned with throwing off the colonization of Native enclaves in the real world are likewise skeptical.

It is perhaps the reality of this conflict of intent in the discipline that has invigorated the threatening and unwanted discussion called "postcoloniality." It brings about questions that can no longer be ignored. *Who, asked Native scholars holding the legacies of their tribal nations sacred, will define the presence of sovereign Native nations in the landscape of twenty-first-century America as the First Nations struggle toward sovereignty? How will sovereign nations of indigenous peoples gain control of their own affairs?* Therein lies the so-called postcolonial dilemma. Will it be left to the colonial mainstream, the "big tent" scholars, the filmmakers, classically trained scientists and academics, or will it be the indigenous nations themselves that will define the future status of these enclaves? What will postcoloniality really mean in the real world? What about indigeneity as the major category of analysis for the future?

At the Minneapolis conference James Riding In, the Pawnee editor of the *Wicazo Sa Review* and longtime professor of Indian studies at Arizona State University, called the "big tent" emphasis "troubling." He suggests instead a disciplinary approach following a "different paradigm," away from the interdisciplinary or diversity approach (i.e., history, literature, and anthropology), and embracing law, politics, land, sovereignty, and specific indigenous issues, which seems much narrower.[8] Though the models of the discipline are varied and eclectic, the one favored by some nationalists in this debate is described as a tribal-nation model. Others, who are somewhat unconnected to the historical development of the discipline of Native studies since 1960–70, have also commented on the debate. The Italian literary theorist Elvira Pulitano, who studied in California and wrote *Toward a Native American Critical Theory* (2003) and whose work takes a rather frontal stance in *Reasoning Together: The Native Critics Collective*, has documented what has been called a "schism" in Native studies, a "separation or division into factions."[9]

This so-called schism is nothing new to longtime observers and participants in the development of Indian studies. It was evident in the field's curricular development as early as 1960, then staged mainly by activist English departments and humanities enclaves. This literary studies collective may be what initiated some of the thinking that moved the American Indian and Indigenous Studies conference, touted mainly by literary scholars, toward "the big tent" approach. There is no question that the ambiguity in literary studies allows for greater diversity than Indian law and federal Indian policy, thus allowing the schism to fester. An emphasis on indigenousness and sovereignty, which is the crux of Indian studies, is rarely the intent of literary studies in terms of problem solving, solutions, and research. Literary studies has been mainly effective in the study of major figures and creative works rather than politics.

Native scholars like Deloria, on the other hand, who was trained in the law and was a political science professor at the University of Colorado, Boulder for many years, were not thinking about literary studies, literary criticism, or a moral world grounded in creative works and anthropology. Nor were they thinking that populations would simply immerse themselves in the mainstream, or go away altogether. History, Deloria always contended in his writings, has proven they will not. He, more than most, knew that problems like forced assimilation and personal memoirs could not find solutions if the same consciousness that created them in the first place continued to seek the answers in the conclusion. That was the basis for his scholarly attacks on anthropology and Christianity.

In the context of such realizations, Native scholars have forged ahead. *Indigeneity as a Category of Critical Analysis* is the title of the significant works of a gathering of scholars at the University of Illinois in 2007.[10] The subject matter seized upon the current controversies concerning the ravages of colonization in this country with the will to ruminate on how these issues seem to be ubiquitous and concurrent and fodder for scholarly conflicts. This gathering, long overdue, was in recognition of the fact that even though such controversies are not new, they seem to be flaring up again in a way that is reminiscent of what some are calling the old McCarthyism of the 1950s. Argument and competition have been the result. The cause for this flare-up is, undoubtedly, the refusal to understand the failed function of colonization on Indian lands, as well as in the academic enclaves around the country. This is true despite the recognition of stunningly relevant third world scholarship.

Yet in Indian studies and ethnic studies and even in literary studies, as well as in much of the international scholarship being done by university scholars these days, it seems to have become dangerous to forcefully challenge the foundations of colonization and forced assimilation in the United States, the three Cs: Christianity, Capitalism, and Civilizing the Indian. It resources hostility to seriously critique the morality of the current colonizing war, the Iraq war, or even to mention the history of the nation of Israel (a surrogate U.S. colonial enclave in the Middle East), which some say is a major source of the current global conflict. If a scholar wishes to delve into these controversial waters in a way connected to Native studies in American universities, he or she may be targeted by those who disagree about the functions of colonization in the modern world and will very likely be exposed as a dissident of the academy or, worse, incompetent and wrong!

For some of these reasons, Indian studies, the seat for indigeneity as a category for analysis, has suffered bureaucratic hostility from the beginning, and it continues today. The denial of tenure to Native scholars at universities across the United States in the past ten years, for example, while apparently under the radar of those who usually research such phenomena, suggests more than mere malfeasance or neglect. It is a clear conflict between the colonized and the colonizer, which makes the "big tent" approach to development at universities all the more safe and comforting. It suggests that colonization in the United States, and in particular the methods by which power-based structures of the nineteenth century claimed Native America, will not be dismissed nor even analyzed in a fair-minded manner by higher education functionaries.

The case of Norman Finkelstein at DePaul University, though unconnected specifically to Indian studies, shockingly reminds us that colonial thought in the academy rules. Finkelstein, called radical by colonial thinkers, was denied tenure when he examined the current relationship between the United States and Israel, and Israel and the Arab countries and concluded that Israel's oppressive colonial power in the Middle East is the major source of hostility in the region. Finkelstein charged Israel with crimes it claims others have perpetuated against it. Israel is no longer the victim, he said; rather, it has itself become the perpetrator of criminal acts toward the Palestinians.[11]

Many Native scholars whose vision of world history conflicts with colonial thought have suffered the same rejection. Many books like Finkelstein's are on the same shelves where Indian studies texts are under devastating attack by right-wingers and antihistorical agents, conservatives, and others who defend democracies with colonial histories. Most Indian-specific books have yet to get decent reviews from classically trained historians, evidence that there is much antagonism toward the relatively new field of Indian studies and the even newer field of postcolonial studies. It is long past time to take seriously indigeneity as a category of critical analysis in an effort to thwart the attack on Native scholarship, especially now, in the academic climate of what is being called "postcolonial reasoning" or "postcoloniality," terms with a variety of unclear meanings attached to them.

Today, as globalization marks the position of the colonial subject, the faulty placement of the Native informant concerning how to move out of the so-called aboriginal period of human history into modernity brings risks to every Indian community in the United States. Make no mistake: American Indians and their nations are the most colonized people and enclaves in the United States and have been for over two hundred years, especially since the passage of the 1934 Reorganization Act.

The hostility that surrounds much of the work in indigenous, American Indian, and Native studies for the past several decades has now forced an examination of the astonishing academic conflicts that have, very subtly, accompanied this work from the beginning. I am referring, of course, to the attack on the freedom to teach and think and write, as reflected in several recent and shocking events: the denial of tenure to Norman Finkelstein at DePaul; the ousting of Ward Churchill from his tenured enclave in ethnic studies at Colorado University, Boulder;[12] the investigations going on at Barnard, the sister school of Harvard University, resulting in the casting of aspersions on the work of Middle Eastern scholars who have written and taught there for decades; and the failure to produce large, effective faculties in the discipline of Indian studies at any major university in the United States. I am also referring to such student unrest as displayed in an organization called the Students for Academic Freedom, who, in their organized effort to stifle dissent in 2007, put out this admonishment: "Your professor shall not make statements about George W. Bush."[13] The mealy-mouthed response to all of this by the American Association of University Professors is disappointing. While the media and conservative alumni groups headed by people like the journalist Robert Novak have denied that such treatment of scholars and programs is about ideology, Novak himself, speaking on a television news programs, claimed, "It's not about ideology but about scholarship." This is defeating to the work expected of public universities.

Presenting a brief analysis of Indian studies and explaining how it is situated in what we now term postcoloniality in the academy may be a serious challenge. Many scholars have found that to talk to Indian studies professionals, students, and audiences about postcoloniality and indigeneity is to see their eyes glaze over as they hunch over their BlackBerrys and answer calls on their cell phones. They don't want to talk about it, and the vocabulary that helps scholars talk about it is lacking.

The situation is even more troubling on the Native homelands, for while what is called Indian Country houses the most colonized enclaves of our time, little assistance in deconstruction is offered to its victims. Colonization on the four hundred or so Indian reservations and enclaves in North America is a real thing. Why else do you suppose poverty is rampant on Indian lands? Why else do you suppose tribes are still in the Dark Ages, clinging to gambling casinos as lifelines, ineligible for municipal or broader private financing and thus crippled in their efforts to enter into the financial marketplace except through rich lobbyists in Washington? Why are these governments not fully recognized by the Securities and

Exchange Commission? Why are there no federal banks on reservations? Why are these governments still victims of institutional racism? Why is title to tribal land still held in bondage by the federal government? Why are treaties not honored? The answers to all of those questions lie in the narratives of the colonial adventures of Europe extended into the New World, which often provide alibis for domination and exploitation, yet there seems to be no hurry to move away from victimization.

How the concept of postcoloniality is situated in indigenous studies is *crucial to the notion that solutions can be found to age-old and seemingly endless conflicts* between indigenous peoples and their colonizers. This must be done through the academic process. It cannot be left up to politicians, the courts, the victims, nor to the press and the Internet mainstream image-makers.

The first thing American scholars must do is come to grips with their own history and treatment of the indigenes, and how they have allowed their interpretation of that history to shape their own cultural identities. This has resulted in a fog of history obscuring the idea that tribal nations are extraconstitutional, meaning that they do not exist as part of the U.S. constitutional structure. These Americans will not acknowledge Indian nations as *separate countries* within a democracy that will not give up its self-congratulatory, nationalistic piety. This failure to come to grips with their own American history prevents the open-mindedness that is the crux of scholarship. The result is the oppressive colonization so noted in this text.

As further evidence of this failure to communicate, Michael Medved, a radio personality and blogger who is hardly a scholar of note, but one who reflects the prevailing American attitude toward Indians and appears regularly on talk shows, recently wrote, "America must reject the Lie of White Genocide against Native Americans."[14] This charge is made by many political and third world scholars. Medved's plea is an antihistorical mantra that is simply untrue and unsupportable by fact and definition, but, incredibly, the facile reason that he gives is this: "A nation (AMERICA) ashamed of its past will fear the future." He speaks for thousands in this country who believe that only the virtuous glory of the United States must be described, never its failure. The function of history as Medved knows it is, unfortunately, the deep historical perspective that underlies the neglect of appropriate scholarship in the field of Indian studies. In spite of what some say about shame, others say that the function of shame in the realm of scholarship and ethics, if not politics, is to be a *moral compass*, and

American historians should pay it sufficient attention. Indeed a military man of our time with a stellar reputation, General Colin Powell, who led the U.S. Army in the Gulf War of 2000, in his recent memoirs said, "A sense of shame is not a bad moral compass."[15]

Medved says that when Indian scholars compare early colonists and settlers in Hitlerian, mass-murder terms, they are engaging in anti-American slander. He is apparently one of those who believe that the killing of six million Jews in the Nazi Holocaust is the *only* model for genocide, when throughout American history the genocide of indigenous peoples has been based in much more subtle tactics, legislation, and colonizing intentions and actions. While American historians have had little taste for the use of the term "genocide" in Indian history, it must be acknowledged as a reality of Indian-white history if justice is to be achieved.

Some historians believe that genocide can occur only when the outside force of a state acts against its own, as in the case of the German race purists against their countrymen and fellow citizens, the German Jews. These scholars claim that because unassimilable treaty Indians, members of their own tribal nations, were not U.S. citizens in the nineteenth century, their destruction could not have amounted to a real genocide. They weren't, after all, Americans. All sorts of excuses have arisen from this wrong assessment of what constitutes genocide.

Today the acknowledgment of genocide as mass murder has found some advocates. In 2005 the United Nations General Assembly adopted the principle known as the "responsibility to protect," imposing on member states an obligation to safeguard their people from mass atrocities, but so far the UN has done virtually nothing to put the principles into action. Unfortunately, this kind of global initiative does little or nothing to protect the indigenous peoples of the United States from the ideological structural devices (federal bureaus of management and economics) of strict colonization on Indian reservations, in place since the 1800s. The genocide recognized here must include death rates due to poverty, ill health, poor living conditions, failing health systems, lack of education and employment, violence, land theft, racism, lack of the opportunity to thrive, and other larger patterns of elimination of an entire people. Is such an extreme moral problem the same as genocide? Some scholars think so.[16]

Treatment of Indians has had all sorts of parallels in American scholarship. "Blacks were not the only race to feel the lash of white hatred," says Lawrence M. Freidman in *A History of American Law*. Freidman says the term "genocide" is "shocking" and has been used "loosely," but grudg-ingly admits, "It comes embarrassingly close to reality when we consider how the white man treated Native Americans. The tribes were driven from their lands; they were hounded and sometimes slaughtered. They had to give way constantly to land-hungry armies of white settlers."[17] To say this is "embarrassingly close" hardly suffices. His is not only a reenactment of what Dee Brown and countless others have documented, but it is also an example of the continued failure to accept the reality of genocide as a U.S. policy in law and legislation toward Native peoples for at least two hun-dred years. The term "genocide" is absent from these narratives.

Though Friedman cringes, Medved denies, and Helen Hunt Jackson fades into history, genocide is what happened and continues to happen to Native Americans. It is not now nor has it ever been just a matter of the physical extermination of a people through mass killings, enslavement or torture, enforced segregation or colonial apartheid. The systematic kill-ing of an entire people by the United States as it has happened through colonization *is the denial of basic human rights by a nationalistic legal, social, and intellectual system that makes it impossible for a domestic nation to express itself collectively and historically in terms of continued self-determination.* This is the genocidal theory and practice that has plagued the telling of the his-tory of the First Nations of America since the beginning. This historical reality is what makes it important to define colonization and postcoloniza-tion in the new epistemology, geography, and legislation that confronts indigenous America, to find new ways to contemplate our futures in the twenty-first century as the First Nations on this continent.

How to contemplate our futures as the First Nations is a moral and political question that looms large. The question of who should come up with the answers continues to plague the accompanying scholarship. Today, following the twentieth-century effort at urbanization of Indians through the Relocation and Termination Acts of the 1950s, a new frac-tured population of American Indians has entered the fray: the urban-ized.[18] There is now the contrast between Westernized Native intellectu-als in urban areas and those who live on the reserved homelands. This twentieth-century apposition is a major barrier to finding solutions and must be carefully worked through by scholars, who often end up just call-ing each other names. Westernized Native intellectuals are often accused by critics in Indian studies of accepting postcoloniality as whatever comes *after colonization is achieved.* They are described as "sellouts" when they behave as though the demise of colonialism has already been achieved. Those who recognize that domestic Indian nations are still in the clutches of the Bureau of Indian Affairs and the Department of the Interior are often called "blanket Indians" by those same critics, and said to be living in a condition of poverty, darkness, continuing colonization, and pessimism. All of this makes it possible to reject the idea that American Indians can be seen properly as postcolonial.

Since the colonization of American Indians began in earnest during the 1800s as the result of the imperial rise of the United States as a world power, and since "postcolonial" is a term that suggests an opposition to the practices of imperial power, Indian scholars will admit that postcoloniality may be a condition of becoming. Because of the nature of the indigenous political structures still in place on reserved or treaty lands, however, it is an ambiguous term useful only with qualifications.

Native American nations, as we all know, have been aggressively colonized since the mid-eighteenth century, when they were assigned by treaty to reservation status by the U.S. government in collusion with their own unfolding, lurching traditional governing systems. Since that time they have been forced *by law* to seek grounding in a white, Europeanized, American world. Colonists often think these groundings are our only histories, though thousands of years of development preceded them.

Nonetheless, anticolonial movements of the nineteenth and twentieth century have somehow occurred. These resistance movements have asked, What came *before* colonial rule? Why has that reality been abandoned? And how may we restore that precedence? Perhaps the most essential effort toward the resistance of a fraudulent postcoloniality, at least politically, was the forming of the National Congress of American Indians (NCAI), a lobbying group settled in the nation's capital as early as 1944, though it did not have any representative standing for at least another decade. Besides, in those days the NCAI was not asking for much of anything except recognition of recently reconstituted tribal governments as real and democratic entities.

Indeed indigenous peoples all over the continent, including the World Council of Indigenous Peoples, organized to promote self-determination and nationalism.[19] A ubiquitous criticism of this political activity has been that it continued to simply reflect the colonist's gaze in order to respond to it for the sake of mere survival. Even now, much of the work being done by indigenous groups at the UN, for example, is directed by reconciliationists and green environmentalists, whose focus is not tribally specific. The tribal activists among these groups, working toward tribal nation land restoration and tribal sovereignty, are the minority voices in those movements.

Many who object to prioritizing global over tribal concerns still hold out the idea that justice must happen (which means the return of lands) before reconciliation can happen, and both must happen before decolonization becomes a reality. Waziyatawin, for example, better known in scholarly circles as Angela Cavender Wilson, is one of only a handful of American Indian PhDs in history now arguing the reality of genocide in the development of the United States, and she says genocide must be acknowledged before progress can be made.[20] She begins *The Struggle for Liberation of the Dakota Homeland* with a preface entitled "Envisioning Justice in Minnesota," as the state of Minnesota celebrated 150 years of statehood. Her first chapter gives the clearest picture of war, exile, diaspora, and colonization (and, yes, genocide) in Indian Country that one can find in area studies. At the center of the drama lies an important creation story of the Bdwakantunwan (Dakotas), which demonstrates indigeneity as a category of analysis seen almost nowhere else in any scholarship readily available. A review of her stunning text appears in the Fall 2009 issue of *Wicazo Sa Review*.[21]

In the ongoing critique of postcolonial reasoning, a major question needs to be posed: Can models of liberal pluralism that seek to reconcile, accommodate, or transcend colonial domination serve to lead tribal nations into the twenty-first century, or must the colonial structures in place for several centuries be abandoned altogether? And if they are, what will the restructuring of tribal-state-federal relations look like? If we choose restructuring, that will mean a fundamental challenge to colonial power, and we can expect continuous conflict and struggle for perhaps the entire century.

For American Indians, then, the unanswered questions continue to be: What happens to colonized enclaves (like American Indian reservations) as a consequence of imperial domination? How can these populations recover, and how can their unique histories be protected? Only in the past ten years have Native scholars written even minimally on these consequences, and only recently, perhaps in the past twenty years, have the terms "colonialism," "neocolonialism," and "postcolonialism" been given useful meaning and standing in American Indian historiography. The reason for the delay is that Native histories and cultures have been in the clutches of the elite, the self-styled academics of sanctioned ignorance, namely, conservative academic departments, classical disciplines, and uninformed faculties. As a strategy toward indigeneity and sovereignty, the real issue in American Indian studies is whether or not colonized or once-colonized or partially colonized nations, those that still stand within a tribal federal treaty paradigm, yet struggle in a so-called trust or fiduciary or domestic or plenary paradigm, can properly be seen as postcolonial. In other words, when did we leave the colonized state? Is "postcolonial" an accurate term to describe the present condition of the long-standing relationship between the Indian nations and the federal government, especially since our treaty lands are still held in trust and tribal governing systems are nonfunctional as tribally focused structures?

Native scholars like David E. Wilkins probably doubt that the term has much agency, because in the closing pages of his text on the Supreme Court he says that to unmask this fraud, "the U.S., but especially the Supreme Court can disavow the use of *plenary* (read: virtually absolute) power and repudiate the despised, outmoded and always inaccurate doctrine of discovery."[22] How soon do you think that is going to happen? Wilkins intimates "not soon," yet this plenary power that he speaks of is simply a claimed colonial power, which is an indication of its treacherousness; it appears nowhere in the U.S. Constitution, but everywhere in Indian law and policy. One might be led to think that it could be dismissed as easily as it was claimed, but history tells a different story.

The truth is, it is getting more difficult every day to protect the extra-constitutional status of the tribes and the citizens of the tribal nations. This is because of the failure of American institutions to believe in the reality of our concomitant histories. Wilkins says this is true because the United States is still in its imperialist mode of the 1800s and refuses to acknowledge in its action that the First Nations of this country were always existing sovereigns, and that they were not parties to the U.S. Constitution or state constitutions.[23]

Not to be forgotten is the effort to subsume Native populations in the twentieth century, when the U.S. Congress passed the 1924 Indian Citizenship Act (many times over the objections of the tribes) in order to assert federal income taxing authority over all tribal citizens, and for other reasons even more outrageous. Major exceptions were income earned from federally recognized treaty fishing activities, particularly in the Northwest, and income from Indian allotments and land claims and judgments. Many law scholars have stated that the Act is in violation of the U.S. Constitution, and in 1980 the Red Lake Band of Chippewa Indians challenged this authority, which resulted in the Supreme Court's describing Congress's power over the tribes in even more aggressive and graphic language than before.

Though the "consent of the tribe" is always the accompanying mantra to these legislative measures, Indians generally see the phrase as merely a cover-up for the United States to exert continuing and absolute power. As in Red Lake case, such legislation often set up a conflict between tribal councils and activists in the 1980s. David Wilkins and K. T. Lomawaima give a clear picture of this dilemma in chapter 3 of their book, *Uneven Ground: American Indian Sovereignty and Federal Law*. If you think all of this has been more or less up in the air even after the Red Lake challenge, you are right, though taxation issues should now be on the front burner for every tribe in the country.

But it is not only the imperialist actions of nations like the United States that muddy these waters. Activist movements throughout the world have too. Rarely have the protest movements, even the powerful mid-twentieth-century American Indian Movement, represented all of the interests of all of the nations; thus the subjective debates concerning how to move into postcolonial realms flourish in academe and elsewhere, producing observable separations we may call "schisms." These schisms, whether they occur in politics or economics or education, can no longer be ignored, because larger postcolonial movements across the globe (in Africa and the Middle East, for example) have taken hold and are influencing all academic enclaves, moving the domestic nations of the United States along with them. American Indian nations must adopt the view of what is called the third world rather than the colonial view of domestic nations or nations-within-a-nation, breaking the bonds of the Marshall decisions of the early nineteenth century. The current push for a clearer sovereign condition vis-à-vis the United States is an imperative focus for the future.

Ania Loomba, a professor at Jawaharlal Nehru University in New Delhi whose work on the English–East Indian history of colonialism parallels much of the focus in the United States as it concerns Native peoples, gives those of us in American Indian studies something to think about when she says, "If the term post-colonial is taken to signify an oppositional position to imperial practices, then it has the effect of collapsing various locations so that specificities of all of them are blurred. . . . Post-colonial theory shifts the focus from locations and institutions to individuals and their subjectivities."[24] This shift from traditional, political, and institutional analysis to cross-cultural criticism embeds itself in the colonial paradigm; unfortunately, this is what has happened in Indian studies enclaves in American universities. As curricular development has veered from disciplinary development to multicultural diversity and reconciliation, there is the assumption that postcolonial discourse is a done deal, that postcoloniality is a real thing, and we should simply remove postcolonial arguments from any kind of reference to and dependence upon the previous colonial condition.

In other words, we should just pretend that the colonial condition is a thing of the past and that the once-colonized populations (such as tribal nations) and the once-colonizing countries (such as the United States) have simply merged. This seems like a practical matter to those who know that in our time and for the past century, colonization has exercised its presence over eighty-five percent of the globe and that little can be done to rectify history. What the populations of American Indian tribal nations need to know and act upon, however, is that even though their indigenous ideologies, practices, and hierarchies have interacted with colonialism only in a minimal way and only in response to forceful oppression, their enclaves have often become the breeding ground for chaos and further subjugation. They look at what is happening to them today on Indian reservations in terms of poverty and disease and domestic violence, and realize that there is profound urgency for drastic change.

To impose a single meaning on the term "postcoloniality," then, or even to suggest that we academics are dazzling ourselves with words, seems ineffectual. The term's usefulness in describing where we go from here in developing curriculum in the discipline of Indian studies is suspect. There is probably agreement that the words "colonialism" and "postcolonialism" need to become more focused, but that is where the agreement ends. Scholars who represent the established cross-cultural school of criticism have suggested that when colonial discourse concentrates on the representation of the colonized and the present condition of the colonized, as is done in multidisciplinary studies and social studies, colonialism and imperialism can be placed in the past and the term "postcoloniality" can take root as tribes move into the future. Those on the other side of that argument, who believe that the question *What came before colonialism?* or *What about indigeneity?* must be foremost, worry that such a focus on the present is mere assimilation, mere ruse, or a delaying tactic. Whatever side you are on in this argument, the discourse goes back to the reality that indigenous nations do exist in the historiography of the United States and have since the beginning. It goes back to the reality that all of the effort of the United States to rid itself of this indigenous past has failed, and it suggests that Indian studies as an academic discipline is, after all, an educational scheme intent upon giving appropriate education to colonial subjects who are in the process of sustaining or the remaking Indian nations as extraconstitutional entities.

Decolonization scholars like Taiaiake Alfred seem to have a clear notion that what came before colonization is manifested in Iroquoian tradition and in governance and land issues for the Mohawks of Kahnawake. But when Taiaiake applies it to all of "Turtle Island's indigenous peoples" as a manifesto, inspiration concerning the "logic of our traditions" gives way to chaos. One must remember that Canada probably has more influence in the Alfred model than does the United States because it has at least tried to redescribe its indigenous populations as First Nations entities. How successful it will be is yet to be determined.

One of the important questions is that of tribal citizenship and identity, a crucial principle of nationhood. Alfred seems to doubt the infallibility of citizenship and "aboriginal capitalism" in the definition of what makes a nation sovereign in today's world, and, as far as the structure of government is concerned, he suggests that leadership "takes the form of guidance and persuasion," which he considers "tribal," rather than structured institutions and policies. The Mohawks, as do other Native groups, traditionally defend what anthropologists have called the "clan" system, finding it more useful to reclaiming those traditions. The problem is that many tribal nations, especially in the Northern Plains of the United States, do not traditionally organize themselves according to clans. This makes the "manifesto" of the Alfred scholarship merely theoretical rather than practical.

It may be true that citizenship is not defined by the colonial state, as Alfred contends, but rather is a concept with its own nationalistic (tribal) integrity. How can a nation (tribe) exist if it does not know who its citizens are? In the same way, how can a nation (tribe) exist if it does not defend its nationalistic borders? It is not necessarily true that economic development as it concerns lands and resources must be seen as the source of expropriation and alienation in the modern world; perhaps, instead, it is a useful concept concerning profit and well-being for entire independent societies. Land and resource development requires new and subtle restructuring, not a return to the blanket days.

The return to tradition is not just a question of "shoulds" and "should nots," nor can we say that the return to tradition occurs in isolation. The real answer, perhaps, in returning to tradition lies in the treaty paradigm as exemplified by the Maori of New Zealand. The Maoris' reorganization of the 1840 Treaty of Waitangi in 1975 required the rehearing of cases going back over a hundred years. While this may seem to be a political matter rather than a cultural return to tradition, these paradigms are inseparable. This return, then, may be the only answer to eventually achieving what can be called postcoloniality. The Maori model must be studied and taken seriously by every indigenous group in North America. In that model, the return of lands is a central principle.

It is an unfortunate fact that Indian treaties are seldom studied in the curricular designs of university enclaves. This means that indigeneity cannot be examined or analyzed for the purpose of finding solutions; thus legal fictions (like the term "domestic dependent nations," which comes out of the 1830 Marshall decision) is how more and more law scholars describe the historical events that Native nationhood has suffered. This means that the overreaching law that is used to determine Native land issues is fictional if what is sought is justice. Most recently, treaties have been the basis for successful litigation concerning land issues in very few cases, yet the Maori model of reform is available to all scholars. The Black Hills land issue, in the courts since 1920, comes to mind as one of those legal fictions. The Maori model and the work of Linda Tuhiwai Smith and Taiaiake Alfred are invaluable for the twenty-first century because both call for actual retribution and the return of stolen lands.[25]

A New Understanding of a Specific Historical Event within the Colonial Paradigm

The So-Called Ghost Dance as a Living Event

To reconstruct a well-known historical event from 1890 is dangerous, and at the same time can be enlightening. In spite of the risks involved, this essay is an attempt to reconstruct a well-known and entrenched event referred to in Lakota history as the "Ghost Dance."

A recent example of the dangerousness of revisionism occurred in 2009, when school board members in Texas revised curricular designs and textbooks in order to teach science seemingly based only in religious belief. The scenario brought up the notion of the claimed neutrality of historians and teachers, citizens, parents, and school boards. What was called into question was whether or not these obviously partisan Texans were acting out of belief or scholarship. Schoolbooks are designed to be in place for ten years, horrified scholars who objected to the change were told. The cultural and political whirlwinds of interpretive audacity (and sometimes dishonesty) called scholarship tend to get academics riled up, and ugly accusations are sometimes made public. Yet the effort to get to essential changes of attitude, which are said by intellectuals and nonintellectuals alike to be observable facts in history, may help us to understand who we are.

Historical revision is a contested terrain, and the meaning of the past in intellectual, political, and cultural life is very much debated in the United States. "Disinterested scholarship," "objective study," and even "balanced judgment" may be the missing elements because most of the early writers of this 1890 event were not historians, or even scholars. In any case, unbiased interpretation has never been a part of the history of the Indian War period, and when Indian scholars, especially those who are not classically trained historians, add their belated voices to the mix, sharp critiques by those invested in the original works are to be expected.

In the case of the genocidal attack by the United States on the Lakotas at Grand River in 1890, driving their ceremony called the Ghost Dance, professionals made what they believe is a dispassionate interpretation. Those professionals were not innocent bystanders to the understanding of colonial thought; they were the makers of it. Taking another look at the events in the face of a changing historical knowledge base may be one of the ways to understand why coloniality as a concept in historiography is flawed, and why indigeneity may be a useful way to look toward new meanings. What the largely Christian writers of the event described as the Sioux response to the events of 1890 was, we can be sure, anything but a "balanced judgment."

Indeed if accommodation is the name of the game in historical writings (which seems to be the thrust of colonial scholarship), it must be that to rationalize this event as an inevitable religious conflagration amounts to a constructing of justification for the rise of U.S. imperialism rather than the accounting of a believable Native history. One way out of this conundrum, if one is dissatisfied with such scholarship, is to understand historical events as a combination of mixed truth and invention, with the idea that to stage a reenactment even on paper can be a revelation. Writing history is not, after all, just an esoteric game to be played as some kind of private enterprise. It has to witness, analyze, and be the voice of a humane conscience.

This essay will attempt to recast what historians have called the Ghost Dance of 1890 in a new definition of purpose, that of the traditional Plains "cry dance," a mourning ceremony advancing indigeneity as an analytical response to catastrophe. It will refute the explanation of Indian behavior on that day as a time when Indians were in the throes of the recognition of their own cultural and nationalistic death.

In postcolonial theory, one of the major difficulties in examining historical events with the intention of understanding Native knowledge is that in the past hundred years the American historian has been constructing a justification using his own personal knowledge of a stereotypical kind of

Indian: "Princess" Pocahontas and Squanto or even Tonto, and certainly the savage as terrorist. To ask what would happen to history without such ubiquitous colonial and imaginative notables would be to recognize that American historians have provided an interpretation designed to protect the colonial version of events.

During the first decades after the major Indian peace treaties were signed in the West (1850–68), the emerging nationalism of the United States allowed and encouraged its scholars to write its imperialist history with the intention of declaring the Indian dead, vanishing, or worse, an accommodating European stereotype. What is forgotten is that tribal peoples were also emerging as nationalists in opposition to the imperial savagery of their enemy. What is forgotten is that they were not Christians, which means that their reaction to this event cannot be placed in that context.

For much of the time of early historical writings, indigenous nations had access to neither their own courts nor to U.S. law and order, nor to their own practical identity or historical perspective as "nations-within-a-nation," a designation that would come into focus only when Native writers and legal thinkers entered the dialogue decades later. Part of the colonial story depended upon the destruction of Native religious practice by merging colonial law with the declining political autonomy for tribal traditions. Non-Native writers focused on their own religious traditions without considering the consequences of massive land thefts for a people for whom the land itself was the religious and spiritual reality.

This story may not have been the focus in the era of the Puritan (1600–1700), since mere survival was a major issue for invading whites during that early period, we are told. The opening of the West in 1800, though, was a different matter. Now it was about land and power, but conscience would not allow the term "theft" to be out in the open. The change in intention brought about by the rise of U.S. imperialism made it practical for historians to center their interests on the encroachment on the making of the constitutional law paradigm, the privileging of the European (white) man, and the use of political language as an instrument of hegemony, all of which was often discussed under the rubric of "the westward movement." This habit of historians has plagued their discipline ever since John Fiske, an advocate of social Darwinism, extolled the Manifest Destiny of the "English race" and Frederick Jackson Turner talked of Natives as the "vanishing race."

One historical event that has been given its due in Indian history as a colonial event is the endless examination of what is called "the Ghost Dance" of 1890,[1] when the Indians of the Northern Plains, called Sioux in the vernacular, resisted the ongoing land thefts. This event has rarely been understood outside of the colonial language of Euro-culture and Ameri-politics, which emerged as quickly as the events unfolded, when such expressions of nationalism by Natives were propagandized as the desperate fantasy of a dying race of religious fanatics. Postmodern theory has had almost no effect on this narrative, yet many of today's scholars are giving lip service to a grudging new look. This new movement in historiography is sometimes called "the new historicism," and it probably began with the work of Vine Deloria, a major voice in Indian studies and political science.

Often the periodical remembering of historical and political histories in Indian Country challenges our ability to monitor our achievements as scholars, both Indian and white; thus scholars deeply committed to a propagandized way of thinking find it difficult to proceed. Moving from tribal and traditional sovereignty to colonial oppression to termination and relocation and then back to tribal sovereignty has been a real and sequential and continuing journey for the first peoples of America, and the scholars who write about them. If we are to seek truth about all of this in a responsible manner, we must examine the history of how it happened, how our cultures changed in the process, and how we can plumb the nature of our present condition.

Homi K. Bhabha, a postcolonial authority of recent decades, has tried in his writings to tell us how to get out of the margins on such historical occasions. He says, " It is one of the salutary features of this postmodern theory to suggest that it is the disjunctive, fragmented, displaced agency of those who have suffered the sentence of history . . . subjugation domination, diaspora, displacement . . . that forces one to think outside the certainty of the sententious."[2] He lets us believe that empowerment and articulation can happen if scholars who care about postcoloniality in cultural studies as well as those who have become historical victims pursue with vigor the latent meaning of the most vivid of real events.

It is in the reexamination of such a historical event as the Ghost Dance that today's postcolonial investigators can come to meaningful intellectual developments beyond the margin. In other words, a reinterpretation of events by today's tribal-oriented scholars can grasp the distinction between tribal truth and postcolonial hegemony in scholarship. From the perspective of affective experience nearly two centuries after the event called the Ghost Dance, which began in the fall months of 1890 and reached its zenith by Christmas on the Standing Rock Reservation, Dakota Territory, the entire movement of what is called the Ghost Dance takes on empowerment rather than loss. When looked at outside of the history of the institutionalization of colonization classical historians attribute to it, Indian intent takes on new meaning. By ignoring this perspective of affective experience, which has informed such writers as John G. Neihardt and his countless followers, the conclusion that "the nation's hoop is broken" and the Indian is a tragic loser is unavoidable but, fortunately, flawed. In the experiential context, then, following the theft of the Black Hills in the Congressional Act of 1877, following the assassination of the great Sicangu chief Spotted Tail, following the unexpected return from Canada to his homelands of Sitting Bull, the war leader of the Hunkpapa, and following the passage of the Allotment Act by the U.S. Congress in 1889, the Sioux resistance movement called the Ghost Dance takes on a perspective of ascendancy toward life and survival rather than a descent into death.

In spite of the continuing attack on the Sioux by scholars who may possess unhelpful cultural and political motives, the Ghost Dance, say many tribal politicians, signaled an eventual "cultural renaissance," not death. Formerly thought of as a metaphor for death, it has recently been seen as an emerging nationalistic event contextualized in such modern activities as the 1970 American Indian Movement and the historical Centennial Ride in 1980 from the Grand River to Wounded Knee commemorating the December event and countless other occurrences on Native lands in the modern world. Led by Lakota/Dakota nationalists who have understood history on their own terms, people like Debra and Alex White Plume, Birgil Kills Straight, Arvol Looking Horse, Lionel Bordeaux, Stanley Red Shirt, Charmaine White Face, Royal Bull Bear, and hundreds of others who know the function of such grieving ceremonies as the misnamed Ghost Dance, come to a different conclusion.

In order to contextualize this event in a nationalistic way, as they do, the Ghost Dance must not be interpreted as it has been, as a religious text, but rather a secular one. This historical event has been described by non-Indian historians as the quintessential religious event marking the "end of the Plains Tribes," the last gasp of a defeated race, a tragic and final effort by a sad and defeated people unable to save themselves from an untimely but inevitable demise, allowing this colonial perspective to fester in historiography to the detriment of the long-term consequences of survival and reconstruction of the Sioux Nation. These non-Indian historians tell us over and over again that the Ghost Dance was a horrifying, iconic, and religious moment of *death to the nations-tribes*. It was that, they say, because it promised a religious outcome for the people—a transcendence and an enlightenment reminiscent of Christian dogma. After Sin comes Redemption. This interpretation is important to Christian America because if it is seen for what it was—the culmination of a hard-fought war for land and resources by invading colonizers—the origin myth of the United States as a benign benefactor of the Indians is insulted. This interpretation does not account for the continuous resistance to colonialism by Native peoples.

To come to the conclusion that the Ghost Dance was about religion and redemption, inspired and demagogic historians had to forget two historical facts: (1) the Sioux, the victims, were not Christians at the time of the event, many of them never becoming converts, thus invalidating the Christianizing of the event; and (2) this ceremony was nothing new to those who participated in it. Indeed it was as old as the Earth itself. The Sioux and many Plains tribes had been practicing this ritual ceremony (euphemistically called the Ghost Dance by white observers) in the West for a very long time. It was known by many of the Great Plains peoples as the cry dance, a mourning ceremony of grief that precedes a cultural regathering and tribal survivance period. There are, perhaps, many versions of the *cheya wacipi*, which may have been lost in the mists of history.

The mistaken settling of this event in the nostalgic and religious mode of imperial and Christian America allows historians to speak of the "moral" imperative, alluding to an epiphany and a redemption embodied in the event rather than tribal reality, survivance, and political authority. To mourn was a sacred responsibility in Plains Indian cultures, and still is. It was, and is, made art of. It was and is ceremonialized relentlessly. Ceremony was and is a communal and tribal survival tactic, having nothing to do with useless death knells.

To think of history in this new way brings up the fact that what may be thought of as radical arguments made by skeptics can be used to reconstruct meaning and responsibility in a way visible to what we know has come to pass: the continuing survival and presence of Indian nationhood in modern America and the continuing strength of today's resistance movements. The Sioux Nation (called the Ocheti Shakowan by Native speakers) has survived, has remained sovereign, and has defended a huge land base as well as a political and ethical conscience. This has been done in the face of enormous backlash because it is a tribal responsibility as old as the tribes themselves.

If historical events like the Ghost Dance are described as rituals signaling death to the nation, there is little chance to think about cultural survival or rebirth. However, such an opportunity presented itself in a symposium on rebirth in 2005, entitled From Termination to Sovereignty: A 50-Year Retrospective on National Indian Policy, held at the University of South Dakota, Vermillion. It was a review of federal Indian policy that required its participants to think of the history that preceded policy as the cause for one crisis after another in Indian life and how to overcome those crises. More than anything, though, it was a chance to think about the fate of the first peoples, their contemporary conditions, what the advisors to the gathering were calling "cultural renaissance," and how to go forward. This exercise in the communal thought of participants and scholars demonstrated ongoing cultural relevance in the Indian world, hardly a commemoration of death to the tribe, or broken hoops, or vanishing Americans.

Cultural renaissance, which some believe is the outcome of the 1890 Ghost Dance, has been a huge concern to contemporary peoples, and it was a huge concern to those who talked of policy issues at this conference. That notion is what ties the idea of resistance and survival rather than death to the Ghost Dance phenomenon I am discussing. "Cultural renaissance" is said to mean a recovery of beliefs, traditions, certainties, and ideas. Many of the participants at tribal gatherings all over the country have privileged the notion that such a rebirth happened after the Ghost Dance and, most important, because of it. No one denies the people's suffering and fear that came about after the assassination of their revered leader, Big Foot, as well as their political and resistance leader, Sitting Bull, nor the terrible massacre that was precipitated. But among Native people all over the world, cultural nationalism has often been a relevant response to the larger struggle for liberation and defense of a nation thousands of years in development. The evidence for that reality is the continuing existence of indigenous peoples on every continent.

When discussing the asserted nationalism brought about by history, scholars talk of the Centennial Rides of 1990–2010, sponsored by several tribal enclaves, when as many as fifty horseback riders from all of the bands of the Sioux Nation retrace the flight from Grand River to the Pine Ridge Indian Reservation in December 1890. The flight was of course a necessary event after the killing of Sitting Bull. The Centennial Ride generally follows or is followed by a gathering of feasting and prayer. This act of remembrance is re-created every December at the killing site in a nationalistic fervor commemorating honor and life and grief. It is not a death event that is celebrated; it is an affirmation of the people and their leaders. The former trail, now called the Big Foot Trail, was developed as Route 79, an offshoot of I-90 in South Dakota, and was established publicly to mark the events of that postcolonial case. The Centennial Ride participants often speak of these matters in third world terms rather than in the colonial piety of the past generation. This means that what was once a private and tribal grievance has now become a public one. It also means that contemporary Indians respect their own interpretation of history. Maps and brochures are distributed and symposia are held at reservation-based community colleges and homes to honor and glorify this history.

Other examples, such as sun dance gatherings and tribal ceremonials, also tell the people of past events. In fact as many as forty summer sun dances are held on the Pine Ridge Indian Reservation in South Dakota. Does this signify death? Life? Or can it be dismissed as just an obsessive manipulation of religion? Because we now have a gambling casino on every reservation and can buy a new car, are we experiencing cultural renaissance or just becoming capitalists? Modernity does not always reflect historical reality, nor does it always signify what seems pertinent. But economic survival and change are certainly part of the future and require a mixture of modernity as well as indigeneity for complete understanding.

What do we mean by "cultural renaissance," then? What is "culture"? Must we accept that Native "cultures" have died or been killed off by our historians and museum keepers? Are some parts of them in need of being born again? Is that why we are talking about "rebirth"? Asking these questions brings up the likelihood that there are many ways to define "culture" and many notions of what those definitions mean to historiography. Is the development of contemporary historiography and the body of criticism and theory quite outside of the reality of events and what they have meant to the people who lived the events?

To avoid errors in theorizing, it's useful to begin by agreeing upon a definition of culture. I propose that presented by Alfonso Ortiz in his 1968 classic text, *Being and Becoming in a Tewa World*. "Culture," says Ortiz, "is a system of *historically* derived meanings and understandings," and it is expressed in all sorts of ways: in language, mythology, religion, lifeways, storytelling, literature, war, politics, and government. Ortiz probably did not think Native cultures were to be expressed in gambling casinos or an exploitation of sun dance rituals, or any of the more obvious capitalist endeavors available in the modern world, but his point is that historical events, how they are written or told or remembered, and how they are perceived by the persons living the events, are a vital component in our discussion of culture, cultural renaissance, colonization, and postcoloniality: "Culture refers to a system of historically derived meanings and conventional understandings embodied in symbols; meanings and understandings which derive from the social order, yet which serve to reinforce and perpetuate that social order; the intellectual aspects of Indian ideas, rules, and principles as they are reflected in mythology, worldview, and ritual."[3]

If we are to examine the cultural renaissance or the rebirth of culture utilizing Ortiz's definition, we must take into account how the historically derived meanings and understandings that make up culture have been portrayed and how the flaws in that portrayal may have impacted the disciplinary narrative. We must also determine whether rebirth is plausible at all. It has always been the position of some critics that cultures rarely, perhaps never, die out. Cultures change, they adapt, they rise and fall, but in the view of many scholars, they never die out completely. Many writers, especially third-worldists, argue that there is a reciprocal relationship between culture and the historical events making up that change. Thus the affirmative notion that cultures are reborn must be looked at with the notion that contesting foreign domination is as much a part of culture as language or custom or religion. It is always good to start out being a bit skeptical. Skepticism, as we all know, is a tradition in every culture that questions our ability to obtain knowledge; even Plato's philosophy left us with an ambiguous legacy that suggests we have to provide some reason for believing as we do. Sifting the facts is a good thing for historians to engage in from time to time.

In the case of one of the significant events of the 1890s, disciplinary and cultural tendencies toward representation of meaning seem to depend on the colonization of the present in the nostalgic mode. This may be the first mistake made by historians, in need of further Native input. While it may be true that the sun dance as it is portrayed on many occasions these days is probably not a rebirth but a signal of resistance unprocessed, there are just as many who believe it to be much more significant than mere remembrance. It has real outcomes for those who participate.

Often wars, treaties, land thefts, deaths, and subsequent bureaucracies signify who indigenous peoples are. Unfortunately, many educational institutions, including the institutes of Native studies, museums, and historical repositories that have been here for decades, have gone along with nostalgia rather than politics. Skepticism, on the other hand, and the denial of privileged archives is what may bring about postcolonial authority in scholarship. The ascendancy of secular texts, symposia of Native scholars, and the authentication of what may be called "the oral traditions" in the discussion of Native events that have heretofore been examined only in a religious context, are particularly significant in developing a new historiography.

An examination of the historical event called the Ghost Dance and how it has been misunderstood and what that misunderstanding has implied about the death of the Native, his culture, his future, his nation, and his intentions can, perhaps, remove the colonial inscription given to it by theorists interested in advancing the most ubiquitous colonial theory of them all, the "vanishing American." While much lip service has been paid to the denial of the vanishing American theory, particularly by the so-called new historians, it still is institutionalized in many precious registers of literary theory and, more dangerously, in public policy.

To set the stage for this discussion it is useful to consider the very recent work of a professor and researcher at Colorado State University in the Department of History, Gregory E. Smoak, who has examined the Ghost Dance of the Shoshones and Bannocks.[4] For our purpose, the suggestion that Smoak's origin study as identity formation and emerging nationalism posits that other Plains tribes share the same political consciousness of the ritual as the Shoshone and Bannocks do is appealing.

As mentioned before, this Sioux historical event has been described by non-Indian historians as the quintessential religious event marking the "end" of the Plains tribes, the last gasp of a defeated race, a tragic and final effort by a pitiful and defeated people unable to save themselves from an untimely but inevitable death. These historians tell us over and over again that the Ghost Dance was a horrifying and iconic moment of death to the tribes, when the Nation of the Dakotapi (Sioux) ceased to exist.

Smoak constructs an argument opposing such a dire conclusion, and it is useful for all researchers to contemplate his position. His work intimates that such a final scenario may be a false conclusion, that rather than a death knell, the ritual became a nineteenth-century vehicle for emerging nationalism. In the face of thriving contemporary Native populations in the twenty-first century, his argument bears much weight.

In the context of other, more recent war-time defeats, the historical imagination of survival can take root. For example, after the dropping of the A-bomb in 1945, surely an "end-all" catastrophe, the Japanese nation did not cease to exist. One of the reasons for this contrast in history making is that a Christian interpretation has not been applied to the Japanese example: unlike the Ghost Dance phenomenon and Native nation decline, the Japanese defeat has not been written about as a religious matter. One supposes that "savages" out on the prairie can hardly be compared to sophisticated modern nations.

For the Indians who took part in the ceremonial, the Ghost Dance was not about death; it was about life. First of all, ghost dancing, as Smoak points out, was not a new thing, as has been implied by many colonial historians and observers. Wovoka, tribal spiritual leaders, and some of the many people who have been asked to interpret the event have failed to express the primordial nature of the ceremony in Plains cultures, since political expediency and Christian fervor have always set limits and maintained pressures in American historiography. Smoak's book *Ghost Dances and Identity: Prophetic Religion and American Indian Ethnogenesis in the Nineteenth Century* gives ample evidence that the Ghost Dance was known and practiced by many tribes in the West for millennia, belonging to what the Sioux call the *o-hu-n-ka-ka* period, the first period of life on Earth. Smoak's research tells us that the Shoshones, Bannocks, Lakotas, Pawnees, Arapahos, Shehelas, Minneconjous, Dakotas, and Paiutes all knew the Ghost Dance because it had taken place ritualistically over hundreds of years in the Northern and Western Plains as a *restorative mourning* ceremony. Many of these tribes called it the cry dance, in Dakota language *wacipi cheya*.

Smoak's interpretation could mean that the Ghost Dance did not symbolize what Robert M. Utley and Dee Brown and countless other mid-century American writers say it did: the Last Days. The dance was not just an appeal to supernatural powers to restore power to the tribes (though that was a persistent theme); it was also a powerful expression of racialized "Indianness", a vehicle for the expression of social identities in the midst of grief and chaos, social identities Indians had always known and defended. It wasn't just a sign of resistance to the invasion of the white man, though it was that too. It was what it had always been: a symbol of tribal identity and tribal culture and a process of nationalism in the face of grief that has always been a facet of Sioux culture.

Smoak writes in his introduction, "The native peoples of west of the Rockies were enmeshed in a culturally rooted and ever-evolving set of religious beliefs which provided a means for understanding the great changes in their lives and gave meaning to emerging identities."[5] He could well be speaking of all of the tribes west of the Minnesota River, even west of the Mississippi. Understanding who these tribes were has been problematic to historians even before Frederick Jackson Turner, who knew nothing of Indian cultures in the West and wanted desperately to put in place the historiographical tools for the "vanishing American" theory. More appropriately, the Ghost Dance was evidence of the use of traditional grief ritual to signify a wrenching and awful cultural change. Cultural change is always wrenching and it is always resisted. American Indians took part then, as they do today, in a process of protesting but shared discourse to defend tribalism, what may now be called nationalism. As they experienced the effects of colonization, epidemics of various diseases, economic dependency, the loss of land, and war, they defined themselves as they had always defined themselves in the context of indigenous presence. They had always been a plural population, indigenous to specific geographies: the Crows lived to the west of the Sioux, the Ojibwes occupied lands along the rivers in Minnesota, the Arapahos and Cheyennes were to the south and west, staunch allies and friends of the Sioux, the Pawnees to the south, and the Bannocks on the great camas prairies. The historically defined meanings and understandings of their lives were as they had always been, in spite of the white man's terrible and violent intrusion; thus they proceeded to perform a mourning ritual known to us today as the Ghost Dance, an interpretation largely perpetuated falsely by classical American historians as a ritual of final death.

While there is no argument that European intrusion brought enormous change to some Indian groups, the truth is many tribal nations live today where they have always lived. They have not vanished, nor have their cultures. Indeed as this manuscript is being written in the summer of 2010, the tribes of what is now called the Sioux Nation are planning a prayer ceremony and spiritual ride at Green Grass to commemorate their histories, for what they call "Opagi," filling the pipe with tobacco to affirm national identity in their own brave and unmistakable way to connect them to their land and the sacred universe. While the United States maintains its advantages, the Great Sioux Nation dedicates itself, as it did during the Ghost Dance period, to understanding its place in the universe during enormous change. It does not signify death. It signifies life.

It was Vine Deloria who always started his talks on politics and law by saying, "The Indian did not vanish. . . . Just his land did!" He meant, among other things, that we cannot dismiss the reality that the land was stolen and colonized. But what does this mean in terms of rebirth? It is not important that there are forty sun dances going on today as an indication of rebirth. What is important is that the Lakotas, today, do not do their sun dance in Cleveland or San Francisco; they do it in the hills of their homelands, as they always have. The Diné today do not sing the *yei-bei-che* in Atlanta; they perform it in the communities where they have lived for a thousand years.

To understand the function of such ritualization of grief as provided by the cry dance is to understand the principle of place or setting in these rituals: the loss of the geographical universe is what the Sioux lamented, not the death of the tribe. What is so difficult to accept in a history written by others (particularly colonists) is what Edward Said told us about the challenged Palestinians in the Middle East years ago, that there has to be recognition of the fact that *citizens with rights* (and who are not movable anonymous populations) are the moral norm in regions where democracy is expected to flourish.[6] That includes the United States, does it not? Why else were Natives made dual citizens of this country? Historians must take that fact to heart. The Sioux Nation has always had a right to live, in spite of the scholarship that says it must die.

If death had happened, as pronounced by the repetitious writers and historians of a wrongful history, there would be little rationale for the struggles of the indigenous nations against what many call a colonial "termination" era of the mid-twentieth and twenty-first century. There would be no militant and sacred response to the federal government's attempts to end the treaty status of the large western tribes and to remove the peoples from their lands through relocation, or eliminate them entirely. Instead of passive acceptance of death, tribal nations fought long and hard against termination. The American Indian Movement of 1960–70 armed its participants with the same fervor that was evident during the Ghost Dance era, when the Indian world was changed and brought to the mainstream, when Indian enclaves sought a better political understanding. In the historical imagination of the one hundred years since the Ghost Dance phenomenon occurred, the argument advances the redemptive message of that time for Indians. The ritual message of unity and identity for the Sioux persists and resonates, not only in the works of today's Native scholars, but in the lives of those on the homelands.

The point is that what we call "death" or "rebirth" is a matter of how we interpret those histories in light of present conditions. The Sioux Nation has not died. Its tribes have not vanished, nor have their cultures or their presence in the world of nations. Institutions and repositories of historiography have an obligation to examine what has happened in educational, intellectual, political, and historical terms.

If we care about the function of history we cannot assume that casino wealth for a few tribes, which is what is going on today, is evidence of a cultural renewal. Our modern obsession with economic development cannot allow us to ignore the appropriate interpretation of our history. Becoming capitalists was not on the minds of the cry dancers in 1890; thus we cannot say that modern becomings signify cultural renewal. Neither can we say that such becomings as economic prosperity are the death of culture. Such an event as the so-called Ghost Dance signifies a moment in time that must be seen in the context of the past. Only a clear undertaking of the past, only open criticism of what is thought to be "settled" theory will allow scholars to put back together an interrupted historical narrative that helps make sense of the present condition of the indigenous case. Thus the Ghost Dance era is not unconnected to the present situations of the living.

The truth is, by examining an event like the Ghost Dance in a new light we are drawn to seeing the future of Indian studies in the context of this new world and in the context of postcoloniality. Many are disappointed in the development of the discipline of Indian studies in the Northern Plains and elsewhere in western universities because they see the same old interpretations of indigenous history taught as dispossession and death.

Departmental status in the discipline has rarely occurred because of the oppressive nature of established departments like history and sociology and literature. Programs and institutes, operating outside of the intellectual debates of Indian Country, carry the indigenous message of colonization rather than self-determination. Ad hoc funding takes place over institutional commitment and investment. Native scholars are rarely asked what they think about the Iraq War; they are only told to send their sons and daughters to fight in foreign lands.

Indian studies is often seen as a collection of courses drifting in and out of women's studies, ethnic studies, how-to courses, and diversity, a little bit from history, more from anthropology. There is little talk of third world decolonization theories about how to rid ourselves of colonization and plenary power and poverty and powerlessness, which should be the thrust of the discipline in most university settings and should be the focus of development. There is only talk of how to run a casino efficiently, how to make countless trips to Washington to testify about poverty and alcoholism and poor housing, how to write 638 grants to run a shambles of a court system that more often than not victimizes its professionals and its clients.

Every generation moves on and does what it can. Great changes are in store as the nationalistic narratives of the indigene replace colonial misinterpretations. Many writers are now challenged to move from colonial discourse studies to indigenous nation studies, in spite of the fact that their institutions and repositories, faculties, deans and provosts, editors and publishers often are not. It is the challenge of modern writers to cast aside the conceptual ordering of the two worlds of America, the colonial world founded on a genocidal or quasi-extermination model vis-à-vis the modern, technological world operating on the notion that the resources of weaker states can be stolen by the powerful with no destructive embrace from practical and logical thinkers. These, they say, should not be the only choices available to us.

Other Eurocentric critiques have been posed as useful ways to restructure what cultural change has wrought. Some institutions, such as museums where there is a plethora of materials concerning the Ghost Dances of the 1800s, are a reminder that death is ever present, not just for Indians but for all mortals. Are the new museums being funded by federal monies both here in our region and on the Mall in Washington evidence of cultural rebirth, or are they evidence of further assimilation in rewriting and restructuring histories? Or are they symbols of death? The failure of historians, museum makers, conference scholars, and others to research the real facts of Sitting Bull's assassination—which triggered the Ghost Dance events—is an example of the restructuring of a colonial history discussed here. He was a major figure during the mourning era, yet his political assassination during that moment in history has been overshadowed

by the American historian's obsession with religion. To continue their ac-
quiescence in writing about his assassination as an accident of history, as
many scholars have done, or, worse, to nostalgically mourn his passing,
disregards how the Sioux have survived the ravages of a colonial history
and violent dispossession. It silences their persistence in speaking for their
own participation in the human strand inherent in all histories. To fail
to critique the genocidal practices by an abusive federal government during the Sitting Bull years, which is evidenced at most modern museums
and repositories, is to fail to admit that this assassination, other deliberate
killings, and the interpretation of the Ghost Dances as death dances are
denials of the right of the Sioux Nation to thrive in the modern world.
When what occurred during a period of the defense of Native values and
rights was at its most fervent goes unexamined, the hegemony of the colonial storytelling maintains its shallow intentions. This omission is almost
as catastrophic as the events themselves. These events should not only be
examined because of the need for the study of the American mind; they
should be studied as examples of the strength of Native culture, revealing
a survival mechanism rather than defeatism.

At some museums there is the constant reminder that death to Indians is ever present. Yet mortality is the ultimate recognition of every
human being, not just Indians. Do the new museums being funded by
federal monies both here in our region and on the Mall in Washington
give evidence of cultural strength, or are they condemned to give evidence
of further assimilation and the structuring of dismal histories? Must they
invent symbols of death as they have invented the Ghost Dance? What is
the function of museum work and scholarship for indigenous peoples in
terms of postcoloniality?

Can the reinterpretation of an event like the Ghost Dance censure a
colonial history? Should it? If such a reinterpretation were to be accepted
in the new dialogue of historicist writings, would the continued occupation of Indian lands and the continuing control by the Congress and the
courts over Native nation sovereignty be confirmed? Or would the fate of
Native peoples indicate a political transition? A renegotiation? It is not a
radicalization of historical thought to move away from the imagined long
and barren death for the indigenes. History is one thing. But what of the
need to address present injustice?

4

Eliminationism

Context for Understanding

Though American historians and political scientists have tended to describe the first years of colonization in any instance as a time of progress, recent political scholars such as Daniel Johan Goldhagen argue with that special assessment. In his latest text, he introduces the term "elimination-ism" in the context of colonization and decolonization studies.[1] He says that the euphemism "amoral utilitarianism" has been used to sustain controversial practices of what many don't want to recognize as genocide and to rationalize a far more savage behavior on the part of imperial nations. He does not exempt the United States from this history.

A few historicists are now concluding that the colonization of indigenous peoples has not been just a disturbing, utilitarian, unfortunate, and unlucky method of imposing a humanistic theory of the development of civilization, as had been accepted in the historical narrative of the United States. The works of Angie Debo and Howard Zinn, perhaps even Patricia Nelson Limerick, come to mind as Native scholars find themselves in agreement with Goldhagen's analysis. Even though American Indians aren't the focus of some of this new work, the research findings certainly support the American Indian experience of devastation and dependency. Some have replaced the loathsome term "genocide" with the term "eliminationism" to describe the cruel and ongoing treatment on the part of the United States toward its indigenous populations.

Goldhagen tells us that the euphemism "amoral utilitarianism" disguises the hatred, racial enmity, and plain savagery behind it, allowing the murders of thousands of unoffending Native populations in defense of the cause of colonization throughout the globe. This doctrine of eliminationism could be said to have been originally promulgated by the early democrat John Stuart Mill, whose "Essay on Liberty" in the mid-1800s was an answer to the question of what to do with a population that does not seem to advance what is good for the majority. Mill was opposed to universal suffrage because of what was considered the extreme unfitness of the working class. Such thinking addressed the problem of finding social balance with a blanket of morality thrown in, but in the end nothing was allowed to threaten the reign of conservative Englishmen (and Americans by extension). There is precedence, therefore, for the elimination of an unwanted people, Goldhagen suggests. Democratizers used terms such as "amoral utilitarianism" to lend an air of retributive justice and compassion to the awful reality of outright mass elimination of an unwanted people. The colonization of Indian nations has become the theory and practice by which the United States has taken over the continent from its unwilling indigenous nations, suggesting that they vanish, and when they did not, making them beggars through elements of economics and irresistible romance. It continues on its path toward eliminationism by law, yet giving lip service to self-determination. Colonization as we know it rarely supports its claim that it teaches public virtues, though in the United States, beginning in kindergarten, colonization is still taught as a form of "progress" and as a method for achieving justice.

The mass murder of Jews by the Nazis, exemplar of twentieth-century eliminationism, is probably the most horrific event of our time, and the theft of American Indian lands—though resulting in endemic poverty and death, along with the relentless rise of aggressive state government power over tribal nation autonomy—seems almost benign by comparison. Evidence of plunder and death in recent cases, however, rendering American Indians the most poverty-stricken and undereducated class in the country, suggests that the elimination of indigenous presence is ongoing, to say nothing of the many episodes of outright massacre of Indians throughout the centuries. This condition of American Indians has been brought about through the use of colonization on what is left of the Indian estate and has been an assault on humanity in general and on American Indians in particular. Just saying that, however, does not mean that colonization will go away, nor will it be described as criminal in the democratic United States.

Instead, the United States continues to be the main colonizer throughout the world and an aggressive assimilator of our era, an example of successful imperial progress toward capitalistic democracy.

American attempts at mass murder and the elimination of American Indians in the first encounter has been rationalized as the necessary acts of a nation trying to be born. Indians were shot on sight by the Pilgrims and settlers even into subsequent centuries. In spite of the Thanksgiving drama so familiar to our children, attempts to rid the scene of Natives were ongoing. The United States spent a couple of centuries devising a strategy to round them up and pen them up (colonize them) as a movement of slow and deliberate elimination. Relocation and control in the nineteenth and twentieth century were inevitable, as colonizers refused to recognize Native America as a land occupied by many indigenous nations for thousands of years.

There are in the course of human history many eras of nationalistic slaughter or murder of unoffending peoples; such acts are "always political," says Goldhagen, and often end in warfare.[2] In writing of these eras in the context of *extermination,* he introduces a vocabulary to clarify what it is that colonialism does, even if its intentions are not clear. Few scholars have gone as far as Goldhagen in this investigation of the *elimination* of unwanted populations, and not many have associated his theory with classical historiography concerning American Indians. He is among those scholars who argue that there is little difference between the eliminations that occurred in previous centuries and those that are occurring in our time, in Germany and Armenia and Africa. The argument has been made that earlier mass murders and eliminations were the result of "imperialist Europeans acting without moral restraint, or amorally, to secure [land for] non-Europeans."[3] If both the perpetrators and the victims inhabit the same country, as in the case of white Americans and Indians, people are happy to excuse elimination in a highly meditative way. What that has meant for American Indians is that their early dispossession and murder, warfare and subsequent colonization can be separated from the "real" criminal act of savage killing. A simple working definition in the name of humanitarian acts can be devised, genocide can be denied, and legislation can go forward as though no crime, amoral or otherwise, has been committed.

The westward movement, which the early crusader Helen Hunt Jackson called "a century of dishonor," is an example of the restraint in the scholarship of the time that has ensued for most of the last two centuries.

Dishonorable, yes. Criminal, no. Genocidal, unutterable. Some historians even suggest that the terms "genocide," "colonization," and "eliminationism" had not been coined when Jackson wrote; thus such terms are inappropriately used now. Yet even though she refrained from using such terms, Jackson managed to provide the central thesis for many histories of later times: that the United States followed an outrageous Indian policy "in defiance of the basic principles of justice and the laws of all nations,"[4] and that it was a policy without honor that should put the early democracy to shame. She even denounced treaty breaking and would have condemned the unconstitutional Allotment Act as a solution to dealing with a troublesome population, legislation that caused dire poverty and death to thousands of indigenous people.

It has been only in the past two or three decades that the national character of the United States and its democracy vis-à-vis its unwanted Native population could be said to be anything more than flawed and regrettable. With the work of such investigators as Goldhagen on the academic scene, it may be considered criminal.

On Looking Westward

Prior to Helen Hunt Jackson, and even with very little anticipation of her work, several theories of democratic rule emerged during the settlement of the West. One largely accepted theory, that of the continued "discovery" of place, was necessary for legalizing the theft of a continent from its indigenous populations. Little was remembered of the pious renderings by early figures who devised "the Law of the Indies,"[1] when the necessity of killing off great populations and occupying lands was considered, albeit with great skepticism, a moral undertaking under the watchful eyes of popes and churches. As everyone from Teddy Roosevelt to George W. Bush and his ilk told us later, the settlement of the West was to become the work of he-men and imperialists.

Politics and law, not morality, took center stage even while President Thomas Jefferson clearly made land acquisition (which is the major function of colonization) the most important feature of his National Indian Policy and therefore set the stage for a nation to go westward not as democratizers, as is often mythologized in history, but as colonists and land seekers. This feature became the major function of colonization. Jefferson, of course, was not the first, nor was he the only executive of this country to do so. His letters suggest that he wanted to buy and occupy land with the consent of Indians who would eventually "vanish," but some historians believe that his letters also show he was not averse to a more aggressive policy that even suggests an eventual extermination policy. There is no question that many early presidents saw no future for blacks or for Indians in the United States, and Jefferson was no exception.

It can probably be said that Jefferson struggled with law-related demo-cratic principles and the ideological interpretations of various doctrines, while Andrew Jackson, Abraham Lincoln, and even Teddy Roosevelt, who were in power decades after the Jeffersonian period, became the real crimi-nals of early American colonization and genocide, deploying federal In-dian policies set up to exterminate indigenous peoples. One of the decisive thinkers of the nineteenth century, Abraham Lincoln is today touted as a great humanitarian, though he continued to set a broad stage for the raw assertion of colonial power. In spite of the short history that encompassed his colonial orders as chief executive, he is often touted as a significant figure in the development of what are considered American ideals, a states-man of high order and the emancipator of African slaves in the late 1860s during his brief presidency. His likeness is blasted into a mountain sacred to the indigenous peoples of the region in what has become the state of South Dakota, and he is today the model for those who believe the first black man elected to the presidency of the United States, Barack Obama, is indebted to the legacy of freedom espoused by Lincoln.

The issue of state power in the West was set in motion prior to the Lincoln presidency, of course, but, with some insight into the long arm of history, it is clear that during his tenure as the most powerful politician in the nation, the most important issue in terms of justice for the indigenous peoples was the issue of states' rights and the usurpation of tribal auton-omy. States' rights was a huge concern to western politicians at the time, even though the Indian Wars were put on the back burner as the Civil War was waged and the Union became the intention of American ideal-ism. Though most of the states in the West were still considered territories and treaties with tribal nations were still being signed even as they were being broken, the move toward statehood, whatever that would mean, was Lincoln's intention as he looked westward.

The sovereign condition of powerful Indian nations in the West and the Northern Plains (specifically Dakota Territory) had to be accounted for by settlers and politicians alike. Since many of the states of the north-ern tier did not become states until after the peace treaties were signed (South Dakota, North Dakota, Idaho, Montana, Washington, Wyoming, and others), a clear principle of "primacy" of Indian law was established. According to Indian law experts such as Felix Cohen, this principle did not apply to New York, Kentucky, and other regions, but it clearly es-tablished Indian nation sovereignty in the West.[2] This was probably not Lincoln's intention, but he was busy with the Civil War and the defense of federalism. Statehood in the western regions, delayed until 1889, was a secondary focus vis-à-vis the powerful tribes of the West still at war with invaders. To get the tribal nations off the battlefield, just as the southerners had to be moved from their protesting of the great union, several legal strategies were used, and so-called peace treaties were among them.

Lincoln is clearly idealized as an American innovator, but a second version has emerged from his minor dealings in Indian Country, indicating that Lincoln was a man of his time, a white supremacist, and a crafty politician. One of the major treaties in the West, the Fort Laramie Treaty of 1868, was not signed until after Lincoln's assassination. In one brief instance, Lincoln's relationship with the Dakota Sioux in the Northern Plains prior to that treaty seems to be a far cry from the expected idealization of this president.

Whatever is accepted or rejected about controversial historical views, Lincoln's relationship with the indigenous peoples of this country and how Lincoln's time forwarded dangerous ideologies about Indians is a forgotten history. And that is a shameful historical oversight, since it might shed some light on the paradox of what the United States has become: an imperialist nation invading weaker countries for their resources using the cover that it is democracy it is seeking. It might even shed light on the continuing conflict between western states and western Indian Nations, which is taken up in every dialogue concerning state-tribal relationships of the nineteenth and twentieth centuries.

In this essay, a brief look at Lincoln and his administration's dealings with the Dakota Sioux Indians illustrates that racism takes many forms and its consequences are far-reaching. It says too that political expediency is a powerful incentive for historical acts as well as historical inaction, and Lincoln, after all, was a political man. Indeed this history can be illustrated with many comparisons. Few historians have described the destruction of Indian America in the 1800s, the time of Lincoln's presidency, as an Indian Holocaust, much like the Jewish Holocaust of Nazi Germany. This is a comparison not well received by many historians in the United States, but a statement that must be taken seriously if a sincere effort to understand the era of the westward movement is to be made. In my introduction to *New Indians, Old Wars,* I say this: "The first nations of America are rather like Israel, a country that exists conditionally."[3] The suggestion is that Israel is hated by its Arab neighbors and has a nuclear arsenal to defend itself second only to that of Russia and the United States. The American Indian is hated to death or loved to death depending on the white man's whim, and has been in the courts since 1940 to defend himself against greed and avarice, racism and discrimination. One can go too far with that thought, though, except to say that neither the Jews of Israel nor the unlucky Palestinians in Arab Country are the Indians of America because there is no question in America who invaded whose lands."

At the beginning of the twenty-first century, engaged as we are in a wounded era of national crisis, it is time to admit that the founding fathers of the United States, like the fathers of all nations, were not just good and wise. They were like all of us, both good and bad. And often not wise. They wanted freedom but owned slaves for two hundred years. Two hundred years! That was not just an error of judgment; that was an intentional federal policy. They wanted equality, but they meant equality exclusively for white male persons and fought a vicious war to defend that idea. They revered the right to religious freedom but empowered exclusively Christianity. They wanted opportunity, optimism, and freedom but devised a system of genocide and chaos for the Native inhabitants of the country, especially during what is now euphemistically called the westward movement, the period following the founding years—to be specific, the nineteenth century, called "a century of dishonor" by that most important historian, Helen Hunt Jackson. Lincoln emerged within this oppressive history and was never completely free of it.

American historians in the nineteenth and twentieth century wrote about the separation from England and the meaning of the frontier in American history, and the Federalists asking for "implied powers" and those involved in various domestic dissensions prior to the present time. These historians gave in to our nationalistic need for whitewashing the awful history of the later period. In reality, it is our charge now to do just the opposite. As scholars and thinkers and citizens, it is our business not just to look with admiration to those times for what we may consider the building of a democracy, but to explain how bad it was during those formative years for people who were overrun by powerful forces. Indeed many of those people—the Indians, the labor groups, and those in contest to defend new territories from those with power—have yet to recover from them.

The responsibility to tell how bad it was should not be left out of the discussion of "Abe Lincoln Looks Westward," which is the title of many writings and academic gatherings these days. In 2009, the bicentennial of Lincoln's birth, we history scholars reviewed his life and tragic assassination, and we reviewed the history of the westward period, wanting desperately to believe that now, in this period of contemporary renewal, when we have elected a black man to the presidency, is very much like the period of renewal that Lincoln sought. We really are loathe to express the reality that at the same time the white man's great civil war was being fought, Indians throughout the country were suffering through a genocidal period as vicious as any known in history. The serial abuses of democratic ideals in the forming of the United States correspond with any of the unspeakable acts of imperialistic impulses throughout the globe, yet the United States still wants to excuse itself. Thus much of the history of the Dakota Sioux is omitted as Lincoln looks westward. Even fiction writers have been on the bandwagon of celebration. A decade ago, for example, Gore Vidal, who ordinarily has nothing good to say about anyone, wrote a bestselling historical novel, *Lincoln,* calling attention to Lincoln's time in the West as he went about his presidency hanging Indians and consorting with his favorite general, Ulysses S. Grant, a dismal little man who became president on the basis of his reputation as an Indian fighter.[4] Together they set the stage for the eventual congressional theft of 7.7 million acres of treaty land from the Sioux Nation in Dakota Territory. Vidal's novel is often called a "novel of empire."

It is the view of some that Indian-hating has always been deeply embedded in the American character. The thinking that Lincoln was no exception, they say, may rationalize his inaction and inability to rein in the settler populations, states' rightists, thieves and criminals who stole the West from the people who had lived there for millennia. Lincoln was a man of his time and place. He was born a Kentuckian and grew up believing, as his countrymen did, that Indians were wild creatures without civilization or honor or government, to be shot down in the forests of the Blue Ridge like quail or squirrel. This was his personal attitude even though he knew, as a scholar and trained lawyer, that the Kentucky-landed Sauk and Fox, among other tribal nations, had lived there in communal and tribal dignity and safety for many decades. He knew that this so-called wilderness into which he was born was never an unoccupied place, as he and others wanted to imagine, yet this idea continued to gain agency during the early years of U.S. settlement.

In 1784 Lincoln's grandfather was killed by unknown persons in this supposedly vacant Kentucky, and naturally Indians were blamed. The old frontiersman's son, Mordecai Lincoln, an uncle of the man who would eventually be president, became a determined Indian hater and Indian stalker. This was not unusual in Kentucky and other western states. Following Miles Standish and Daniel Boone, one of the first fictional he-men to whitewash this national style of killing Indians was James Fenimore Cooper's Natty Bumppo. Many believe *The Last of the Mohicans* is sympathetic to Indians, yet it is clear that there is no place in the United States for them. The "vanishing American" is a major figure in the novel, which is still taught in every American literature course with little historical evaluation of it as outdated colonial thought.

That Indians were nomads, stateless and without government or civilization, luckless primitives to be "removed" in whatever way possible, was the thinking of Lincoln and his compatriots and accounts for the treatment of Natives in his time. To make a people unaccountable and stateless, political scholars will tell you, is the first step taken by colonists, invaders, imperialists and, yes, even democratizers, and is a tactic of genocide. Indeed Hannah Arendt, the revered Jewish scholar of the twentieth century, wrote in her essays on understanding the nature of totalitarianism, "[The] first step in the Nazis' destruction of the Jews was to make them stateless."[5] Since 1951 her papers have been available in the Library of Congress. Likewise, the United States made a mockery of the treaty process it undertook with American Indian nations and passed laws very much like the Nuremberg laws of Nazi Germany, stripping Indians of laws to protect them, such as in the 1883 *ex parte Crow Dog* case and the 1889 unconstitutional Allotment Act. These actions, which followed Lincoln's tragic and brief presidency, were presaged and not unconnected to the general climate of his time. For a very long period of Lincoln's adulthood he believed that whites were destined to possess this new land, that blacks should be colonized elsewhere (they had no place in the United States), and that Indians should be removed in whatever ways were palatable to the general public. Neither blacks nor browns had a place in the United States, as Lincoln had been taught by his forebears, and the euphemism "removal" would become a vicious federal policy that would last many decades.

Thus Lincoln and others in power in the United States acted on the belief that people with no stake in the political community of their new country had no right to the protection of its laws. Laws that did not protect Indians were promulgated during most of the nineteenth century. Blacks were to become citizens only after the bloody Civil War, while

Indians were to be forced onto reservations in the West as early as 1830. Blacks had no civil rights in this country for many decades because of the thinking of the general public of that time, and until the twentieth century were held in social and economic bondage. Indians did not receive the dual citizenship they now possess until they had struggled through sixty years of warfare and genocide in their own lands. Only after 1924 could they vote in this country as dual citizens (American and tribal nation citizens). By this time, they had lost two-thirds of their treaty-protected lands and have been colonized in endemic poverty ever since. This is an ugly history, and unfortunately Abraham Lincoln, busy with the Civil War, is often seen by historians as a tragic figure whose life was cut short by assassination but who is heroic for emancipating African slaves. Little is said of his acts toward the indigenous nations.

Anyone aspiring to political office in Lincoln's time had to win credits in Indian-white conflicts, which meant that young Lincoln, nephew of an Indian stalker, enthusiastically enlisted as an Indian fighter early on. He achieved success in the Indian Wars and, in his later writings, claimed his war experience was part and parcel of his political qualifications. Efforts at denying the right to tribal nation self-government and the civil rights of Natives as well as the lack of protection of the laws of the country began, of course, a century earlier than Lincoln's time, but became codified in the most inhumane way during the westward movement in the United States in which Lincoln was a major political force. Evidence of this is told by Native historians concerning the Black Hawk War and the Sauk and Fox, who were treaty Indians with citizenship rights to govern themselves and to live and hunt in their homelands, Lincoln's birthplace. In the *Collected Works of Abraham Lincoln*, Lincoln is shown to be a representative of his time and place, which meant, among other things, that he was unable to see the inchoate U.S. government, rather than a tool for justice for all mankind, as a capitalistic tool, its main function to gain and protect property.[6]

During Lincoln's time there were many exhibitions of "strange peoples," among them the "vanishing aborigines," the Inuit, and Geronimo. Like U.S. Presidents Theodore Roosevelt, Ronald Reagan, Jackson, and Grant, Lincoln came to love the notion of Indians no longer among the living and embraced the romantic myth of the United States "conquering" the indigenes. Their love of the "empty wilderness" was unbounded. As he took up the law, Lincoln learned to move on from the military to romanticize the past with the purpose of perpetuating the myth of the "vanishing" peoples. Colonization was the solution to those surviving such myths. When, during Lincoln's presidency, the United States was confronted not only by the Civil War but also by powerful Plains Indian nations like the Santee Sioux, rather than by smaller, more reticent tribes on the frontiers, Lincoln's notion of the U.S. government as the protector of property informed his actions. In 1862 the United States had acquired by grudging agreement all Santee Sioux lands except a strip ten miles wide and 150 miles long beside the Minnesota River in what is now the state of Minnesota. By this time, the familiar pattern of rigged treaties and invasion followed treaty making, and the Santees, who had lived in this area for hundreds of years, were beleaguered by encroaching whites. Their treaty payments did not come, and they starved and died of disease by the thousands. The Dakotas, having signed treaties in good faith, never lost an occasion to send imploring messages to the "great father" in Washington, asking for protection and advice, but Lincoln did nothing. Wars continued and horrific slaughters took place. The reformer Helen Hunt Jackson would be appalled several decades later, when she reviewed this period. She wrote, "The record of the massacres of that summer is scarcely equaled in the history of Indian Wars."[7]

The Sioux went to war. In Little Crow's War (often called "the outbreak" in Minnesota history) thousands were killed. It ended in "trials" and the largest public hanging in U.S. history of what might now be called "enemy combatants," at a frontier town called New Ulm, filled with immigrants from Denmark and Germany. After the war, President Lincoln was sent the names of 303 condemned Santees. He refused to authorize the immediate hanging of all of them because of lack of evidence, only a select few, but the Sioux have never been grateful for the reprieve. To this day, Dakota survivors say, they were not murderers or rapists or criminals and did not deserve hanging; they were Dakota patriots engaged in battle to save their lives and lands and to defend the treaties made with the United States. Thus Dakotas do not revere Lincoln for his authorization that sent thirty-eight Dakotas to be hanged as murderers and criminals. The Indians also do not believe that sending thousands more Dakotas to prison for life because they defended their homelands was an act of democratic ideals on the part of the Lincoln administration. Thus, they say, Lincoln is no hero for the treatment of their people, with whom the United States had signed solemn treaties. In the light of this history, they condemn the acts that saw their Dakota Sioux reservation, established by treaty, wiped off the map of the new state of Minnesota, They say there is no denying that it was done with the help of the "man of conscience," Abraham Lincoln, whose likeness is part of the "shrine of democracy" at Mount Rushmore in what is now the state of South Dakota.

The Sioux have husbanded a silent history of this time and note that they have lived on the Northern Plains from the Platte through the Dakotas to the upper Missouri for millennia. Fear had come to the Plains country, though, during the invasion of the West, when volunteer units of immigrants and U.S. citizens came rushing in to defend the invasion, citizen soldiers who had the same callous frontier attitude toward Indians that the Lincoln Kentuckians had. Some believe that the Indian-hating of the frontier Kentuckians prevails there even today.

Others wish to credit Lincoln as a man trained in the law when he was reported to have asked for a "complete record of the convictions" shortly after the Little Crow War ended in chaos and racial hatred. They say that he had his staff examine the cases to determine who was a murderer and who was engaged in battle, and that as a result of his intervention, only thirty-eight out of 303 condemned Dakotas were hanged. The remaining 1,700 Dakotas, accused of no crime except to be born Dakota, were sent to Fort Snelling, Minnesota, the Guantánamo Bay retention center of its day, to be stoned, clubbed, tortured, and held captive for years, some never returning to their homelands; some were even killed there. Their so-called trials were military tribunals, not courts of democratic law.

Stragglers and survivors of the Little Crow War were sent to Crow Creek and Nebraska Territory and Flandreau, where they languished in poverty for many years. In *Bury My Heart at Wounded Knee* Dee Brown details the consequences of federal Indian policy of the time and suggests that in spite of Lincoln's legal intervention, a policy that cannot yet be called a genocidal policy, a characteristic of the Lincoln years, prevailed for decades: "Among the visitors at Crow Creek much later was a young Teton Sioux. He looked with pity upon his Santee cousins and listened to their stories of the Americans who had taken their land and driven them away. Truly, he thought, that nation of white men is like a spring freshet that overruns its banks and destroys all who are in its path. Soon they would take the buffalo country unless the hearts of Indians were strong enough to hold it. He resolved he would fight to hold it. His name was Tatanka Yotanka, the Sitting Bull."[8]

This young man had twenty years to live before he was shot down by U.S. government troops on his own homeland, a few steps away from the Grand River in what would become the state of South Dakota. The policy of assassinating leaders of Native dissension and protest on the American frontier continued for many years, although no writer of the period called these deaths either murder or assassination. Indeed the killing of nearly three hundred unarmed Lakotas at Wounded Knee in 1890 was described as a "battle" for nearly a hundred years.

The federal policy of extermination, influenced by the presidency of Abraham Lincoln, the freer of African slaves, has been kept in motion and continues today in many places and in many ways. In spite of the conferences held during the first years of the new twenty-first century, the bicentennial of Lincoln's birth, it is the charge of Native historians everywhere to say that it is not appropriate to maintain a historiography suggesting that Lincoln was an innocent bystander to this tragedy. In the context of this past, historians must reassess their responsibility to the future. It is true that this terrible history cannot be changed. Yet if it is our responsibility to write, research, and reclaim the American Indian voice and experience outside of the colonial narrative that has been so destructive and pervasive, we have a great challenge to reclaim the meaning of past events.

Two native historians, Susan Miller (Seminole) and James Riding In (Pawnee), are doing just that. They have prepared a new anthology, *Native Historians Write Back*, published by Texas Tech University Press. These scholars have been influential in directing Indian studies as an academic discipline at Arizona State University, Tempe, for several years. Their collection, which grew out of conferences held at many U.S. universities in the past two decades, is an important contribution and should be on every scholar's library shelf. It was occasioned by an explosion of interest in cultural studies and is probably meant to offer a kind of user's guide to teachers and intellectuals who want to understand the political underpinnings of Indian-white relations in a postmodern age. These Native writers are attempting to develop a unique set of methodological practices in accordance with the disciplinary forces and theories of Native American studies.

A local South Dakota magazine editor and journalist, Florestine Kiyukanpi Renville, a Sisseton Wahpeton Dakota scholar living on the Lake Traverse Reservation, edited a journal called *Ikce Wicasta* for ten years.[9] In each issue, she saved a page to print the names of the thirty-eight Dakotapi who were hanged in Mankato in 1862: Tihdonica, Hepida, Mahpiya Ain-azin, Sunka Ska . . . The names, like most of the names of the indigenous victims of the United States, are forgotten and unknown to most of the residents of this region, with the exception of the Dakota nationalists and ancestors. Their legacy as defenders of the land are honored by Kiyukanpi Renville. A Dakota Commemorative March has been held by all of the Dakota communities in Minnesota and Dakota every year since 2002.

Closer to hand, and available since the spring of 2007, and, perhaps more regional in its approach, is a new Minnesota Dakota history, *What Does Justice Look Like?*, by Angela Cavender Wilson, a Cornell University scholar born and raised at the Dakota Yellow Medicine Village in Minnesota. Wilson tells us how Lincoln's administration responded to Native tribes and lands as he looked westward, and it is not a pretty picture. She says this about history and the historical institutions in the region: "The Minnesota Historical Society continues to resist using appropriate and accurate terminology such as 'genocide' and 'ethnic cleansing' and 'concentration camp,' preferring instead more benign terms that diminish the horror of Minnesota History. . . . It is not a reflection of ignorance, since The Minnesota History Society houses a lot of evidence within its archives." It is a deliberate historiography of omission and whitewash, Wilson asserts, perpetuated by one of the significant academic institutions in the region. Furthermore, she says, the Society, founded by a former state governor, Alexander Ramsey, is steadfastly upholding its corrupt legacy of democratic ideals cloaked in generations of racist and colonial policy toward the Dakotas. It does so without almost any critical assessment from other historical establishments, The question Wilson asks in her significant historical work would be asked of indigenous policy across the country, initiated when President Thomas Jefferson in 1807 advocated extermination of the tribes by declaring, "If we are to be constrained to lift the hatchet against any tribe we will not lay it down until that tribe is exterminated," and again in 1813 when he wrote, "The American Government has no other choice before it than to pursue the Indians to extermination." In these lines, Wilson tells us, is a sense of the vicious, collective anti-Indian policy that precedes even Lincoln's Kentuckian roots of Indian hating. She tells us that historians from the beginning have failed to make appropriate interpretations, and they continue to do so. Many of the new texts by Native scholars tell us outright that the "extermination" of Indians was the policy of the United States regardless of who was president in the 1800s, when

Lincoln was looking westward. Clearly, "What does justice look like?" is a question many non-Native historians refuse to ponder.

As more and more Native writers tell their true histories, and as the United States goes forward as a powerful global force invading and occupying other nations, we are forced to say "Shame on you." Realistic responses to the Lincoln period must occur. We must ask: Would it harm the United States to recognize its genocidal past to indigenous peoples with the intent to rectify historical crimes? To know them? To acknowledge them? What would happen to our pride in ourselves? Is it our fear that we will have to give up our fantasies of innocence and empire? Perhaps.

The divisive and dangerous years in American history I have described are very much like the awful years of any great nation. It takes all of us to acknowledge our concomitant histories to put things into perspective. It is useful to reiterate that one of the most influential military men of our time, General Colin Powell, in taking stock of the more recent colonial war, wrote, "A sense of shame is not a bad moral compass." He, like many others, can speak of massive mistakes made during the political eras just past and tells us that America's shame can be a vital force in redemption, if only we are brave enough to interpret and research the real history that we all share. Powell's comment suggests that if the United States continues to look at itself only with prideful admiration, we will not learn from the past.

If Lincoln, too, is viewed only in the hope that he was something other than he really was, if scholars continue to ignore the worst traits of his character, which might be his innate, hidden racism against indigenous peoples, the United States will probably not be led to the understanding of this nation's history necessary for the future nor the moral clarity that is sought.

Law

The Task of Justification

Because of twentieth-century studies in law and politics heralded by the Dakota Sioux scholar Vine Deloria, Jr., it is possible to move away from fantasies of history into such grinding topics as "tribal self-determination and the federal trust responsibility: collaboration or conflict," one of the subjects taken up in recent meetings of the Federal Bar Association, Indian studies enclaves, and elsewhere. This kind of subject matter has recently taken the place of Dee Brown's sorrowful *Bury My Heart at Wounded Knee* and Robert Utley's *Last Days of the Sioux Nation,* because there is a sense in Indian Country that their plight as people within a colonized government can, at last, seek attention from scholars who know what the score is, admit it, and move toward reconsideration.

Looking at the work of the historian Thomas Biolsi, we are reminded of where the real trouble lies. His book's title, *Deadliest Enemies*, comes from this 1886 Supreme Court phrase: "Because of local ill feeling, the people of the United States where Indian tribes are found and Indians themselves are often the deadliest of enemies."[1] That is worth repeating: "Because of local ill feeling, the people of the United States where Indian tribes are found and Indians themselves are often the *deadliest of enemies.*" In legal terms this means that *states* and Indian *tribes* are the deadliest of enemies. Biolsi suggests that state governments might be held responsible for their actions. Anyone who has examined the trajectory of Indian law of the past two centuries knows that states' rights, state governmental and legislative influence, is at the heart of anti-Indian law, as Biolsi documents. The erosion of the trust responsibility of the federal government and the erosion of treaty law has been and still is a consequence of statehood. Certainly as the history of the West unfolds, the organization of state governments beginning in the mid-1800s in Indian Country has been a flawed and racist development vis-à-vis Indian nationhood.

The year 1886, from which Biolsi's quote is taken, marks the Civil War, the fight for states' rights, the rise of state law, and a genocidal policy outlined in the U.S. Congress. The quote, buried as it is in legal wranglings, takes on importance in today's understandings of the function of the law. It was written mere decades after many treaties in the West were signed between the federal government and tribal governments, one year before Congress passed the Allotment Act, and four years before the largest massacre in this country, of hundreds of unarmed Minneconjou Lakotas at Wounded Knee, Dakota Territory.

Few serious scholars deny that the policies of 1886 reflected the aftereffects of thirty years of warfare with the western tribal nations and the setting forth of a federal policy of silence and neglect toward indigenous peoples. It was after the Civil War and after much anti-Indian legislation was passed to remove Indians from their homelands, during illegal settler occupation of Native lands; it was a time ripe for the dismantling of Indian nation autonomy, sustaining a period of genocide and poverty and ultimate extermination initiated in previous decades.

Few historians, even today, write clearly and unambiguously about this history and this policy of genocide. Some historians, from the scholars in the South Dakota Historical Society to Robert M. Utley, who writes for the Jefferson National Expansion Historical Association (*Indian, Soldier, and Settler*, 1979), have given voice to a larger mainstream voice that says tepees must be pulled down and Indians must disappear from the American scene. Musings by state and locals politicians who would remain largely unknown were taken up in the context of the morality of the legal thinking of the day. In the same year the commissioner's quote emerges in official documents, other documents, such as "Miscellaneous Document from the 40th Congress" appeared, stating, "Indians are to go upon said reservations. . . . They have no alternative but to choose between this policy of the government and extermination."[2] The "ill feeling" of local people identified by the Supreme Court was in agreement with the congressional policy, as evidenced in local newspapers. L. Frank Baum, the editor of the *Aberdeen Saturday Pioneer* in the northern city of Aberdeen, South Dakota, said, nine days before the Wounded Knee Massacre, three hundred miles to the south, "The Whites, by law of conquest, by justice of civilization, are masters of the American continent and the best safety of the frontier settlers will be secured by the total annihilation of the few remaining Indians." Five days after the Massacre, on January 4, 1890, he wrote in the *Pioneer*, "We have declared that our safety depends upon the total extermination of the Indians. . . . Wipe these untamed and untamable creatures from the face of the earth." He went on to write the most sweet-natured American story of them all, *The Wizard of Oz*.

These sentiments have been repeated throughout Indian Country, in spite of the mainstream fantasy that things are getting better. Today when we discuss the issues surrounding decolonization, which surely means tribal self-determination and the responsibility of honoring treaties, we must talk about them in terms of conflict, not collaboration. Because the policies set forth in this history have been codified in law in the courts of the land and are meant to be historicized as legal activity we must talk about these matters in terms of what happens when law itself becomes illegal and goes unchallenged.

As previously mentioned, this history has rarely been called genocide by American historians. Perhaps it has never been called genocide by law scholars either. Because that is probable, we come to the discussion at hand concerning trust with our ideas confused in an endless and unanswerable debate. This means that one of the important tasks of any Indian in the contemporary academic world is to force an examination of the question, *For how long will the courts and academia and the intelligentsia of this country refuse to describe this history as genocide?* And what is the consequence of that denial? If these events are not understood as genocide, then the question we are asking ourselves today about trust being collaboration or conflict is a moot question. Moot, as you all know, is an imaginary case argued by law students in a mock court, just an academic exercise without substance.

If history or events of history are rendered moot (or imaginary), then the discussion of postcoloniality remains a meaningless exercise as well. This is the dilemma of Indian law today: when history is falsified, denied, fantasized, or deliberately misunderstood for the sake of avoiding conflict, or when voices fall silent for any number of unnamed reasons, the events, even horrific ones, like massacres and land thefts, are without legal significance. The connection between accurate and fair history and just law is undeniable. In a colonized world, Indian land thefts carry particular significance and are the events most likely to suffer from historical malfeasance.

Some Native scholars have been writing on these subjects for thirty years, so it is useful to say a couple of things about the function of writers in the examination of such dilemmas as just mentioned. The function of writers can be useful if for no other reason than to try to direct the dialogue; thus it is important for writers to be part of the dialogue at gatherings of the Federal Bar Association, as directors of Indian studies enclaves at universities, and as politicians. It is not up to writers just in the legal profession to be part of the dialogue; writers from many other related disciplines must also participate.

The truth is, though, all sorts of writers write about politics and the law, and even though they are not lawyers many have had significant things to say. As an example, almost all classical literature, such as the marvelous Greek dramas—*Antigone, Oedipus,* the *Iliad,* with the Greek chorus going up and down the aisle chanting the appropriate interpretation of Greek law—are about politics and the law and justice. Shakespeare's plays, Victorian novels: these are political writings explaining the law.

Even today, novels such as *The Bonfire of the Vanities* and Richard Wright's *Native Son* are works concerning the law. I certainly consider my work, even my fiction, a common literary reaction to law. My first published novella, *From The River's Edge,* examined the illegal flooding of hundreds of thousands of acres of treaty-protected land all up and down the Missouri River and the struggle by the Sioux Nation to survive despite the U.S. government, the law, and American justice.[3]

These works and many others are about the tragic consequences of politics and the law. It would seem that as far as literature is concerned the law has a lot to answer for. The experience of the Sioux, described in *From the River's Edge,* tells us this: The failure of the federal government's trust responsibility to the Sioux Tribe concerning the theft of lands and rights, and to all the tribal nations of this country is a notorious failure, has been for generations and continues to be. A book I wrote with the Oglala lawyer Mario Gonzalez entitled *The Politics of Hallowed Ground: Wounded Knee and the Struggle for Indian Sovereignty* documents in specific terms that land, the loss of land, and the theft of land is at the heart of the decisive and dangerous U.S. law as it applies to Native nationhood. It is land theft that has declared for all to see that Native nations without statehood, without government, and without law necessary to protect them will not survive the coming centuries. That is why the study of law in Indian studies, as it applies to land cases particularly, should be a primary focus. That is why colonization, which begins with the taking of land from others, must be described as criminal behavior, regardless of the promulgation of laws that make it seem to be a reasonable enterprise.

While some may argue that much of this dilemma has been attended to by recent legislation and state government action, specifically by state-tribal compacts and various agreements, coalitions recently established, reconciliation movements, and various law remedies, there is little evidence that the law can correct itself without massive upheaval and land return. The return of lands to tribal nations is being contemplated by federal government planners, as far as can be discerned in discussions of the law and American Indians, but only because of vigorous political action by tribal officials.

Yet schemes to take even more land from Indians are always on the planning board. Recently the U.S. Congress has been examining what is being called "land transfer" legislation for the Northern Plains. The bill has been promoted by Congressman Bill Janklow, previously a four-term governor of South Dakota, who conspired with many but certainly with the longtime senator from South Dakota, Tom Daschle, to put in front of the public what is called the South Dakota Land Transfer and Wildlife Habitat Mitigation Act of 1997. It sounded to the public like a good idea. They were told that this is good law concerning the Missouri River, but it is really designed to diminish Sioux Nation tribal sovereign status in the arena of law, to claim land for the state, and to claim jurisdiction over hunting, fishing, and tourism. Looking at that legislation carefully (put together by very clever lawyers and politicians), one will see that it is another land grab by the state and that it will benefit no band of the Sioux tribe along the Missouri River on a long-range basis. *It is wrong law and it is wrong history.* Yet it is touted as a measure to (as the governor and congressmen have said) "put to rest" all jurisdictional conflicts and troubling questions over water and hunting and fishing and tourism. It will, the bill's initiators said, "put to rest all jurisdictional questions," a panacea. Tribal leaders have concluded that it is a way for the federal government to get out of its trust responsibility to Native peoples, and give land, once protected by treaty, to the state of South Dakota.

The false claim that conflict can be avoided through heavy-handed federal legislation fails to recognize this reality of history: the tribes do not need this legislation to protect water rights, nor to reserve and protect Native hunting and fishing rights along the river. These rights are implicit in treaty and history. According to treaty negotiations of past decades, tribal nations have the right to use, to administer, to control, and to exercise their property rights independent of state control and interference.

In a previous work, I wrote:

> The kind of legislation that prevails, unfortunately, brought to bear by pressure from state officials, the Secretary of Interior, and officials of the federal government, should be recognized for what it is, a failure of the "fiduciary" responsibility of the federal government and an effort to drastically limit the claims of Indians. In the kinds of "reconciliation" legislation offered here, something called "settlements" are undertaken. These "settlements" attempt to convince the tribes that their rights are being preserved and protected. But, in actuality, their rights are being sacrificed over and over again in the furtherance of the needs of greedy water monopolists and states' rightists. Non-reservation based farmers. Hog producers. Cattlemen. We should know that. And we do know that. The deception practiced by the Secretary of the Interior to seize the invaluable reserved rights to the use of water from the tribes was known when the Great Sioux Nation lost its rights in the Pick-Sloan plan. Indeed, that was a superb example of the kind of manipulation in native/states/federal relations that we are so accustomed to. No one should feel that the future is secured by the now-agreed-upon Mni Sosa Water Coalition because what that coalition does in actuality is it denies the *sovereign* rights of native water holders and does nothing at all to ensure an economically sound future for Indian Reservation long-term development.[4]

If this kind of legislation is put into the context of colonization, or decolonization, or postcoloniality, as much of the academic world is wont to do, it is clear that such terms have no meaning. These acts are not acts that can assist in throwing off the bondage of colonialism because they do nothing to assist an Indian nation toward autonomy, nothing to lessen economic and fiscal and governmental dependency, and nothing to clarify the situation of federal enclaves placing federal law at the pinnacle of the powerbase for the future.

Not long ago, I was at a meeting in Denver, pointing out some of this history to an audience, and a young white man, a graduate student, asked, "Well, what do you want us to do?" This is a guy probably getting an MBA, or, worse yet, a Master's of Fine Arts, and so the question what do you want us to do is surely a rhetorical one from his point of view. Truth is, though, I don't want that young man to do anything *except to know this history.* His generation must know this history, and he must know that much of what results from this history in terms of the law *is wrong*— politically, ethically, morally, and legally. In truth, what must be said to this young man is, *little can be done about history except to know it.* History is past, but as an American citizen, his question is pertinent. What Indians want is a fair playing field, and this young man must access historical archives to know that there is nothing "fair" in a colonial and imperialistic history that oppresses Native populations. Rather, this history expresses elimination as a solution. It is a throwback to the "vanishing American" theory we long thought had been rendered unworkable.

The law is present. It is ongoing. It is an organic thing. It can change and rehear itself. It is like eating: we can't stop eating as we cannot stop the law if we expect to live and be healthy. We must have food. Like any sustenance, the law cannot be stopped; if we expect to live and be healthy we must have the law. Yet much of Indian law is simply wrongheaded and unhealthy. It is interesting that one is urged not to say it is immoral. The concept of moral wrong has no agency in the law itself, many scholars have said, because morality is a religious matter. Thus, there is no way to address morality in the law because it is a religious matter.

Many who have lived the colonial existence of indigenous nationhood, however, have witnessed moral wrong. Some, especially those who have suffered as victims of rigid colonialism, know that the concept of moral wrong exists in Indian law. Those people say that it was wrong to snatch Indian children away from their parents and force them by law into federal boarding schools, prisons really, thousands of miles away from home and family. It was wrong to force the Allotment Act upon communal societies to express individualism rather than tribalism. It was wrong to massacre unarmed Minneconjou men and women and children at Wounded Knee who were protesting land theft, and give the murderers medals of honor. More medals were awarded to those killers than were awarded in World War II, the reason being that the massacre had to be described in history as a "battle" rather than a massacre of unarmed people.

If we accept the concept of moral wrong in Indian law, we are forced to confront the *task of justification*. The *task of justification*, it often seems, is what Indian law is all about. As is often mentioned, it is also the task of American history. Many observers of the American scene know that wrong law toward Indians has been justified, not only in academics and history, not only at Wounded Knee, but in the courtrooms of this country as well. The United States makes and enforces laws all the time that are prima facie undesirable for those who are stripped of the power to resist. These laws are undesirable because they involve the curtailment of some of the most fundamental of human values, such as freedom, national autonomy, and self-determination as a people. Federal Indian law has curtailed the values of the Sioux Nation, the Ocheti Shakowan, by outlawing traditional ways of behaving and replacing them with something formal and foreign.

How, then, and why are these laws justified? The answer lies in a European, Western, Christian mode of justice.

First, such laws are justified by the principle underlying an accepted mode of reasoning. Rational thinking is, after all, the mode by which civilizations can thrive. Ironically, when the Greeks put Socrates to death for his protests against what he considered wrong thinking, when they fought a twenty-seven-year war with Sparta and then made slaves of Spartans and put to death all Spartan male children, they justified and defended the law by saying, *We are called a democracy and we must have law that does the most good for the most people. We must have law that defends our style of life, which is refined above all others. The law secures equal justice to all alike because we are a democracy. The fruits of the whole earth flow in upon us,* or words to that effect.

For the Western mind, then, and perhaps for all the world, this thinking justifies the death of millions across the globe. It justifies massacre and war. It justifies the curtailment of human values. It justifies the wrongness of the legal process. And for American Indians, it has justified their colonization for several centuries.

Second, such laws are justified because it has been demonstrated that the employment of this reasoning is superior to other kinds of reasoning. Often the rationale is given that while democracy is not a perfect form of government it is better than any alternative, and what is done in the name of democracy is not done in self-interest, but in the interest of civilization itself. This is still the mantra of public and journalistic expression as we look at the current wars in the Middle East.

The military and their civilian counterparts can always find excuses for their sworn obligations. "We hated to kill those savages but it was for the good of mankind," said the military men at the graves of Wounded Knee. Many newspapers of the time did not express such communal regret, calling Sitting Bull, the major opponent of the Allotment Act, a "greasy savage," a description that has gone down in historical archives so readily that one even forgets where it originated. These are the ways that the moral wrongness of the law persists.

As we know, there was a time when it was not morally wrong in this country for one person to own another person (a black person, of course) for profit. This was justified in law. When it could no longer be justified, it became illegal. Not without argument, you understand. Legal argument. But *a certain reasoning to right a wrong became superior* in the argument and overruled other kinds of arguments, economic ones, for example. This is the way that the law of a particular civilization meets new obligations.

As far as Indian law and Indian justice are concerned, no one need be told that the Indian First Nations of America are the most rigidly colonized enclaves in this country or in many other democratic societies. There are no banks and few businesses on Indian reservations. Land is held "in trust" by the federal government. There is no tribal tax system. Law has said that enforced colonization for Indians is legal, and the federal government has primacy over its colonies. And so the legacy of colonization, poverty, and apathy is everywhere in Indian law and history. Colonial strategies are the basis for the Mitigation Act and the basis for the theft of the Black Hills, the basis for the killing of eighty million Indians on this continent in fewer than a hundred years. Recently the flooding of thousands of acres of Native homelands for hydropower enriched the state and others, but not the Indian tribes. These are just a few of the details of how it is for colonies of the federal government.

There are literally thousands of cases in Indian Country justified by the legacy of colonization. Schools. Religious practice. The most important legacy of colonial thinking directed toward the indigenous peoples, say many scholars, is about land and it is this: the United States really owns the land.[5] Therefore, the reasoning goes, the U.S. government will hold the land "in trust" and will keep a colonial government in place in perpetuity.

What has happened to the law in the American Indian experience is that enforced colonization by law and colonial practice has resulted in the reality that the colonial legacy has been justified. It is justified in almost every case that the tribes take to court these days. It is embedded in a claimed concept called "plenary power" of the U.S. Congress.

There are no easy answers, but the most obvious wrong in Indian law and the most ubiquitous failure of the trust responsibility toward Indian nations is the misuse of political authority. Natives can vote to express what they think about how they are governed, but their minority voices are seldom heard. It is not useful to use these arguments to bash lawyers and the law because this political authority, we are told, comes from "the people." If you agree with that argument, the Indian minority vote can be said to be a part of the "democratic process." Congress has made attempts to rectify this problem by passing civil rights legislation since the 1970s, yet most of that was an attempt to further restrict tribal governments vis-à-vis their own constituents, rather than give the minority colonial Indian voice power in a system that holds out little hope for political survival.

To reverse the prima facie wrongness of Indian law and the trust matters involved in Indian law, I offer the following suggestions. These are actions to be called for by ordinary people, not by lawyers, who are trained to uphold the law.

Thinking people everywhere can, first, disobey some specific laws, as the treaty Indian fishermen did in Washington State in 1970. They managed to change sixty years of wrongful laws against them. People could, one supposes, stage a revolution or a coup d'état; the Indians in Peru have not had much luck with that, but ask the Pueblos. One should remember, though, that civil disobedience and political agitation in the mode of the midcentury American Indian Movement can be effective. Indeed in the 1960s and 1970s, AIM changed wrongful attitudes and laws that had been in place for decades. Amendments to the Constitution could be written, as some law historians have suggested. There is more about this in part IV of this text.

Failing these efforts, it is important that scholars continue to write and practice law. One of the most important Indian scholars, David E. Wilkins, gives us one of the most important suggestions to date. In the final pages his book *American Indian Sovereignty and the U.S. Supreme Court*, concerning law and Indians, he writes, "We must somehow work to disavow the use of plenary power and repudiate the despised, outmoded, and always inaccurate doctrine of discovery."[6] That must be done within the parameters of treaty law, and it must be done because these ideas are the basis for the wrongness in Indian law. Wrongness, Wilkins notes, is built into Indian law because of these aforementioned concepts, and in every case, in every examination of history and experience, it is good to remember that democracies (no matter how virtuous or how flawed) cannot last if the law is unjust. This is not a threat; this is a historical reality. Unless this democracy corrects its flaws and fantasies concerning indigenous law, outdated, ill-founded, and unworkable discriminations throughout the law profession will fester.

Knowing that, the future of the United States, one of the important democracies ever known to humanity, can learn much from its failures in Indian law—if it chooses to do so. The wobbly nature of democracy at this very moment is witness to the U.S. government's "preemptory invasion" of a nation thousands of years old on the other side of the world, attesting to that reality. The unaccountable invasion of Iraq is perhaps the most obscene, cruel, and violent imperialist invasion since Custer elbowed his way into the sacred Sioux lands for gold, a vision of democracy forever corrupted.

To go about teaching, writing, and committing our work to public scrutiny for legal reorganization and justice there is hope: everywhere in the Indian world there remains a fierce commitment to the principle that the tribal nation must remain the primary forum for collective self-government and moral law. This means that the larger state does *not* define Native nationhood. And this means that there are many conflicts ahead. It is unwise and illogical to think otherwise.

The final consideration of the function of the law vis-à-vis this country's indigene is its unconscionable acceptance of America's five centuries of fraud by lawyers, political leaders, and scholars alike. This reality was expressed most recently in an op-ed piece in the Native newspaper *Indian Country Today*, a newspaper located in Canastota, New York; the columnist, Peter d'Errico, a man few of us have heard of publicly over the years but a writer of considerable merit, a consulting attorney on indigenous issues and a man well-known in the legal professions who has taught legal studies at Amherst for many years, indicated in this op-ed that it is time to overrule some of these wrongful precedents in Indian law.[7] He writes in this article as well as in other venues about the wrongful precedents in Indian law, accusing Supreme Court Justice Antonin Scalia of showing his contempt for indigenous rights (in the *Carcieri v. Salazar* decision) by parroting the colonial mantra, "The U.S. has a right to rule over Indians by 'conquest.'" In this remarkable falsehood, d'Errico says, Scalia is pretending the same thing the United States has been pretending since John Marshall first pretended it in 1823 in *Johnson v. McIntosh*, the "pretension of converting the discovery of an inhabited country into conquest." D'Errico goes on to say, "The actual basis of federal Indian law, as Marshall's quote shows, is not conquest, but the 'pretense of conquest' based on 'Christian Discovery' and 'ultimate dominion.' This is what Scalia's comment covers up. Marshall, at least, had the honesty to call it what it was."

D'Errico is not the first scholar to come to these conclusions and to say these things publicly. Certainly Vine Deloria, as a mentor to such Native voices as Tom Holm, David Wilkins, Edward Valandra, leaders of the National Congress of American Indians, and countless others throughout academia, espoused these principles for decades and wrote many books useful to teaching indigenous law as it was meant to be taught by justice seekers. What makes d'Errico's manifesto concerning the infamous Marshall decision and the resultant body of law of the past century so incendiary is the fact that he calls out John Echohawk, the executive director of the Native American Rights Fund (NARF), for his seeming "acceptance" of this pretense. D'Errico charges that the "culture of acceptance" pervades law offices both Indian and white, as well as law schools, and it is a charge that has been whispered in the halls of tribal offices for years.

According to d'Errico, when an interviewer from *Indian Country Today* asked Echohawk in 2009 whether or not there was a challenge to Congress's claim to "plenary power," he responded, "Yes, but of course under the law of this country, the way all that's been interpreted and the way it has been litigated as the tribes are 'domestic dependent nations' and that's just the way things are and you go to court and that's what they'll tell you."

D'Errico says that NARF's acceptance of the "pretense of conquest" in this particular instance, saying "that's just the way things are," is an ominous sign, but predictable. D'Errico says this means the "most widely recognized group of Indian lawyers is not arguing against the basic discrimination in federal law." Everyone reading this exchange knows that this reality is not just unfortunate. It is a reflection of a deep and unthinkable continuation of domination in federal law.

D'Errico's charge: "The culture of acceptance of the pretense of federal Indian law prevails not only at NARF, but also in law schools, even in Indian law programs." This has been talked about in private conversations on Indian reservations for years by those who have never seen the inside of a law school, but of course, these kinds of tacit protests are most often dismissed as rumors, unhelpful and spiteful remarks, with no bearing on the reality of the stubbornness of U.S. law toward the indigenes. Everyone will agree with this scholar, however, who says what we all know: "Federal Indian law is still bound by racist others who often agree with the assessment of these matters." D'Errico graduated from Yale Law School in 1968, was staff attorney in Dinebeiina Nahiilna Be Agaditahe Navajo Legal Services from 1968 until 1970.

In 2009, with the nomination of Sonia Sotomayor to the Supreme Court of the United States, the sacredness of "the law," which may be at the heart of this dismissal d'Errico speaks of, pervades the hearings that are publicized on television and in subsequent writings. The nominee, bombarded with questions of her "philosophy of the law," was adamant in her claim that as a judge in the federal system for over a dozen years, she has honored precedent and follows the law according to the facts of the case, that she is not an advocate, nor is she, heaven forbid, an activist. In an American legal system based on European, colonial precedents (i.e., the Norman Conquest and all that), sharing a vocabulary and so making such concepts easily translatable, this steadfast adherence to "the law" by barristers of all stripes in the so-called New World is troubling to some who desire change in the law.

The conclusion reached by many, including this writer, is that federal Indian law as it has developed over the centuries is really colonial law developed over the years by a capitalist society mainly interested in the acquisition and protection of land title and assets. That it does not protect the welfare of indigenous landlords is a given. The law protects the law, not Indians. Having said that, however, most scholars will admit that there is no question that legal protections for the indigenes are necessary in what exists as the struggle for primacy in the federal-tribal-state paradigm of jurisdiction in the law. These matters are usually centered in treaty agreements. The legal paradigm of nations-with-a-nation is a fragile concept with massive possibilities for corruption of democratic ideals, especially when examined within the constant legal battle between federalists and states'-rightists so characteristic of U.S. policy since the late 1800s. To cling to such colonial-based law is probably a rationalization (in self-flattering ways) that all is well in the seeking of justice.

When young Indian legal professionals are confronted with this perception, long silences follow, and one feels only compassion for law students who need to have teaching institutions spend more time developing cause-and-effect models using indigeneity as a category of analysis. That silence will continue until law schools determine that a revolution in how they teach the law is essential.

"No more," says d'Errico, "should anyone say that 'plenary power' is just 'the way it is.' No more should anyone be afraid to tell a court that the 'pretense of conquest by discovery' is 'outdated, ill-founded, unworkable, or otherwise legitimately vulnerable to serious reconsideration.'"

Law in a perfect world based in democracy adapts to experience and greater understanding, we are told, but too often that ideal is not met in the reading and teaching of Indian law.[8]

Part II

Imponderables

"Imponderables," we are told by definers of words, are those matters that are incapable of being measured or verified with precision. Part II, then, is a respite from the call for justice of the first part of this text, a move away from theories and encounters that have to do with the law and into the challenges of what some call modernism, taking up the facts of an academic life and the fate of all of us who try to go in two opposed and, in my opinion, ridiculous directions at once.

7

Just a Thought

When I was ten years old, a French Algerian named Albert Camus was writing "The Myth of Sisyphus," all the while wondering about the existence of God. He was enduring the Nazi occupation of his country in the midst of two wars, double twentieth-century disasters in Europe, and I was living with relatives near a *kudwichacha sma sma* creek that had been a tributary to the Missouri River for thousands of years. We probably weren't wondering about God, but we, too, knew about war, living as we were on an Indian reservation that began as a concentration camp for the Eastern Sioux Dakotas who in 1862 had fought the same tyranny in the Little Crow War and later at the Big Horn. We too, perhaps, were *existentialists*, like Camus, finding meaning in disaster.

Years later, when I began to understand the poverty of where I came from and knew that the law did not protect my people, the Dakotas, I read Camus's essays in college classes and wondered if the gods had condemned the American Indian in the same way that he had condemned Sisyphus. Then I wrote:

At the time when descendants of Goethe had begun their massive, secret march through Belgium, in those years before the United States entered World War I, there lived near Fort Pierre one Joseph Shields, a fifty-year-old Sioux Indian who in his own way knew something of the rise of brutal doctrines, something of the destruction of ancient civilizations, something of a change of worlds. Though the tyranny of those years would be evident to the world by the crushing of innocent people all over Europe, the perilous-ness of them seemed remote to old Shields, not at all like the years he remembered from the shadows of his past when his family hid out in caves along the river, the Mni Sosa, surreptitiously kept watch on the movements of the U.S. Army troops, wondered aloud about the business of the Seventh Cavalry, Sibley, Thompson, Sheridan, about the new troops they could not identify, who they were and what they wanted here in Sioux Country.[1]

Since that time, I've tried to follow Camus's impulse: "As soon as the mind reflects on itself, its first step is to distinguish what is true from what is false." There are limits, of course. There are vicious circles and, often, as he says, "the mind gets lost in a giddy whirling."[2]

8

Citizen! Citizen!

. . . . the Absurdist . . . . 2009 A.D.

. . . . preface to foolishness, vagaries and blunders;
farce, even.

A month after I was given an award called "An Indian Living Treasure" by the governor of the state of South Dakota (who knew?), I
was asked to speak at the Naturalization Ceremony for twenty-five
new Americans at the U.S. District Court in downtown Rapid City. Apparently feeling smug about my new status, and thinking that dead writers
are often "treasures" but living ones seldom are, I reluctantly accepted the
invitation. Is there some responsibility, perhaps, in being a "treasure"?

As I entered the room, the potential citizens were seated in jury-like
seats in front of me, looking like this whole impending drama was an
ordeal, scary and uncomfortable. The kiss of death. They were from places like China, Cuba, the Dominican Republic, Mexico, Russia. Names
like Gonzalez and Grimley, Silvana and Vladimir were on the applicant
sheets.

I was introduced by Judge D. as a Crow Creek Sioux poet, novelist,
and scholar. The judge said it was her "great privilege" and that I had been
born at Fort Thompson, South Dakota.

I looked about apprehensively. I said a few words to them in my tribal
language to welcome them: "Nape ciyuzapi do. Mitakuyapi, owasin cante
wasteya" (I come before you and shake hands with a good heart).

Then, what next?

I was sure they had never read a word of the six or eight books I had written.

Lining the walls were black-and-white photos of white male judges who had presided there since 1860.

I shuffled my notes. To begin, I distributed an indigenous map and said, "This is what America looked like before it was America."

The applicants put the map on their laps and studied it as though they would be given a posttest.

"Surely you know," I went on, "that there are indigenous peoples all over the world, and up there [pointing], near what is the Canadian border, is the Sioux Nation, called there Dakota, Nakota, Lakota. Yes. They are called on this map Santee, Yankton, Teton. That indicates the three dialects of our language," I explained.

I named the nine Indian reservations in the state, slowly and carefully. "They make up the Seven Council Fires of the Sioux Nation."

"You know too, perhaps," I went on, "that a true democracy like ours here in the U.S. is troubled by the presence of Native peoples."

The twenty-five potential citizens stared. They seemed genuinely puzzled.

Should I mention thirty years of warfare right here where we stand, the theft of seven million acres of treaty land, genocide, poverty?

They looked at me and again at the map.

What? What? We want to be citizens.

"It's because," I said apologetically, "tribes are organized by blood, by clans, *tiospayes*, bands, not one man–one vote, not individualism, not equality, not colonization.

"You know, former President George Bush has said, 'As Americans, we are not united by blood. . . . We are not united by religion or geography. We are united because we are dedicated to freedom.'"

Silence.

"Obama says it too.

"But American Indians have reason to think carefully about that statement . . . yes, very carefully," I managed, as the twenty-five began to frown.

How did I get here? Standing in front of twenty-five supplicants to America and a hundred of their relatives in seats behind us.

I plunged on.

"Now, you have probably been taught about the Civil War, slavery, about America's brave fight for independence from England, a brave and founding epoch, a landmark for America's marvelous beginning. Yes? But you have been taught very little about the cruelty of land theft, the breaking of treaties, the cruelty of colonization.

"Is that so?"

I looked about the room, the stricken judge, the little stubby man from the Order of Elks holding twenty-five small flags, the Daughters of the American Revolution representative, who was all of a sudden examining her shoes. The pre-citizens sat politely.

I said some more things, about history, about the Congressional Act of 1924 that made the Sioux citizens of the United States.

"My father was a full-blooded Santee Sioux. He was in the army in World War I before he was a citizen," I told them. "Thousands of Indians have fought for this country, this land."

I didn't mention that my grandson has been in Fallujah, Iraq, in the Marines for a nearly a year.

I talked about the traits of a democracy, the Constitution, and then said, "You know, in the beginning, citizenship was just for white males who owned property. Women could not vote. Blacks could not vote. Indians were exempt from the Constitution and the Bill of Rights.

"Now, though, yes, we've come a long way."

My mouth was dry, and I felt desperate.

"Um-m . . . well, maybe I can tell you a funny little story about the Crazy Horse Monument. You've all been there, surely, at the mountain." My voice trailed off as though I had asked a question.

"Everybody goes there, to the monument."

An elderly white woman in a long unbuttoned tweed coat, nodded. So I smiled.

They say this:
"Keyapi: on the mountain, Crazy Horse is pointing
to a place 'over there, where my dead lie buried,'
in response to the white man sculptor's question:
'Where are your homelands?' Just then, the
white man made a mistake. He set the dynamite
under the pointing finger of Crazy Horse and,
accidentally, he blew the finger clean off. Now,

in response to the question, Crazy Horse simply
lifts his chin and points with his lips."

The twenty-five looked at me as though I had lost my mind. Sympathy oozed from them collectively.

The judge, fiddling with her pen, paled. The chubby little man from the Order of Elks stood gamely by, clutching his twenty-five small American flags ready for distribution, waiting for me either to implode or cry. One by one, sixth graders from Riverside School were introduced, and they each read their poems, all entitled "What America Means to Me." Finally, four elderly white men billed as "a Shining Democracy Barbershop Quartet" marched to the front of the courtroom and sang "God Bless America."

Mercifully, the honor guard retired the flags.

Later the Altrusa Club ladies served refreshments in an anteroom. One of the coffee servers said, "I think I didn't get it. About Crazy Horse. Was he nodding because he didn't want to point?"

A pale skinny girl with lanky blond hair came over to me with her coffee cup in her hand, introduced herself as the granddaughter of the long-deceased sculptor of the Crazy Horse Monument, and asked without a smile, "What did Crazy Horse have to do with . . . with . . . this?"

A young man wearing a jacket stamped with the logo U.S. ARMY shook my hand and said, "I really liked your speech. I'm from the Philippines, you know. I think what you said was very interesting." He put on his cap and left without speaking to anyone else, clutching his citizenship papers.

One of the sixth graders, chomping a cookie, smiled up at me.

"You did good," he said.[1]

9

The Cynical Tourist

Middle English tells us that the base of *tourist* is "a turning." The French *tour*
comes from "turn," or a "circepiguit." From Latin the base word is *tornus*, a
tool for drawing a circle, which means, perhaps, that
you end up where you started?

If not "citizens," "settlers," or "immigrants," who want something for
"free" in Indian Country, then the person most ubiquitous on the road
these days is the one who is traveling unknown lands "for pleasure." Ah,
yes, the tourist. For "free."

In order for the tourist to take a comprehensive trip with visits to places
of established interest, colonialism, as a policy by which a nation (in this
case, the United States) maintains or extends its control over foreign dependencies (the tribal nation governments all across the land), is essential.

There is nothing more cynical in the coloniality suffered for centuries
by the tribal nations than the issue of tourism in Indian Country. The pathetic efforts of contemporary American Indian leaders initiating economic projects under the oppressive influence of the bureaucracies of the U.S.
government is beyond scornful. Beyond mocking. The absurd notion that
the feds hold lands and resources "in trust," requiring constant monitoring and overt supervision, all the while mouthing notions of Native nation
sovereignty, should not be taken seriously by anyone who understands the
genius of selfishness and greed in a capitalist democracy.

I am often asked to sit in on discussions of economic development in the cities and towns and villages surrounding the nine enclaves of the Sioux Nation (called Indian reservations) and am given the chance to witness the practices of domination, subordination, antagonism, conflict, and outrageous compliance by people of goodwill inherent in the colonial condition of American Indian bureaucracies.

The following narrative stems from a conference I attended in Denver at the Renaissance Hotel in the fall of 2005. It was called the Denver Conference on Tourism, and I was there at the invitation of a friend connected with urban-tribal affairs. The issues facing the Indian nations of North America as we go into the twenty-first century are not very different from those of the past two hundred years (how to make a living now that the buffalo are gone), but on this day we were assigned to discuss the session titled "Tourism Attractions or Sacred Sites? Badlands, Sand Creek and Grand Canyon." The conflict needed little explication since experienced veterans of the economic and political wars were there. John Yellowbird Steele from the Oglala Sioux Tribe of Pine Ridge, South Dakota, was in attendance. Alexxa Roberts of the National Park Service of Colorado and Ed Natay of the National Park Service of New Mexico were there, and a select group of Native bureaucrats as well as entrepreneurs were on hand. They were gathered together at the invitation of some entity called the Native Tourism Alliance.

I chaired the session and made introductions. By way of getting started I introduced myself and said, the truth is, I have almost nothing good to say about the bureaucracies of the United States of America as they apply to Native life, and even less to say about the virtues of tourism. I admitted that I talk about tourism almost in the same way that I talk about strip mining in the Northwest and uranium mining across the country, the destructive dam building in my part of the country, and a hundred other outrages. This introduction did not endear me to the participants, who really were there to make some positive headway. They looked at me dismissively.

The conference began, and there were many important speakers and points of view. What I gathered from the speakers' interests was nothing new. For me, the relationship of the tribal nations to the bureaucracies of the United States of America, and in this case, and for this conference, was dominated by the need to say who was in charge. It became obvious during the presentations that the tribal nation relationship to the National

Park Services vis-à-vis tourism demonstrated what has always been the historical reality. It is a relationship in which the U.S. bureaucracy needs to legitimize its claim to primacy, and the tribal nation needs to establish its legacy. This is not a pleasant thing to think about, especially in this era of the rise of sovereignty in tribal nationalism, but it is true, and everyone in the room knew it.

Because of their beginnings during the U.S. expansionist eras following the treaty-making period, these U.S. bureaucracies have struggled for power over Indian land and resources in spite of the lip service they give to their role as protectorate. As most knowledgeable people recognize, in 1905, during Teddy Roosevelt's "big stick" tenure, the policy toward Indians and their lands was disenfranchisement and genocide. It wasn't merely to diminish tribal nation power and achieve primacy, it was also to promote the "vanishing American" theory. Congress created the National Park Service about ten years later, in 1916, and together these federal entities worked to "open up" in any way possible Indian lands protected by treaty. It was a period of incredible greed, theft, and subsequent legislative violence and criminality. These bureaucratic entities, as we know, followed on the heels of the criminal period called the Allotment Period.

There is an awful reality to this history. In the process of developing these federal bureaucracies Native Americans have been deprived of land and deprived of their relationship with homelands across the country. Yet if you read anything on this matter, even *American Indians and National Parks* or *National Parks: The American Experience,* there is little expression and no definition of "ancestral lands" and "sacred sites," two concepts at the heart of this controversy.[1] Two federal departments, agriculture and interior, are the seats of power for all of this, and their dialogue with Congress concerns day-to-day management. It does not seriously include sacred lands or ancestral lands, and seldom is there mention of indigenous rights of tribes.

In a book that I wrote with the Oglala attorney Mario Gonzalez, *The Politics of Hallowed Ground,* we had this to say:

> The Institution of the National Park Service came into existence in 1916. The Forest Service was instituted in 1904 as the result of the expansionist policies of Teddy Roosevelt who was then the president of the United States. These Agencies have a long and troubling history of intervention and public service actions. They are accused by the tribes across

the country of taking lands ostensibly for "public domain" but for many other unstated reasons, giving out ecologically questionable leasing permits and grazing permits, developing tree farms instead of forests, selling the timber which should be a major asset for tribes, building roads for tourists and illegal hunting, and a hundred other violations.[2]

The argument goes on.

Of late, there is the issue of ancestral bones and burial remains, and laws have been promulgated, ostensibly, to protect Indians, but more often than not they protect other interests. The Kennewick Man issue in Washington State is an example of protecting science against the Umatillas. The theft of a Tyrannosaurus rex is an example of protecting "personal property rights" and "museum rights" instead of the indigenous rights of the Cheyenne River Sioux Tribe in South Dakota. There are blatant examples that litter this history, dozens more one could name. To connect the dots, these complaints mean that the "colonization" of American Indian rights and resources is ongoing, perpetrated by bureaucracies with profit margins in mind. People like to talk these days about the "postcolonial," but those of us who attend these kinds of tourism conferences know that the United States has never become postcolonial in its relationship with Indians. Thus a colonial and paternalistic condition is what tribal nations and tribal people must attempt to utilize for their own survival.

Two of the most persistent unresolved issues as far as Indian nations are concerned are "ancestral lands" and "sacred sites," the subjects most troublesome to those who promote economic tourism on Indian lands. In fact, the confusion over these matters is profound and emerges in the most unexpected places. It was brought home to me just a couple of years ago, when I attended an oversight hearing in Rapid City before the Senate Committee on Indian Affairs. All the South Dakota tribes were there to designate their goals and priorities. Even though there was no mention of these bureaucracies and tourism (it was mostly about health issues), I heard Senator Daniel Inouye say, "The ancestral lands business is nonsense as far as I'm concerned."

This was said in connection with his talk on the status of tribes, treaties, nonratified treaties, and the relocation of dozens of tribes in the 1800s, a rather long narrative that turned out to be Inouye's review of history. The dismissal of indigeneity was shocking to many in the mostly Indian audience. We shook our heads as we listened. Inouye is perhaps our only true friend on that committee, and this is what he has to say? *The ancestral lands business is nonsense.* These are words that come out of a colonial history, and they must be challenged. Does Inouye know what he is saying? First, how does he define what those terms mean? What are sacred sites? What are ancestral lands? Is there any writing out there that will assist us in defining these terms?

Unfortunately, most of the information we have about sacred sites is given in law. It is unfortunate because sacredness is not a matter of law. Nor is it economics. But to know the contemporary and mainstream usage, you have to read about specific cases brought to the attention of the courts. This reading of specific cases tells us what the federal bureaucracies know about sacred sites, cases involving the Devil's Tower, the Grand Canyon, Wounded Knee, Blue Lake, Pipestone, and dozens more. What we can see as we look at specific cases is that the issue of natural resources (which always boils down to fisheries, mining, timber, and money and tourism) is always given primacy over human resources and cultural history (which simply means that the role of religion and tribal knowledge and ancestral places is diminished). The Inyan Tower, Grand Canyon, and Blue Lake are important because the holy people have revealed themselves to the people in those places; Pipestone is sacred because that is where the sacred pipe, the essential object of religion for the Sioux, was formed from stone. This information is told and remembered in all of the creation mythologies of the tribes, and is expressed in ritual and ceremony.

Traditionally speaking, most of the important Native sacred sites are situated in the landscape naturally; they are often integrated into the landscape and in many cases even concealed by the landscape. There are sometimes powerful shapes that are natural sites, and their sacredness is noted through the recognition and intensity of the general population who possessed the site, knew of the holy personages (i.e., spirits) who resided there for a thousand years, and enacted ceremonials there for religious reasons. Like the site north of Rapid City (Butte Bear), for example. Sacred sites are those places where the holy deities brought cultural knowledge to the people, which means that the holy deities possess the site; they live there and they are accessible to the people in those places. There is little evidence of Native architectural and sculptural edifices associated with sacredness in America, except in the case of the Mayan and Incan civilizations to the south. Thus landscape features such as sacred peaks, caves, and rivers, forms of the landscape itself, are the ancestral places of origin, and sacred.

The truth is, Native Americans cannot expect that either the legislature or the courts will defend the sacred places with any degree of enthusiasm. Past experience tells us of that reality. The courts, some would like to think, have been put in place to provide a protective shield in Indian Country, but that has seldom been the case. During the Rehnquist years, in fact, the courts have become instead the avowed enemy of Native rights in almost all respects, and some would argue that they have been that since the beginning. In *Lyng v. Northwest Indian Cemetery Protective Association*, (1988), as a recent example, the Court's majority opinion found that the Constitution's Free Exercise clause did not prevent governmental destruction of sacred sites in California, and, like most opinions, it has been used to defend the U.S. Forest Service's activities throughout the country. Chief Justice Rehnquist (along with a Republican Congress) has led a crusade to strip Native governing bodies throughout the United States of any jurisdiction over white people on Indian lands. While legal scholars interested in structural injustices should be making efforts to reverse these wrongful and injurious forms of the law, they are instead plotting further destruction. The Rehnquist Court has become the most important anti-Indian court since the early 1800s.

Fighting off the ongoing assault on Native rights by the bureaucracies that have charged up the tourist economy on reserved lands should be the essential thrust of tribal governments, yet there is little taste for such a battle in reservation-based thinking since Natives, in too many cases, have learned well the artful wiles of being beggars. Working hand in hand with the tourist officials have been the casino and gambling tribes. Consequently, several Indian tribes have been bilked of tens of millions of dollars, all the while begging for decent health services and protection of their sacred places.

Tensions about power and economics and subjectivity have become the focus of the study of colonialism and postcoloniality, yet Native communities, which house among the poorest populations in the country, are still in the process of mending broken systems. It has been an unusually long period of transition in which there is a particularly insidious contract between the new tribal governments based in settler-imperial histories, the courts, and political legislative activity.

As I think about such conferences as this one in Denver, I know that we all must challenge ourselves to add to our thinking the appropriate vocabulary to defend ourselves, to inform ourselves, to assist in defining the presence of sovereign nations-within-a-nation in the landscape of the twenty-first century. And, yes, to react negatively to those ideas and systems that diminish our ancestral presence on these lands.

This particular conference, like many others, ended with uncomfortable wranglings between the executives of the bureaucracies and the tribal governments. Nothing was settled. As I moved through the glass doors of Denver's gorgeous Renaissance Hotel, with its gold appointments and marble floors, toward the parking lot, I felt haunted by the presences of the restless spirits who know what the risks are but have no ideal way to inhabit the world that makes up our new lives. As I listened to my footfalls on the pavement, I imagined my grandmother's soft steps toward the creek where she lived in her little one-room house, when she would ask me to pay attention to the cottonwood trees that lined the shore, saying, "If you know the right songs, they will reveal themselves to you as human beings."

I could not remember how to sing her songs. At that moment, I had no words to express the crucial absence of her spirit.

10

What about Violence?

No book is complete without a comment concerning the fate of women, Native women in particular, even though most writers, including this one, have no notion of feminism as it applies to tribal societies in general and cannot really demonstrate that his or her views are anything but insular, professing the troubling ideology of the middle-brow to which we are all subject these days.

No discussion about women is complete without the harrowing exposure to violence, which, they say, is rising on Indian reservations and has been for several decades, perhaps for all of the twentieth century. Some cynics suggest that several structures are most responsible for the violence and domestic chaos on these reserved lands, and, as a matter of observation, the Christian churches, forced onto traditional societies as a matter of governmental policy, are high on that list for some of us.

The destruction of the Sioux *tiospaye* system of plural marriage and child rearing, for example, mandated by the federal government through Christian missionaries in the 1800s, has been the subject of controversy on Indian reservations since the beginning. Plural marriage was at the heart of the *tiospaye* system and, in spite of the criticism of it from such disciplines as religion and anthropology, may have been a buffer against the violence in today's Indian societies. It makes sense to think that if a man had several wives and they were, perhaps, all related to each other, his use of control and violence would be much diminished. There is much evidence in anthropological works that Native women were the home owners and major figures in child rearing.

The second influence on a more violent society today are the gun lobbyists, who believe it is a Second Amendment right for ten-year-olds to have firearm licenses to learn the protocols for hunting wild animals for sport. Violence begins early, according to the people in opposition to the motives and actions of gun enthusiasts.

Another influence has been the use and abuse of the innovations in communications, the talk shows, the Internet, the blogs and tweets, and the websites. The Internet has come to the Indian world big-time, as a dubious indoctrination process for the young, which means that there is not a federal grant given to any indigenous community for any reason (especially in the schools) without the distribution of massive numbers of free computers. Sometimes they go to reservation and rural homes where there is not even electricity to provide the slightest accommodation, yet computers are there.

For many, it seems that world churches and ubiquitous religiosity in the modern world are most responsible for the hard-right stance toward the protection of people, women in particular. Reproductive freedom for women since *Roe v. Wade* in 1973 has been under vicious attack from the churches and the right-wing political structures since the beginning. In Indian Country, movements toward that kind of liberation were largely clustered around political and legislative needs rather than personal freedom for women or religion, but violence toward women's rights has been the subject of controversy as modern thinking has influenced tradition.

A characteristic of feminism, as a white women's movement of liberation that emerged in all segments of society, is the tension between women as females and the communities at large. Often this tension leads to violence, observers on Indian reservations tell us. Most Native women are not feminists in that sense because they do not perceive tension between their own struggles and the community at large. The struggles of the individual and the community, according to traditionalists, are probably one and the same, and may not be the major cause of overt violence.

There is alienation, though. Anticolonial movements such as the male-dominated American Indian Movement of the mid-1960s did little to defend what may be called women's rights. Indeed some have said that the movement continued the exclusion of women from full membership, as had been the unconscious and unthinking result of the Christianizing and political influences of the previous century. Native women, as an example from that history, rarely signed treaties with white politicians and rarely took to the public pulpits as traditional participants of their societies. Thus women leaders working for their own needs and desires in the American Indian Movement were a rarity. Women of All Red Nations (WARN), which organized during the militant era, has tried to make a case for their participation in the movement, and spokespersons like Madonna Thunder Hawk, though she has written and published very little, has continued her work as an icon for Native women's interests. She sees feminist theory as a colonial assault on indigenous cultures.

Models of the relationship between feminism and violence described in the context of colonization and imperialism of the modern world are a study in complexity. In the context of power and powerlessness, these models become even more shadowy. To suggest that postcolonial hierarchies have liberated Native women is another contradiction in Native communities, since the violence displayed in modern venues is inflicted on the self or the individual rather than a move toward changing the broader community. Some, especially socially conscious researchers, have suggested that Native women accept violence as a means of self-flagellation or communal harmony, but not as a means to personal liberty. Can this be called feminism? Probably not, since most of the female population on any Indian reservation have not accepted the label and often refuse to be drawn into the debate. You often hear the statement "I am not a feminist," especially from the young.

How is it that violence is ordinarily expected to be displayed in feminist ideology if power to the powerless is the objective? Some suggest, for example, that Harriet Tubman, the black woman who organized an underground railroad for runaway slaves in the middle of the nineteenth century, was a feminist because she was an *advocate for* the use of violence in pursuit of freedom. She was said to be a violent woman because she was armed and she threatened to shoot any slave who quit the journey and preferred to go back to the home plantation. She just plain snuffed out the life of a black person who willingly rejected what she thought of as the Journey to Liberation in the North. Apparently Tubman, a woman out to save herself and her people, did resort to violence, with no apologies. She shouldered her rifle and simply shot those slaves who wanted to turn back. Yes, she liberated many slaves, but she was not opposed to acts of violence in the name of that liberation. While much of the scholarship on Tubman has been done in the name of antislavery movements, not enough has been done in the name of feminism. This is true in American Indian studies as well, as its relationship to feminism is geared toward what white feminist scholars have been interested in, expressed in a comparison model. Some of the violence occurring in the world today is challenging colonialism, but little of it can be described as the kind of feminism exemplified by Harriet Tubman. Indeed most of the violence experienced in today's world, and the way it is described in behavioral studies, is male-oriented, as well as in white woman Americanisms, rather than tribal custom.

Some moderns would instead suggest that violence is in the eye of the beholder. The sling-shot violence of the Palestinians against the Israeli Army in the Middle East, some say, is not violence, and even the organized Intifada is nonviolent because they just throw rocks, a random activity rather than institutionalized. It is worth noting that Arab women are not excluded from this violence, benignly described as "resistance," as they too have become rock-throwers and car-bombers. But such studies seem rather incomplete and random.

Even in our time, Rashid Khalidi, a professor at Columbia University and an advocate for Palestinian rights (in fact, he is said to have been a former PLO operative), who watched the Palestinian national identity slowly morph into violence, and who could have, perhaps, predicted the militancy, recognizes it as a national trauma. But because of his knowledge of history, he is ambivalent toward violence and is reluctant to condemn it. He is called by right-wingers "a racist terrorist," which, of course, he is not.[1] He has had little to say about the participation of women, though, in the resistance against colonization, except to acknowledge that they display, as a gender, little estrangement or tension from the community itself, as is often acknowledged in the white American feminist movement.

Khalidi's major contribution to the interests of Native women feminists occurred when he addressed American Arab antidiscrimination conferences both in Madrid and Washington, and in his lectures on campus in 2002. He said, "Killing civilians is a war crime." He has been a critic of Hamas on that basis, as have some proponents and critics of the 1980s American Indian Movement, who also recognized the possibility of violence toward women as a feature of all-male political strategies.

Thoreau believed that civil disobedience, that is, deliberately ignoring the laws of the community, was nonviolent, but anyone who participated in the 1960s antiwar events knows it is not. People were killed violently; bombs were thrown. Men and women were armed to the teeth, and the gun lobby came to own the politicians in Washington. Mahatma Gandhi believed that refusing to acknowledge colonial power systems was nonviolent, though the British believed the opposite, jailed him, and threatened him with death. His followers were stoned. Today, on the Indian reservations where the American Indian Movement shot out car tires, took over churches, burned homes and businesses in the villages, and is now being held responsible for killing two FBI agents, some sympathizers are asking, "How long did it take us to get here?" Their concern is not violence, just "How long?" Many Indians tacitly condone such disobedience to what they recognize as unjust law.

What constitutes violence, then? Does it matter how we define violence in the United States or in Native enclaves? Is it important to say that contemporary Native feminism, if it exists at all, is not characterized by public acts of violence? Is violence in the United States always based in fear? What is the difference between violence and resistance? In the context of federal Indian policy, put in place on Indian reservation homelands in the early 1800s, the recognition of colonial violence toward Natives seems essential to understanding the causes for stricken and chaotic homelands, troubled tribal lives, failed justice, and uncertainty in the future of tribal societies. Are the white settlers on Indian lands to be seen as invading colonists, violent and greedy capitalists who pay their taxes to the warring states in which they live and refuse to obey the criminal laws of the tribe, or are they to be accepted as nonpartisan neighbors in an established white supremacy narrative for the sake of nonviolence? Much more writing and research must go into the examination of useful answers to these questions.

Texas, among many other places, is an example of how a state defines violence within the context of a settler society. Texas was a place full of indigenous peoples long before the longhorns and cowboys moved in, before it became a state in 1845, and today it has become notorious for its violence toward citizens and noncitizens alike. Statehood, always an enemy of tribal law, was a long and drawn-out affair in Texas, as it was throughout the West, with long and drawn-out consequences and a construct of violence based in fear. An active Indian-white conflict went on for forty or fifty years. In order to "ethnically cleanse" the area, in a place where the perpetrators and victims had known each other for a long time, it was argued and determined (*by law*) that "nomads," such as the unfortunate Comanches, could be "removed" and ultimately exterminated (violently? nonviolently?) because they were "will-o-the wisps," on the move and dangerous. But the Choctaws were allowed to remain because they were settled and worthy communities.

Even today many Texans refuse to accept diversity in the population based on the so-called Southern Code of racial practicalities, and they often refuse to take into account the nationalism of tribes that signed treaties and were treated, even in the beginning, as nations-within-a-nation. If you read the papers today in places where there are large populations of Indians, and if you listen to what the National Congress of American Indians had to say at their last meeting, they are applauding a new initiative to plow more money into a "crime initiative" on reserved lands, hiring more police and upgrading legal services. This has to be a good thing, unless one remembers that crime initiatives in the past have always been followed by a crackdown on pathetic wife abusers, helpless alcoholics, drug users, the homeless, and activist tribal leaders. Rarely does a crime initiative on Indian reservations mean that non-Indians, grave robbers, stupid criminal legislators, greedy and crooked businessmen, and federal government functionaries will be given substantial prosecutorial attention.

One of the latest challenges of the law as it concerns ordinary people occurred in 2006. It was a moment when violence against feminist thought and philosophy clarified its position in the state of South Dakota. It was a moment not to be forgotten, as the rights of Native women were challenged, not only by the state, but also by tribal law. A sixty-year-old Oglala Sioux tribal member, Cecelia Fire Thunder, the first woman to be elected to the governmental structure called the Tribal Council of the Oglala Sioux Tribe in the two-hundred-year history of the tribal nation, tangled with the state of South Dakota. She opposed a state legislative ban on abortion rights of all women in the state, a ban that was said to be legal on Indian reservations, where law and order theories are often mere fiction or satire, depending on one's point of view.

Fire Thunder's opposition to what she believed was an attack on women, both Indian and white, was based, she said, in her belief that to restrict the reproductive rights of Native women, and to take away from them the sacred right and responsibility of making their own decisions concerning childbearing, was an act of violence against them.

Within months Fire Thunder was impeached by her own, mostly male council. The reason given: "malfeasance in office." It ended her political career as a duly elected tribal politician. Many believe her demise as a tribal leader probably began because a contemporary tribal society now invaded by white male and Christian attitudes brought by enforced religiosity and education opposed abortion rights, even though there is no evidence of traditional opposition to such laws. Some even suggested that male dominance during the treaty period influenced the matter and that the treaties tribes made with the U.S. government exempted Native female participation in governmental affairs. Prominent tribal men during the Fire Thunder fiasco spoke out against women in leadership roles even as the community resented that position.

Treaties by Natives with white men say nothing about whether or not Native women could have leadership roles in their own tribal self-determination, though all treaties throughout time have probably utilized the male gender in their dialogues. There is little need to dismantle what the treaties have said simply because the texts are male-oriented. All treaties are male-oriented, with the exception, perhaps, of the treaties signed by such personages as Queen Isabella of Spain in her colonial conquests of the indigene, or Elizabeth I in her quest to rule her colonial empire.

The state ban on making abortions inaccessible to all women was turned back by the voters of the state of South Dakota in the next election cycle, but the political career of one of the most exceptional Native women leaders of our time was cut short. Fire Thunder, a woman known to have exceptional skills in political maneuvering, found herself outdone by righteous Christians.

To accuse the federal government or the various states of the United States of passing laws that create violence on Indian reservations is probably not a gross misunderstanding of what goes on at the tribal-federal-state levels of law. Since the Fire Thunder moment, however, another Native tribal woman long involved in state politics, who has been largely silent on women's issues, was elected to the highest office of the Oglala Nation government, perhaps as a backlash measure.

Sharp criticism of the political and religious influence of U.S. governmental policies of the twentieth century has been promulgated by many Native writers and intellectuals, in the form of activism and education. Because of the emergence of Indian studies, these matters are attracting considerable attention and outside scrutiny. In examining the case of Fire Thunder's fate, however briefly, it is important to say that once-colonized and presently colonized peoples, in spite of their struggle to free themselves, often continue to be subjects of the oppressions put in place by colonization.

The Politics of Misogyny

Authoritarianism is the seat of violence in any society, and authoritarianism is a significant trait defined and redefined throughout colonial histories.

The colonial wars being fought across the globe suggest that systems of governance linked to powerful belief systems and authoritarianism are at the heart of violence. If we accuse the Christian churches of being perpetrators of violence on today's Indian reservations, remember that they were placed in positions of power in Native enclaves by the U.S. Congress as early as 1850 to bring the Native peoples out of their state of "savagery" and into the mainstream, where, activists have said, everybody drowns. By U.S. law, Christianity and Christian churches became the instruments of total assimilation and, failing that, imperial rule on reservation lands. The use of religious authority was a significant tactic of colonization and, ultimately, land theft, and, finally, violence in the most extreme sense.

There are few governance systems more rigid in their search for power and control than colonial systems, and there are no more rigidly colonized governance systems in the United States than the so-called governance systems of indigenous populations, that is, Indian reservation governments. Why are we surprised, then, at the violence present in these enclaves? Why don't we understand that governing systems are at the heart of it?

There is no more troubling manifestation of violence in these systems than the violence against women, a condition that was often held in check in traditional egalitarian societies, we are told by some anthropologists who are probably out of the mainstream of the discipline, and others, through carefully monitored societal and cultural systems.

Varied arguments about all of this in tribal enclaves may come and go, but in too many places contemporary misogyny remains an incorrigible function of today's power systems. Maybe the hatred between women and men has been so for as long as the Bible was accepted as Christian probity and instruction in the United States. Perhaps it has been the function of many societies. Perhaps it has been so even before the recent fiasco in the Middle East, during which American writers have preached about the intolerant Middle Eastern cultural views of women of ancient societies. Contemporary life and society suggests a long tenure of misogyny in all kinds of societies and civilizations.

Presently, though, misogyny, defined as hatred of women, is said by people who make a study of these things to be escalating. It is one of the oddities of our times that, just as the hatred of women is intensifying, hot wars throughout the globe, in Africa, the Middle East, and elsewhere, are heating up too. In the public response, it is suggested that fearful peoples throughout the globe have the right to go to war to defend themselves. President George W. Bush, an authoritarian by belief and training and a colonist by historical precedence, even mandates that "first-strike" war, never before accepted as a tenet in the democratic development of justice in a democratic society, is an option in defense. This idea of "first strike," now called "the Bush doctrine" in foreign policy circles, seems to be an escalation almost unprecedented in the making of war by the United States. It is useful for those of us in Indian studies to ponder the following questions: What does this new war policy have to do with violence toward women in the United States? What does it have to do with violence on Indian reservations? What does it have to do with the colonization and oppression of societies?

If we are seeking answers only to domestic policies, we may conclude that fear is a major influence in all conflicts, especially those conflicts between powerful national entities If it is possible that in the conflict between those who hate women and those who don't, *fear is at the heart of the dilemma,* is it too broad a jump to say that therefore fear may be at the heart of foreign attack strategies? Bush says we must not wait to be struck again after the attack on the Twin Towers in New York years ago; we must strike them before they strike us again. He is afraid. He is a violent man who condones invasion, massacre, and torture, revealing himself, some suggest, to be the quintessential American, the mano-a-mano cowboy who fought Indians, striking them in their villages in the dark of night, the fearful colonist who shot Indians on sight, no questions asked, the born-again Puritan who is in bed with his wife at nine o'clock but who cannot tolerate either a national policy of hesitation nor a policy for women to own their special realism.

We cannot allow women to be equal to men, says the misogynist who fears for his safety in the marital contract; we must pass laws that restrict a fearful power potential. And in both cases, Bush's war and the misogynist's war, lies must be told, reason must be abandoned, and troops must descend onto the ground of battle. This behavior will surely end in self-destruction.

It is one of the realities of embracing violence as a means of settling disputes that a primary power strategy in getting people to follow you onto the battlefield is to challenge the power and status of the enemy, the feared ones, the "lesser" peoples, and to describe them in terms of deprivation and savagery. Women in all cultures are among those feared groups. The word "misogyny" comes from the Greek *miso*, indicating "hatred" or "hated," but the dictionary gives us no rationale for that hatred. That is to be expected, one supposes, since it is an old variant of classical thought that hate is an irrational emotion, a human emotion without basis. Shakespeare raised that idea to its zenith in the creation of the villain Iago. Iago doesn't really hate Othello or Desdemona or anyone else; he simply hates, thoroughly and irrationally.

There is very little reliable scholarship on the existence of misogyny and the rationale for its existence in tribal societies. The dialogue is couched mostly in the language of law and order. With the rise of violence toward tribal women, one can't help but conclude that Christian ideologies and colonization ideologies forced upon tribal societies may have helped to devastate tribal societies in the past two hundred years. Some researchers suggest that the dreadful poverty brought about by colonial practices, and the resultant degraded status of Indians in general, brings about structural violence that is based on sex, male-versus-female power structures previously unknown in egalitarian tribal societies. Violence, then, is the result of colonization, in which men and women, equally powerless, learn to be violent toward one another while failing to cope with intrusive changes as they become more difficult and demanding. This thinking leads us to the belief that colonization is a cause for conflict between men and women, misogyny being a function of colonization more than a function of culture.

In many ways, colonization is just a matter of control for control's sake. In that case, violence toward women in colonial Indian history is even more predictable. After listening to the dialogue concerning abortion rights in the country, particularly in South Dakota, for the past decade—all of it during the Bush administration, as a matter of fact—one realizes that governmental intrusion into the private lives of private citizens everywhere has reached a crisis stage, and as it often does, it reaches into diverse communities.

There is nothing new about that, but it does bring up the point that it's not just Indian women we're talking about now as regards violence and control. It's Everywoman. These intrusions, of course, with the suspension of habeas corpus in the first months of the twenty-first century and the torture at Guantánamo Bay incarceration center during the hot war period, should have been predicted, perhaps, since religiosity has become the common thread of Americanism in the past several decades.

The domestic ideology of the Bush regime, which escalated violence throughout the country, seems to be fostered by the born-again revisionists, because they are the ones who know how to control. The idea that life begins "at the moment of conception" would seem to be an extremely dangerous notion because it has clashed with opposing ideologies. The resultant need to control and promote the idea, then, seems to have been a function of the belligerence in foreign policy that hasn't been seen since the Indian Wars. This notion makes it okay to invade and control women's lives in the same way that it is okay to occupy other countries across the globe in the name of religious values. This is something Indians know about, since their experience in colonization has been a matter of violence and control.

There is no question that the ban on a woman's reproductive rights occurring in the twenty-first century is a violence reminiscent of the master colonial narrative focused on male superiority. A little bit of history and the law as it concerns the abortion issue is often left out of the *Roe v. Wade* controversy. The South Dakota legislature, like many bureaucracies in the 2008 political climate, brought about its own Initiative 11 to ban all abortions. It was a referendum on the ballot of one of the reddest states in the nation in 2006 but was reflected in all of the red states of this first decade of the twenty-first century. It was a sustained effort to challenge what we all thought was "settled law," *Roe v. Wade*.

The movement to make an abortion safe and legal, which is what *Roe v. Wade* did in the 1970s, was only part of the picture, historically. It in fact tied in with other movements of liberation that were going on at the same time, movements in which many contemporary scholars participated. In 1973, when *Roe v. Wade* became the law of the land, other movements of liberation were afoot. It wasn't just about women, then, nor is it presently. It was about civil rights, and in the 1970s women came late to the civil rights movement. Civil rights was about all of the people looking for justice and protection—women, the Black Power Movement, La Raza, the American Indian Movement, religious practitioners, schoolteachers, labor leaders, gays.

These movements, including the feminist movement, arose in response to repressive law, failed justice, discrimination, endemic poverty, the war, corruption in government, second-class citizenship for large numbers of people in the United States, and aggressive religiosity. It was a time when people stood up to certain fascist trends throughout the world, and it was a time that will not be seen again in our lifetime. It was a time called "the sixties," and, it was a time for the American Indian Movement. Indians all over the country began to say, "We have rights! We will define them. We will fight for them." Affirmative action, which rose out of that period, was a policy of hope; the Black Hills land case went to court (again), and the Supremes said, for the first time in history, Yes, your land in the Black Hills was *stolen*. The Indian Community College system throughout the United States (beginning in Arizona) had its origins in those years. Indian studies enclaves throughout academia began to thrive.

The time of *Roe v. Wade* and the emergence of all those movements was perhaps the most important social and political time in the twentieth century. The backlash to those freedom movements by right-wing moralists and power-hungry religionists has now, decades later, gained huge competing support systems. Books being published now trash the sixties and condemn the American Indian Movement,[1] and now scholars and politicians and loud-mouth radio jocks label the people who gained their rights in those times "baby killers" and "terrorists." Violence is the theme of these issues and debates, manifesting itself in inappropriate legislative efforts and unrest.

The years of militancy in the sixties were important years of freedom for oppressed people in the United States. It was a time when women recognized that they, too, had civil rights, that they were full citizens within an organized society that protected their individuality. Abortion was thought of as a civil rights matter in those days and, frankly, that part of the discussion has been lost recently because the private religious part of the narrative has gained public supremacy. Now we ask questions like "When does life begin?" And John McCain, the powerful senator from Arizona, answers on national television, "Life begins at the moment of conception," rubber-stamping the mantra of today's Republicanism and today's religious fanatics.

The latest public discourse to restrict women's access to abortion predicts a philosophy or a system of government that can be called fascism and offers a dictatorship of the extreme right, a type of belligerent nationalism for the few that can only be called violent. In the process of this fascist wave, the chance to influence politics has been given to people like Karl Rove and Sean Hannity, whose primary interest is winning power for power's sake. The radio talking-head Rush Limbaugh and other like-minded men dominate the air waves with misogynist foolishness. Native women have been largely silent in this debate, which usually indicates opposition in Native cultures, but non-Native women have joined the fray. Sarah Palin, when she was governor of Alaska, for example, wanted to censor libraries, and now refuses to talk of individual decisions in reproductive rights activity, is against gay rights and condoms, and rises to political prominence in 2008.

Few people who call themselves conservatives are saying out loud these days that women have the right to make private decisions without the intrusion of the government. Few are saying that the Constitution guarantees citizens that the government must be very careful about its intrusion into personal lives. Few are remembering the feminists who fought for civil rights, going back to the prior influence of Elizabeth Cady Stanton, who died in 1902, and Gloria Steinem in the sixties, and all the rest. Young people aren't told that their mothers and grandmothers fought to overcome the repression of their humanness and to demand their constitutional right to "privacy," which really began in the 1920s and lasted until *Roe v. Wade.* No one tells anyone that the Equal Rights Amendment, equally hard fought for during those years, could not pass in the male-dominated Congress because of the backlash of the ignorant, pretentious, insincere, and empty language of misogyny.

For some, this has never been an argument about saving babies, nor is it a religious matter for public scrutiny, as is suggested by those who call themselves "pro-lifers." This matter of what a woman does about her reproductive life has always been a civil rights issue, never a religious matter. It was always a recognition that when systems of government get off-track, they often turn toward advocating a dictatorship of the extreme right. It is one of the hazards of a free society. Thus the extreme right has adopted a fascist ideology. When that happens, the civil rights in the public arena are in jeopardy. When that happens, state and business and religious matters are formed into an ideology that crushes individual rights, the human spirit, and the intrinsic freedoms of human beings.

To stop this government intrusion into the civil rights of all citizens, it is useful for all to realize that making slaves and doormats of American women, and South Dakota women and Native women in particular, over the issue of reproductive rights, just like the bombing of innocent civilians whose governments we do not like, will not make this a better country. Taking away the civil rights of half the population of the United States will not make happier families. It will not make a better people. How do we know this? We know it because the Constitution has said for over two hundred years that in the United States, citizens, even female and indigenous ones, have the right to privacy. And the law will protect that sacred right. We have freedom from human bondage. That's what the Fourth Amendment gave us. All U.S. citizens have a Fourth Amendment protection, a constitutional right to privacy. That is the right that *Roe v. Wade* protects. Just because a woman gets pregnant, she does not lose that right. She is, like the rest of us, protected against "unwarranted search." She has the right and responsibility and the obligation to make her own decisions concerning many private matters, most of all about her reproductive life.

We've heard about how a zygote is a human being, about how "life begins at the moment of conception," about "saving babies," about "what my church tells me," and about "my conscience." We've heard about god and religious beliefs and morality until we've come away thinking that making second-class citizens again of women, half the population of this country, will be a good thing. It will not. We must recognize that these moral absolutes really shut off dialogue. This worst attack on a women's civil and human rights in forty years dangerously creates and defends the moral absolutes from which twentieth-century intellectuals have tried to extricate themselves in the name of freedom of thought and expression.

In recent years, civil rights matters have been challenged in the courts and by our elected governments in too many ways to count: unwarranted wiretapping, investigations of all kinds, even of library repository materials, torturing, throwing people into Guantánamo prisons for years without charge or legal representation. And, yes, from my Dakota/Lakota point of view, stealing and occupying other people's lands for profit.

And now there is an effort to mandate civil and criminal laws to say that a woman's constitutional right to privacy is not retained for the nine months of gestation. She is no longer protected by the Constitution. In the name of what is now being called "fetal rights" a movement to abrogate the rights of women during pregnancy has gained support among our citizens, though there is no such thing as "fetal rights." This is the fantasy of religious zealots who wish to conquer and dominate women's lives. It is one of the most aggressive and strategically placed expansions of the law in this country, since slavery, since the theft of the Black Hills, since the invasion of a Middle Eastern country, as old as the law itself. We should all be alarmed at these obscene and wrongful expansions of the law. Why aren't we talking about the wrong, disembodied, immoral treatment of our female citizens?

In Indian Country, the treatment of women, as we all recognize, is no longer what it was in "traditional" times. According to people of my grandparents' generation, it would have been unheard of in traditional Native societies for men and governments and religious people to have interfered with the reproductive lives of women. Indigenous women's societies possessed knowledge concerning all manner of child bearing and reproduction. Their tribal customs and behaviors reflected that knowledge without interference from men and their societies and their religious leaders. This was women's business, and the use of that knowledge was what contributed to tribal strength and growth.

Since the late 1800s, enforced Christianity has had a huge and deleterious effect on how Native women can express their tribal knowledge. Aggressive Christianity, which destroyed indigenous knowledge systems with a vengeance, brought about male-dominated societies, and we are still paying the price for the loss of Native women's culture. It is one of the sorrows of the American Indian Movement that it, too, had a damaging influence on how large numbers of Native women defined themselves in a new and political tribal context. They saw abortion is a function of genocide, which meant that a woman's right to reproduce was a way to fight off the genocide encountered over generations. Beatrice Medicine wrote and gave many lectures on these subjects and disparaged the male-oriented political movement of AIM and its treatment of women.[2] She spoke of AIM's "concubinage" of young Native women during the 1970s and called for a reassessment. The truth is, tribal women have yet to recover from these intrusions.

Because of long-standing dogmas arising from historical experience, the religious, faith-based communities will never allow the point of view that a woman can choose whether or not to reproduce. Christian faith is a powerful thing. It overcomes enlightenment, it overcomes reason, it overcomes logic. Ever since *Roe v. Wade* was passed, faith-based opponents have not come to terms with the reality that there can be an opposing point of view. Religions are established to codify what is right and wrong according to established dogma. When *Roe v. Wade* became law, the ideals of Christian faith stemming from church-mandated strongholds suffered scars of loss that they could not get rid of, and they began to nurture a revenge strategy that has gained much power. Those who fought for reproductive rights in the 1960s and thought they had won their freedoms became complacent, and let the power over individual rights thrive.

In order for political movements to thrive in modern democracies, it is important to build coalitions. If a woman's right to an abortion is a middle-class, white woman's movement, it must reach out from the experience of a largely privileged and educated class to join with every woman who someday, somewhere will need a public voice, a force she can count on, to defend her civil and human rights. It is essential that women learn to frame solutions to what is right for humanity. It will not be a quick fix. Years of complacency have begun to erase the gains of the past decades in the arena of personal freedoms, and it will take years to recover.

12

The Dilemma of Language and the Art of Political Persuasion

The most important dilemma of all reproductive rights arguments in this country is how to use language in an argument that is paradoxical. The paradox is this: we desire justice, but we also desire to curtail the civil rights of women. Two opposing desires.

It is tempting to believe, especially for a scholar like myself, who spent dozens of years trying to become efficient using the English language to enter into scholarly discussions that concern all peoples, that through rational, logical, and unemotional discussion one can persuade an audience to truthful thinking. That belief is based on the notion that people in general can think rationally, that they can reason their way to truth if they use language well. Because of the religiosity of power systems on the rise across many divides, though, the benefits of such self-delusion may be dangerous. Most people these days use language to comfortably masquerade as solutions or compromises to dilemmas. The instrument of language, long thought to be the instrument of mediation and rationality, is quickly losing its agency. No solutions are found, and what is left is raw emotion.

Based on emotion, people who see the manipulation of a woman's reproductive rights as the way to power, or abortion as "killing babies," say "I am pro-life," or "I vote my conscience," or "Life begins at the moment of conception," or "Abortion is murder." These are static statements, no ambiguity allowed. The notion that thinking is conscious, logical, and unemotional and that women as human beings with civil rights are capable of it as a way to make individual decisions is obviously absent. Unsubstantiated opinion and rash emotion and religious fervor prevent a two-way dialogue. One can no longer believe that talking and thinking are processes of conscious reason. Instead they are sensorimotor systems that only react to emotional or static moral appeals. Talking and thinking, then, respond to bundles of ideas, narratives, emotions, values, and images that stem from the unconscious brain. Why are we moderns surprised at that? Surely we know that's why the advertising of goods and services on television is so powerful in our societies today.

What can one say, then, about the unconscious brain? For our purpose here, one must say that the unconscious brain handles about ninety-eight percent of the information it faces that can be absorbed. It is in that place of the unconscious that deep-seated worldviews about morality and politics are formed. What is morality, and where does it come from? It comes from the unconscious brain, which absorbs ninety-eight percent of the millions of pieces of information it gets every minute. It is the unconscious brain, we are told by linguists and all kinds of scholars, that is the seat of morality and political views.

The conscious brain, on the other hand, where logic and reason reside, absorbs only two percent of the information it receives. The conscious brain gets to deal with only two percent of its data, which the critic presumes is enough to move toward substantive conclusion. Even disinterested folks must find this a caution.

What does this mean to the political and legal conversation that relies on logic to assure that women are to sustain their human rights during pregnancy and child-bearing years? In the face of the emotional data the brain receives, can we be assured? Emotions will be placed at the center of any strategy by antiwoman theorists unless we, in the defense of women, learn *the art of framing dialogues,* using metaphors and images and pictures, to influence political and legal decisions. In the process, we have to get over the idea that politics is an intellectual pursuit based in logic. It is not easy to give up that cherished ideal. When I was a journalism student at the University of South Dakota, I took only one course in advertising (the art of framing dialogue through emotion) and thirty courses in rhetoric and fact finding and statistics and writing craftsmanship, in pursuit of the idea that the craft of writing was always an effort to be coherent and logical. Must I at long last abandon it all? Must I get over my love affair with Noam Chomsky, the linguist who taught me that people think in a conscious, logical, and unemotional way in order to be civil? Must I get over the idea that human rationality is a real thing, and force myself to rally to the idea that human beings aren't rational at all? The pathetic and emotional and influential political dialogue of today almost proves the fallibility of my previous belief that logic will out.

Because emotional political thinking leads to chaos and victimhood not only for women, but for many communities throughout the country, one can go into any Indian community today and hear women saying repeatedly, "I would never have an abortion. I would never have an abortion." This is a defensible position for many, and it is a position we all should protect. Yet it is not a defensible position for a society to base laws and restrictions for all women upon.

If I hear one more old Lakota/Dakota grandmother say "We are all mothers. We love our children," I am going to run over the hills and prairies screaming. Of course we love our children. If I hear one more Lakota politician, male or female, say, as they did during the illegal and immoral and very sad Cecelia Fire Thunder impeachment process in 2006, "A woman cannot be elected to tribal office," I may give up entirely. When that is said, I know that rational ideas and conscious thought are *not* a part of the process that is going on. Such talk can only contribute to a woman's oppression, her victimization, hatred toward one another, and continuing conflicts.

The ideas that fuel this conflict are emotional ones. They are unreliable and, ultimately, unworkable. Whether you personally would have an abortion or you would not is irrelevant because it is an emotional response. Agreement from other individuals or the broader society is not assured. Without consensus, such thinking permits those who agree and are powerful enough and influential in the political process to attempt to pass unjust laws. Often that is the result.

The reasonable point to make is that no society should base its rules, its values, its long-term future on such fragile and marginal emotional appeals. To maintain a woman's reproductive rights in a society is to maintain her personhood, her citizenship, and her responsibilities as a fellow human being. All U.S. citizens and all tribal citizens, even pregnant ones, possess civil rights and, hopefully, the capacity for logical thinking. In traditional times, women of the Plains cultures were most often in charge of their reproductive lives, just as they should be in modern times. Such autonomy of personhood was what made the communal life possible and what made Lakota/Dakota peoples among the most resilient of all tribal nations.

13

Balancing Acts for Academic Risk Takers

I'm currently on leave from the University, she says, on an appointment as a Visiting Scholar in the School of Social Welfare. The intent of the appointment is to provide me with the opportunity to advance my research and scholarship on Violence and Abuse Against Indigenous Women. I have a book contract to convert my dissertation into a book and am spending the bulk of my time on additional data collection.

The above personal narrative is from a Native woman, an incomparable assistant professor, who has been teaching indigenous studies courses at a university in the Midwest for twelve years. This is the commentary of a Native woman who, like dozens of other scholars across the country, has achieved tenured status in a "related" departmental discipline, all the while putting enormous effort into influencing the forming of a Native studies enclave with departmental status at her institution.

This is a personal note from a Native scholar who has been on a collision course with the administration of her university and with the new directives (since 2003) of the institution, which no longer accommodates or supports work in indigenous theory and course development. She says the "intent" of the research appointment, for which she is grateful, is to advance her research, but there are unspoken problems with accepting this rationale, and she knows it: (1) the research she is expected to advance is in sociology, not indigenous studies; (2) she is no longer in the classroom, leaving an incalculable vacuum; (3) she will no longer be a critic of the status quo in the affairs of the university, nor will she advance the development of Indian studies as an academic discipline. Some might say it is surely a calculated move by the administration to remove an obstacle, namely, a competent professor and brilliant Native scholar who wants to move toward the development of the ideals of a newly forming discipline. Moreover the likelihood of her returning to her assistant professorship when she finishes this project is slim, since the courses she designed and taught are being phased out. This is an all too familiar pattern for young Native professionals in university settings.

The emergence of Indian studies as an academic discipline in the past three decades has suffered no more severe tragedy than the failure to establish and support large, fertile faculties in the discipline at key universities, tenured, stable male and female intellectuals with citizenship credentials in indigenous nations dedicated to academic enterprises that are identified with and in support of the constituencies called First Nations or indigenous peoples.

It is in academic faculties, after all, in the organizations of scholars where great ideas and change and innovation, research and publications flourish. It is in the faculty circle where scholars reproduce themselves as Native intellectuals. And it is in these faculties that antagonistic, colonial powers find ways to close the doors to a new historicism in the United States. What has happened in Indian studies development is, first, the denial of departmental status for the discipline, resulting in the "Lone Ranger" approach to faculty development; second, and more vicious in its result, is the deliberate factionalizing and colonizing of the professoriate. Factionalizing and colonizing have indeed been among the outcomes of graduate school study, where the content of Indian studies and its subsequent practice is fractionated, minimized, or worse, omitted entirely. This leads to self-serving competitiveness, identity issues, an unrequited process for dissension by tenured individuals, a focus on various other knee-jerk conundrums in faculty enclaves, and finally, the offer to do postgrad work in a related discipline as a way out of the Native studies classroom.

The "Lone Ranger" approach to faculty development, when a young scholar is the only Indian faculty person on staff, has led some Native PhDs to think they are the first of their kind, the front-line defenders of an intellectual pursuit in the field they believe has been long lost or unheard of in academic history, something omitted or unknown. They are rarely taught that for nearly thirty years Native scholars have gone before them, that there are vast bibliographies in Indian studies research available to them, because these accounts are often dismissed in graduate studies protocols.

Often young scholars go on and on about academic freedom and personal traumas, when instead they should be assisted in professionalism, disciplined to do the ordinary work of academics everywhere, meet classes and students daily, develop appropriate courses, do research and publish, serve on committees, do the work of departments, and be fully aware that departments and deans are free to do what they sometimes do: deny faculty lines, take away graduate programs, and in all other ways carry out the duties of running the university according to some long-range plans that may not include them.

The trick is to remember that administrations and faculties are often hostile adversarial forces. This is nothing new, and professors of every stripe, even Native American professors, must develop appropriate skills to not only dissent and survive, but to thrive amid the good ideas of their own and others in the field. The acceptance of a research grant may be seen as a way to get one's research organized and published, but it may also be a waiting game. The right moment may come.

Surely, we who have been grateful and even surprised by our unaccountable entrance into academe in the middle of the twentieth century, when affirmative action was a real thing, have been blissfully unaware of how the structures of our programs and institutes, largely in humanities and sociology and anthropology management systems, would work against us. It was not until the beginning of the twenty-first century that the overpowering intention to colonize the teaching workforce in Indian studies became too obvious to ignore and the results untenable. What we have learned is that curricular development, degree achievement, career advancement, useful research, and appropriate publishing cannot occur without the support of large, influential faculty systems in our discipline, the one source for empowerment and enrichment in academe that has been systematically denied Indian studies. It has been denied through hiring practices, structural mechanisms, and advancement protocols.

By whom? one may ask.

Of course, the first culprit to blame is the recent administrative transition of academic centers into global labor enclaves run by CEOs and employers from the business sector rather than intellectually qualified professionals who know what the academic process requires. The so-called private sector with its competitive wage and bargaining dialogue so enthusiastically accepted by those who control state and private academies in this country presents the dire problem of financial concerns and job security.

In the process of this transition, accommodations have been made not only by business-type executives but also by the professors who sit on committees, who spend their days in the classrooms and at research tables. We all must take some responsibility as we ask the question, How have some of the methods of colonization of the workforce in academic centers flourished even as we watched and participated? A brief list of how this is accomplished follows:

1. The hiring of adjunct rather than faculty members on tenure track in the discipline.
2. The intrusion of anthropology, history, and literature scholars into the discipline of Indian studies.
3. The hiring of CEOs as chairpersons of the campuswide department or program.
4. The hiring of people who are adept only at seeking government grants.
5. Vocationalism.
6. The rise of occupational training centers encouraged by the Bureau of Indian Affairs.
7. The development of policy centers utilized, largely, for the purpose of economic management on reservations.

First of all, the issue of adjunct teaching assignments in Indian studies is a huge category for inquiry and criticism. Much of the subject matter of the discipline is taught by adjuncts, graduate students, visiting professors, and interdisciplinary scholars from other fields, though no thorough study documenting the numbers is readily available. What we know is that there has been little input by professionals in the field of Indian studies that has been given agency in the hiring practices of any academic center. Most of the hirings of the professorate at any state university have been made by administrative bodies whose boards, as a rule, are not made up of Native professors or scholars. When Native professors and scholars are on these boards, they are often overruled by administrative needs, which take precedence.

Adjuncts who do the yeoman's work of teaching classes and grading papers rarely sit on committees that regulate the business of the university and never gather in the enclaves where curricular designs and degree programs are articulated. Yet they regularly teach what we call the "gatekeeper" courses, that is, the "introduction to the discipline" courses, as well as the core, while the professors are pursuing their favorite interests. In 2009 an article in the *Chronicle of Higher Education* reported that the American Educational Research Association meeting in New York at the close of the year documented an alarming fact: "First-year students drop out if their high-stakes 'gatekeeper courses' are taught by part-time instructors." The article concluded that "part-time instructors can be detrimental to a student's well being."[1] If this is so, what must be said about the well-being of the course of study itself? In the case of the inchoate field of Indian studies, that question is significant.

"Gatekeeper" courses are defined as any large introductory class (sometimes enrolling fifty to a hundred students) that students must pass in order to move forward in the field. In smaller enclaves, gatekeeper courses are often thought to be "remedial" in some respects. When I started teaching in Indian studies as a visiting professor at Arizona State University in 1995, I was astonished to learn that there was no introductory course in Indian studies. In subsequent inquiries, I learned that many (no, most) Indian studies degree programs throughout the state university systems in the United States did not ever offer an introduction to the discipline course. When I spoke to a director at a regional liberal arts college near where I live, I was told that his discipline was law and, therefore, law courses are in the forefront of what is offered, mostly to upper-class persons; thus, he said, an intro to the discipline of Indian studies was thought to be redundant. He is one of two faculty members in the field at that university. The second faculty member teaches anthropology courses. Yet this midwestern university advertises the availability of a complete Indian studies regimen and even offers a major.

On further inquiry around the country, I also found that if an introduction to the discipline of Indian studies is offered, it is taught by an adjunct, or a visiting prof, or a part-timer. Full professors and associate professors in Indian studies at most large universities do not deign to teach the gatekeeper courses! This reminds one of a lot of English departments, where writing and rhetoric courses are taught by graduate students. This is a common pattern that may leave one of three impressions: introductory courses are for morons and a waste of time for students as well as their professors; or Indian studies is not an academic discipline and, therefore needs no gatekeeper course—just plunge in with an anthro course, a literature or law course, and proceed to history; or the body of knowledge of Indian studies, like first-year writing courses, are for the remedial student. A more likely impression is that the Indian studies curriculum as the development of an autonomous discipline will not bring in a government grant, nor will it lead to a contract in resource development on reservation lands, or a Washington consultancy for the professor.

Liberating Indian studies from anthropology is a central tenet of the dialogue about the discipline begun by Vine Deloria decades ago, a dialogue that has become both controversial and political. The charge is that Indian studies is politicizing rather than academizing, with activists who often have massive personal identity issues, leading the academic world to think that Native scholars are indoctrinating students and rewriting history according to their own prejudices. Do they analyze or proselytize? is a question still asked by outsiders, in spite of evidence that makes the question abusive and racist. Many unknowing and uninformed academics still believe that indigenous studies in the United States have no place in a college classroom, something like "creative writing," which is still considered suspect by the uninformed yet has become an academic force of great substance. This bias has thwarted the development of large and influential faculties in Indian studies.

It is becoming apparent that young Native professionals are being dissuaded from continuing in the field. As public colleges and universities go for the gold, hiring the stars (now a little long in the tooth), raiding each other for the scarce number of published, tenured PhDs who have made it, there is little or no effort to add to the tenured field or work with those Native professionals who are just starting out, having recently acquired the skills to do the academic work of research and publishing necessary to advance the discipline. There is little attempt on the part of the decision makers to keep faculty members who have other offers; thus the attempt to build a firm foundational faculty at any given institution is left to chance.

Raiding the field is called "poaching." It is a ubiquitous technique that accounts for a fly-by-night approach to developing learning centers and stable faculties. Except in some instances, such as science and technology, surprisingly it doesn't always have to do with money. Most often it is simply the result of the laziness of search committees or lack of knowledge of resource centers from which Native scholars may be emerging. In addition, those resource fields have dried up in the past decade, due to the lack of funding suffered by dwindling affirmative action enclaves, which in the past decade have become places where administrators are simply occupying space rather than behaving as the activist centers they once were purported to be. It is still true that Native scholars are not the most visible to the outside world, and it takes ingenuity, networking, and proactive dedication on the part of universities to seek them out, hire them, and assist them in their development as scholars.

An unarticulated and unspoken problem in finding Native talent and keeping it is that the top priority of many of the young professionals in the field of Indian studies is the need, desire, and chance to do the work (much of it political, legal, and economic) of their own tribal nations. Many Native scholars in the discipline wish to rewrite the dominant ideology from within, to produce a different version of reality. They recognize that rewriting the long-standing colonial ideology prevalent at most U.S. universities will not be easy, and they recognize that it is not the work of one scholar or writer. To promote indigenous access to power through the academy without negating indigenous difference will take large, stable faculties at important learning centers. It is the work of many.

Other scholars, unconnected to the base of reserved lands and treaty status, move from university to university, from bureaucratic positions in Washington to law schools, from one faculty position without tenure to the next faculty position without tenure, or, worse, find several overlapping teaching posts in an urban setting, driving from one campus to another, filling in the gaps and stitching together a paycheck rather than a career, in places that have little interest in developing the discipline. It goes without saying that there is little interest and almost no encouragement in mainstream public universities in such endeavors since Native enclaves seem isolated, often do not offer industry a pass, ignore global financial markets, and are often separated in myriad ways from other segments of the population. U.S. universities, with their colonialist and capitalist mindsets, have still not come to terms with what must be done to offer indigenous populations and intellectuals a seat at the table, and any young Indian scholar in this milieu is trapped in trying to accommodate ways for his or her educational mission to be realized. Often beginning scholars find very quickly that their scholarly or academic interests cannot be met; they move on to other pastures, which, sadly, turn out to be just as infertile as the first.

Is there an answer to this dilemma? Probably not, if one is looking for a panacea. However, when all is said and done, it is not realistic to expect that universities are going to systematically and quickly overhaul their long-held power enclaves in order to make a place for the long-neglected study of the indigenes in any place other than anthropology. That's the bad news. On the other hand, some genuinely momentous changes have taken place, when the thrust of affirmative action as a federal policy was in place. Another of the encouraging bits of news is the increasing numbers of Indian students from our communities who are seeking higher education.

The *Chronicle of Higher Education* reported that in 2009, fifteen percent of the racial and ethnic distribution of enrollments in colleges and universities in Alaska were American Indians; in California 22,334 American Indians were enrolled in public universities; 11,677 American Indians were in colleges in New Mexico (though, oddly, the high school dropout rate there is ten percent); and in Arizona enrollment of American Indians in higher education reached 18,241. This is phenomenal when one considers that the number of American Indians in many higher education institutions in the 1940s and 1950s could be counted on one hand, even with the return of World War II veterans.[2]

These new statistics are encouraging even though some of the other statistics concerning success give us more dismal information; dropout rates are one example. Current and former leaders of the Native nations across the country and the Native academics who are toiling away in the graduate and undergraduate vineyards of university life must know that this is where the tools for nation building will be designed.

14

Taku Inichiapi? What's in a Name?

Theorizing about aggressive nationalistic (read, tribal) discourse is getting more acceptable in Indian studies these days, and it is in constant opposition to the passive acceptance of coloniality in past historical thought. Native scholars have contributed to the theoretical debate in the hopes that Native peoples can transcend the present condition of colonialism and that tribal nationalism as a concept will thrive in the modern world. Yet the reality remains clear: too often the colonizer has the power to control the imagination and, just as often, controls the aspirations of the colonized. This is done through deception, fraud, and swindle as much as it is done in defense of conscience.

There is plenty of evidence for the notion that colonials control the colonized in this matter, some of the more pessimistic thinkers contend, as they look to the media, educational facilities, and cultural trends. That power-based tendencies of the mainstream often lead to bizarre chapters of identity fraud and deception is all too common. Throughout the twentieth century, when Americans really began to encounter the contemporary American Indian, images of Indians and Americans as they interacted with the newcomer settlers brought about what we now call "identity issues."

If it is true that the colonizer tries to be in control of what we imagine, it goes without saying that pretending to be an Indian in the United States, as Philip Deloria has indicated in his examination of historical trends, is a double-edged sword, emerging as a relationship that is both structurally political and subjective.[1] This relationship, say those like Homi Bhabha who have studied this phenomenon relentlessly and whose work is now available in U.S. college courses, becomes one of "constant, if implicit contestation and opposition."[2] This is more true, perhaps, in a country of settlers and émigrés like the United States than in any other place. The United States is probably more fraught with its own fantasies than many other enclaves simply because of its immigrant-settler nature.

Intruders into the New World celebrated themselves in whatever ways were useful, in a world of unknowns where European travelers with decadent tastes ventured freely, speaking only of their own discoveries. Non-tribal people in the United States, then, have had a long history of acting as imposters to gain authenticity among themselves as well as from the Native peoples they encountered. In the past century many turned the fraud of the claim of Indianness into a lucrative career, and these frauds usually emerge against the modern background of the legal breakdown of the cultural and political systems of the tribal First Nations of America, the result of colonization and oppression. These frauds also emerge as the West struggles with its own catastrophes, such as world wars and economic and religious breakdown. Social chaos of years past destroyed an abiding tribal authenticity, which rendered Natives, without power to claim their own rights, largely silent on this fraud until very recent times.

War and civil unrest and the conflicts of social change have been and continue to be among the causes of the prevalence of these frauds in many instances, which means that such phenomena are not unheard of in global history. We've known, for example, that many of the hereditary societies of Europe have been plagued by this phenomenon as far back as the Middle Ages. The reason for such historical activity is that these aristocracies legitimized authority through lineage and principles of hereditary. If this sounds familiar it is because in many of the tribal nations of the United States transmission of power is also based in blood and a belief in inherited authority and family origin. Tribal enclaves in the United States find, therefore, that they, too, are the hotbeds of such fraud in the modern world. Lots of it occurs under the compelling rationale of foreigners trying to get access to natural resources and indigenous rights.

The shape of the historical record for those frauds in Indian Country has been meager when compared to the historical record for European incidents of this same crime of pretending to be someone other than who one really is. Byzantine politics mixed with the power of the clergy, and church offices in England and France contributed in the Middle Ages to claims of royal birth, the declaration of self as Christ figures, going so far as to perform miracles and milking various potentates for money.

Finally, the incidence of such crimes became so pervasive that rulers like Elizabeth I of England prepared what were called "sumptuary laws," intended to defend royalty, but they did little except tell people what they could wear and what their status in society meant, along with many other petty personal restrictions. These laws put in place some tentative punishments, but these restrictions largely pertained to regulating personal behavior on moral or religious grounds.

Since the laws of the United States are not supposed to be oppressively concerned with morality or religion, such laws have not applied to the frauds in colonial Indian societies. The closest Natives have come to passing a sumptuary law was in 1978, when the Indian tribes in the United States got the federal government to pass the Indian "arts and craft laws," preventing non-Indians from pawning off their arts and crafts as "authentic Indian-made" goods, and requiring that such works be identified as either Native- or non-Native-made. Tribal citizenship papers were required for exhibitions. This was a modern attempt to protect identity from those masqueraders who dyed their hair black and wore braids, beads, and moccasins when they attended the premier art shows in Arizona, South Dakota, and Oklahoma.

Since such sumptuary laws generally do not exist in Indian law, "fraud" is the term used to define the behavior of identity theft, and it was seldom described as a crime in Indian Country in the early years. It is defined in the law today as "a deception deliberately practiced in order to secure unfair or unlawful gain" and left at that. It stands to reason, one supposes, that since there is little chance of being beheaded or burned in oil for pretending to be someone else, as was the case in the Middle Ages, modern people engage in such behavior ubiquitously and without fear.

Just as Giannino di Guccio Baglioni proclaimed himself king of France in 1350 to gain status and power, so, some say, did the white American educator Ward Churchill centuries later, in order to be hired as a professor at the University of Colorado in Boulder, start dressing himself in buckskin, growing his hair long like an Indian, and declaring himself to be a Cherokee Indian for status and power. He seized this opportunity, as did many others in the 1970s academic climate, the success of which depended almost entirely on the credulity or gullibility of the audience. Unlike many of the fables of Europe's Middle Ages, though, which often possessed an element of truth, the Churchill fraud was proven to have none. According to the news organizations that investigated the phenomenon, he was most certainly born a white man of immigrant legacy in the United States, claiming with no evidence to be an indigenous person. As it turned out, he was ousted from his long-standing arrangement as the Indian expert and spokesperson of the ethnic studies enclave at Boulder after a lengthy trial for academic malfeasance other than identity theft. He sued for recompense, and in a touch of irony was awarded one dollar. The willingness to believe, despite claims that are simply ridiculous, contributes mightily to this kind of deception in Indian Country. Often one hears such biased rationales as "Well, he looks Indian."

In the hereditary monarchies of Europe is a long history of imposters. With the exception of the Anastasia poseur claiming to be that Russian aristocrat some forty years ago, whose intentions have never been satisfactorily exposed, such fraudulent deception is recognized as being deliberately practiced in order to secure unfair or unlawful gain.

That motivation was recently revealed in the case of a white American woman who called herself Sasaoleiah Bluespruce and wore her long dyed black hair in braids to "become" Indian for unlawful gain. Though she was never able to present evidence that she had ever been a member of any tribe in the United States, she claimed to be three-quarters Indian by birth in order to be hired by the Cheyenne River Sioux Tribe of South Dakota as chief judge in their tribal court system and to claim eligibility for health benefits from the Indian Health Service, a treaty right of Native Americans that requires tribal citizenship credentials. She was an attorney admitted to practice before the state and federal courts in South Dakota, so her claims were considered deliberate deceptions by the courts that finally exposed her and charged her with fraud

This crime started prior to her arrival at the Cheyenne River Reservation, when she applied for admission to Seton Hall University Law School at a time when law schools, in an effort to promote diversity and affirmative action, were looking for minority-race students. She changed her legal name, Lisa Refert. The document she submitted was not a tribal enrollment document, but apparently the university was uninterested. She claimed she was "regarded as an Indian" in her community, which would arise under 42 C.F.R. 136.12, a federal regulation that was used at the time by the Indian Health Service to provide health services to unenrolled Natives who are linear descendants. Even this claim was found to be false. She was found guilty of fraud by a federal court in Pierre, South Dakota, and dismissed from her job. She hasn't been heard of since in Eagle Butte. Proof, though, that such frauds, incomprehensible and defective as they seem, are not without record, her weather-beaten Blue Spruce Law Office sign continues to stand vigil on a lonely road entering Lantry, South Dakota.

A more egregious example of fraud was perpetrated in 2004 by a man named Charles Roger Leo Adams, Jr., who used the name of a dead man at Pine Ridge Reservation, among the following aliases: Leo Wolfslayer, Charlie Wolf, Wolf Slayer, Charlie Wolf Slayer, Charlie Smoke, Sunkmanitu Tanka Isnala Najin, and Leo Chico Adams. It has been documented that this fraudulent Indian was born in Memphis, Tennessee, to non-Indian parents. He was charged with spouse abuse, a criminal charge that was dismissed for lack of jurisdiction, thanks to the Washington State *Oliphant* case, which in 1976 ruled that tribes could not have power over white people on Indian lands. This law still stands as one of the most important attacks on Native sovereignty in the twentieth century. The Oglala Sioux Tribal Court ordered the imposter to "cease and desist using the name of Charlie Smoke, which is not his real name but is, instead, the real name of a deceased member of the Oglala Sioux Tribe and has no authority to use the name." Adams had appropriated the name after the death of the real Charlie Smoke, an Oglala Sioux citizen with whom he had become acquainted. Since the tribe lacks criminal jurisdiction over non-Indians, Adams was transported to Hot Springs and excluded from the reservation but was never criminally punished. It goes without saying that such frauds as this are perpetrated constantly in Indian Country today, and the erosion of the tribal nation's ability to defend its citizenry is at constant risk.

There have been many uncomfortable controversies in areas other than these kinds of cases for employment and power on Indian lands. The contemporary writing world, as an example, is filled with frauds, and Native writer frauds are no exception. These are usually called "literary forgeries" rather than identity "frauds" and are often dismissed as insignificant. They are not considered crimes at all, and therefore there are scant legal remedies. Buffalo Child Long Lance, Grey Owl, and Carlos Castaneda had brief literary careers based on their "authenticity" as Indian personages. Their books are still on the shelves under the rubric of Native American studies.

These frauds occur not just in Indian literary venues, but in all kinds of situations. J. T. Leroy, for example, who was actually Laura Albert, wrote the novel *Sarah* when she was twenty in order to sell her "authentic" memoir as an underground voice to the movies. Albert's defense was that she "really believed that he was inside of her."[3] A memoirist calling himself Nasdijj, published by Ballantine and Houghton Mifflin, claimed to be a Navajo Indian in order to be published as an "authentic native voice," but was eventually exposed as a white porn author named Timothy Patrick Barrus. There is little case law regarding claims for damages on these literary occasions, and often consumers of these literary works, if they want to make a case of it, have to provide proof of purchase and a sworn statement that they would not have purchased the books if they had known that they was not authentic.

Punishment for such imposters is imposed, we are told, in direct correlation to what can be assessed as threat or harm. In the monarchies of Europe, to claim identity other than your own in a nation based in royal precedence was serious business, as there was no question that the authority of the kings and queens of the realm was at risk, along with their entire kingdoms if such frauds were believed. Because of the fear of the relentless fracturing of the national polity in the Middle Ages, imposters to the throne were sometimes sentenced to death and butchered in the most inhumane way. Some were arrested, handed over to the authorities, and never heard of again. Many who were caught were publicly hanged and mutilated, some were paraded around the city's streets in shame, some were given a royal pardon, and some were even held up as harmless madmen and treated as a joke. It all depended on whether or not the imposter could conceivably construct apparatuses elaborate enough to throw off legitimate ruling class powers thousands of years old. To cast doubt on the legitimacy of the powerful ruling class of Europe was not just a bad review, it was a crime of the first order.

Executing white Americans who pose as Indians or killing them in some obscure prison cell is probably the wrong way to go, but mere banishment from powerful positions in Indian Country and the imposition of a tacky little fine, which is today's punishment, hardly seems adequate. The reason for indigenous nations in the United States to be calling for more severe action is that the ongoing struggle for recognition of tribal nation sovereignty and citizenship rights is one of the more advanced survival issues of the twenty-first century. This reality check is what makes the Churchill case more than mere gossip and personal opinion.

Also, there have been long periods in Indian-white history that have combined overt governmental action against political legitimacy with the human misery of the colonial condition, preventing powerless tribes and their delegitimized leaders from making their own decisions. The struggle to do so while faced with inadequate and corrupt law and justice systems continues.

It is a fact that the use of lineage and principles of heredity or blood and the belief in family origins for authority and power has always been an actual and even primary criterion for influence and power in tribal enclaves. It was deemed controversial and unreliable to the colonizers of American Indians, who wanted to deplete and diminish long-standing power centers, often themselves creating "chiefs" who would sign on the dotted line.

To fail to understand that the belief in lineage is a matter of indigeneity, statehood, and nationalism has always been the colonist's unfortunate, deliberately illegitimate grasp of Nativeness. Most will admit that the future of Indian Country is in the land, yet blood, race, and sovereignty provide political power and status that has been a survival mechanism since before the first colonizer stepped on these shores. Indigeneity is a complex concept, and the denial of its legitimacy has always been the American colonist's intellectual but politically powerful flaw. Settler-immigrant nations like the United States find it useful to dismiss summarily indigeneity as a category of influence since it often calls into question the settler's legitimacy as he claims the land and his own presence.

One of the reasons for the failure to sustain the charge of fraud against imposters in Indian Country, we are told, is that fraud as it is currently defined in the law has to be based not only in deception, but it also *has to cause harm.* It is one of the reasons that the university did not take it up in their legal remedies, because the professionals who are in charge of the university's mandates do not comprehend the harm done to Native nationhood; even if they did, it is not high on their scholarly or political or moral agendas. Had the defense of indigenous nationalism, citizenship, and history been among the principles of established practices of the university, they would not have hired Churchill in the first place, nor would they have promoted him throughout his career. It is a well-known fact that several Native scholars objected to the hiring of Churchill at the University of Colorado at the beginning of his efforts to claim professional credentials and tribal identity. These Native protestations were not considered valuable, according to university hiring processes.

The harm to the aristocracies of Europe seemed sensible enough to Western thinkers, yet the harm to tribal nationalism and citizenship rights fails to transcend such long-standing logic because tribes were wrongly described in early histories as savage and without government or law. If U.S. law requires documentation showing to whom imposing false identity is harmful, Indians have apparently failed to make their case to the satisfaction of the U.S. courts. Indeed the deception of those who are claiming falsely to be Indian seems to be a matter of indifference to the law.

Yet history suggests that the destruction of *a people*, illustrated by the destruction of the Jewish population in Germany, starts out by making them stateless, without citizenship. To do this and sustain it is a function of genocide, as the Nuremberg trials after World War II documented. The German example serves as the most primal case of historical genocide, bringing with it dispossession, expulsion, dispersal, massacres, occupation, discrimination, denial of dignity, assassination of leaders, endemic colonized poverty, and, eventually, the ovens.

The harm done by the denial of tribal citizenship, which is a sovereign right recognized by the tribes since time immemorial and never renounced in spite of massive and implacable tinkering of the laws to force that denial, is impossible to calculate. Since 1934 and the passage of the Indian Reorganization Act, formalized ways to identify tribal citizens have been codified—sloppily, to be sure—in tribal law. But there it is, in contemporary tribal law. Qualification as a tribal citizen is based on kinship rules and recognition of tribal sovereignty and treaties, among other things. This means that gratuitous, self-serving declarations, for whatever reasons, must be considered unlawful. Without question, citizenship is a legal concept, and it cannot be simply ignored in the case of American Indians who possess dual citizenship.

Whole chunks of the following text are taken from the letter reprinted in the appendix to this book. This issue is of prime importance to the future of Indian nationhood, so repetition can bring rare insight to a very controversial postcolonial matter that requires attention from Native scholars. This may be the perfect moment for Indian studies scholars throughout the country to demand that American universities and other institutions stand by the side of the indigenous populations of this country in defense of dual citizenship (First Nation and U.S.) and against fraudulent claims to Indianness. The defense of citizenship is, after all, one of the most important functions of any sovereign nation. It may be time for educational and governmental structures to become real democratic institutions and stop perpetuating authoritarian and colonial rule against indigeneity, by preventing people from pretending to be Indians when they are not. Penalties for Native nation citizenship fraud must be just as severe as the penalties for impersonating a citizen of France or Russia, or even a priest or policeman. Tribal identity is not a manifestation of social relationships or innate characteristics. It is a legal status that is cultural and political and must be defended.

In the final analysis, the struggle for tribal nation citizenship rights has never been thought of as a valuable democratic ideal in the United States. It is not as though these tribes are aristocracies or nations, is the wrongful thinking that feeds into the dilemma. Indeed to know of that denial and its consequences is to understand how important a tribal model of Indian studies as an academic discipline has become in the First Nations' comeback from the cultural near-death of the past two centuries. It is in the academic discipline of Indian studies, after all, that indigenousness and sovereignty are taught as essential concepts of American history, not argued about or equivocated, but examined as historical principles embedded in culture and history.

In the Churchill case, the idea that his claim to Indian identity was fraudulent was hardly a blip on the radar screen of those who wanted to defend American ideals of free speech. Freedom of speech in the United States is much more significant as an ideal than Native nation citizenship. Why? Because most Americans, even Churchill, see Indians as ghosts of the past, forever gone like wisps of the wind, or, if they must face the fact of their presence, as distorted images of themselves.

Indeed there seemed to be a dreadful lack of understanding of the contested issues in Native affairs by the most astute of academic and intellectual persons when a full-page advertisement appeared in the April 2007 issue of the *New York Review of Books*. It deplored the dismissal of Ward Churchill as an attack on his academic freedom to have an unpopular opinion (reference to a controversial essay), which it indicated is "the oxygen of the life of the mind." It was signed by such notables as Noam Chomsky at the Massachusetts Institute of Technology; Derrick Bell, visiting professor of law at the NYU School of Law; Howard Zinn, then professor emeritus of Boston University; and even Rashid Khalidi, Edward Said Professor of Arab Studies at Columbia, among many others.

In their "defense of critical thinking" these folks fail to see the absurdity of assaulting and humiliating indigenous distinctions in history and culture by dominating the thinking process itself with what they believe to be their own broad interests. Their failure to examine the bitter misfortune of their own intellectuals' trashing the rights of America's First Nations can only be seen as an enslavement to their own denial. Defense of critical thinking in this instance is an oxymoron. There is no excuse for this coterie of U.S. scholars to trample on the large issue of Native rights in defense of a man whose work does not deserve their amicable or shallow or radical dispositions. What motivated a few scattered Native scholars to defend him, like my friend and colleague Michael Yellow Bird, who was, at the time of the controversy, the indigenous program director at Kansas State University, remains even more inexplicable.[4]

The truth is, it's not only democratizers who are the problem; it is law scholars too, who are complicit in this denial. To attend Federal Bar Association meetings is an exercise in understanding that confusion and apathy is the heart of the citizenship and imposter and fraud controversy of recent months. In that august body, there is little effort and absolutely no interest in reviewing policies and imposing a factual historical order. The banality that passes for law theory in this regard is illustrated by such anonymous comments as this: "I really hope tribes can get away from this notion of blood as the essence of Indian identity," and "There might be some kind of long-term benefit for Indian Country if we can adopt some kind of expansive notion of Indian Country," and "We need other blood in our cultures."

The emailing and blogging by Native scholars that went on during the Churchill controversy was a signal that the more that is known of that case, the more polarizing it becomes, and the phenomenon of fraud itself will probably not be examined with any clarity. "Will it accomplish anything to register our objections?" or "We don't need to prove anything!" or "We must stop using the term 'tribe' because anthros and other scientists have taken the term to mean 'one-state,'" or "It's really all about money."

American contemporary society emphasizes the attraction, indeed the seductiveness of taking on an imaginary persona, and the American Indian, an indigenous anomaly, a deviation, like a planet divergent from its perihelion, helps the settler American from another world take his false version of history and transform it into an "experience" that is tolerable. It is another way to rewrite the invader's history of imperialism and arrogance, which is difficult to acknowledge in the midst of platitudes and piety that often pass for historiography. Finally, it is the quintessential method by which the colonial United States, the essential nation in global affairs, sustains itself as a colonial power even in the face of a powerful and ubiquitous Native population.

Part III

Two Case Studies

What follows are two case studies demonstrating how it is that colonial power has deprived American Natives of not only the terrain called "homeland," but the will to imagine the self and the people. There are many such case studies, many patterns of legal systems and educational systems based in the colonizer approach to human rights and defensive resource rights, indigenousness, economies, and intentions. Much of what has happened to the indigenes in the United States is hidden in actions and lies, flawed legislation, and the colonial practices of settlement and dominance.

Today, decolonization requires the recognition that there are no perfect histories in the development of modern democracies, only those that *we can overcome.* These two brief essays provide patterns for decolonizing critiques of materials long thought to be merely a part of the vagaries of history and therefore without need of examination for bias and debate. One is legislative, the other literary.

Case Study 1

The Assault on a Nation through the Political Applications of Colonization (1888)

1888 Sioux delegation to Washington, DC.
Courtesy of the South Dakota Historical Society, Pierre, South Dakota.

This 1888 U.S. government photo may be one of the saddest photos in all of Indian history, imaging the relentless emaciation or weakening of a people, the Dakotapi of the Northern Plains, by an aggressor government intent upon genocide. It shows the leaders of a people whose economic systems have been destroyed by invaders, a people who are starving by the thousands, displaced and weary of war, now asked to agree to their enforced colonization. It is a photo that precedes the so-called Ghost Dance by a couple of years.

Hauntingly, these Natives, to a man, wear their traditional moccasins as they stand for the photo, and a couple of them even carry a sacred pipe as indications that they are the defenders of their own legacy. Reflected in their faces is a collective expression of profound grief. They know that they are what is left of a stunningly effective Indian military that won more wars than it ever lost over many generations, signed a "peace" treaty with the country whose military they had just vanquished on the Powder River and the Little Big Horn, put a modicum of faith in a document (the Fort Laramie Treaty of 1868) they believed protected their boundaries, which stated in writing that no white man could ever again enter their nation without their permission.

Without weapons, they stand for the photo, twenty years after their victory and their signing for peace, knowing they now must face aggressive legislators, white educators, Christian proselytizers, and hostile neighbors. This sad photo is posed, an indication that colonization by a determined aggressor can subdue and subjugate even the most elite defenders of the land through complex and multivalent schemes.

When this photo was taken, 7.7 million acres of Sioux treaty lands had been stolen by U.S. legislative action, a congressional fiat, called the Black Hills Act of 1877. Broken up as a tribal nation, assigned to several separate reserved enclaves, they look into the camera a decade later from the steps of an imposing building in Washington, D.C., where they are now being forced to accept another land theft, called the Allotment Act (the Dawes Severalty Act of 1889). They recognize they are to be robbed of much of what they thought was protected by the treaty of 1868—in the end, two-thirds of their estate—and they know this is their last stand. They know they have no access to the courts, and thus no access to justice. But they know, too, that their historical location is within a non-Native culture deeply embedded in imperial domination and that they must somehow go on. They are two years away from a stunning massacre of their women and children at Wounded Knee.

This history has been described as "a tragedy" by most historians, simply illustrating the vagaries of war. Others call the period of the 1800s an era of genocide, for which there are patterns and analyses from scholars impelled by moral and political accounts. Most recently, the contemporary historian Daniel Jonah Goldhagen published a volume in which he says that genocide and eliminationism are crimes notable in the modern and ancient worlds, and that the two words are synonymous.[1] Goldhagen and many other writers believe that mass elimination and its mass murder variants must be included in the definition of "genocide," no matter the stage of warfare, no matter the moral blindness that requires of American historians (and others) a cleansing of the Indian War period.

While many historians place such an obvious example of genocide as the Jewish Holocaust outside of history, Goldhagen points out that such a placement is not acceptable to thinking scholars, that instead, such a history must be used as a reference point. The reason for that is that the institutions associated with the Jewish Holocaust have been shaped by the perpetrators' ideology, their needs, and their views of the victims, as U.S. institutions are also shaped by the perpetrators of a different ideology. Those institutions carry that ideology into the future, in law and policy, even after the genocide has ended, to act as patterns that have occurred in a variety of instances and must be acknowledged and understood.

Native historians who believe that a holocaust happened here in the United States as well as the rest of the Western Hemisphere and that the U.S. government is guilty of genocide during what is called the Indian War period utilize those institutional patterns to back their legitimization of the use of the term "genocide" to describe what has happened to American Indians. The camps, the "removals," the death marches, the dismissal of treaty agreements, the roving killing squads made up not only of military, but of guardsmen and community patrols: when Goldhagen says that these methods have been used by all of the nations accused of genocide—Russia, China, colonial Kenya, Guatemala—he forces the United States to analyze its behavior toward indigenous peoples. Looking at these patterns of eliminationism, we know that hundreds of thousands have died by these institutional means; therefore, structural eliminations cannot be ignored in the discussion of genocide if there is ever to be the responsibility of nations to act and safeguard weaker peoples.

The first step is to acknowledge genocide as a pattern of the policy toward American Indians, which the American intelligentsia in general terms has refused to do for centuries as it goes about what it considers its alternative to elimination, that is, colonization. To acknowledge genocide on the part of the government not only rejects the ideas of "national interest" or "building a democracy" or "fulfilling the nation's destiny," which are used to rationalize the United States; more important, such acknowledgment would reject the basis for the brutal colonization of a population that could not be eliminated by warfare, a population that has always had resources (land, timber, gold, water), necessary for the making of the invading nation. Colonization is not just the invasion and inhabiting of a place owned by others; it is the setting up of laws to legitimize the power of occupancy and ownership. This is the dilemma of saying that the unspeakable policy toward Indians actually constitutes genocide. It requires the admission of criminal behavior. The United States has always omitted itself from the international treaties on genocide and continues to do so in the international law of the modern world. American scholars of democracy consider U.S. laws necessary to good governance and a stable society. On Indian reservations even today, the writing and enforcement of the laws of colonization are always charted by the federal system, often without the consent of the governed. One thinks immediately of the mid-twentieth-century Missouri River project, which, through federal law, destroyed millions of acres of treaty-protected land for hydropower over the objections of citizens who lived there.

Such laws, say some anti-historian scholars,[2] turn out to be a legitimizing factor for the notion that patterns of genocide depend upon the motives and actions of the colonizers. If the motives are acceptable, structural features of suffering and violence can be overlooked. The federal government and legal institutions defend federal Indian policy by means of the principle of the responsibility to protect ("trust") and safeguard the people. This has turned out to be a shield for further plunder and oppression.

When this photo was taken in 1888, these Sioux leaders, as well as many others from many tribes across the nation, were expected to approve what came to be called the Allotment Act, the doling out of small parcels of treaty land to individual Indians as a way to further break treaty agreements and to make Indian land available to white settlers and ultimately to rob the tribes of two-thirds of their treaty lands. To achieve this and to further the "vanishing American" theory of history, an assimilationist policy, a tactic of genocide that starved and weakened thousands of its victims, is rarely thought of by some historians as anything but a necessity to democratic ideals. The people in this photo did not sign anything at that time, even though it was another "sign or starve" command they'd heard before, and many agreements would eventually be forced.

This photo reflects an effort at genocide by a colonial government that has never admitted to its aggression, its illegality, or its racism. Those attitudes continue even today, in efforts to culturally and politically emasculate a subjugated group in order for the colonist to entrench himself and his claimed power. This policy started during a lengthy phase of immense conflict and ended in the U.S. legislature and federal courts, in which Indian nations had no standing. Indian tribes had no access to U.S. courts or international bodies for land issues until 1940, more than fifty years later. That is a long time to wait for help to come.

This photo poses tribal leaders, confined for decades to Indian reservations, under the control of powerful bureaucrats, interpreters, Christian educators, and police in an effort to get them to forget their authentic indigenous identity and agree to an unlawful taking of treaty lands. No one in the photo agreed; there were no signatures obtained at this time. Nonetheless, even without tribal sanction, the Dawes Severalty Act was passed by congressional authorization the following year. Many such laws were passed subsequently, and governmental photos like this one have been utilized by historians ever since to signify the Indians' agreement.

In the photo are famous Lakota, Dakota, and Nakota names in English translation: American Horse, He-Dog, Gall, Standing Soldier, Bowed Head, Fire Thunder, Little Wound, Hairy Chin, Yellow Hair, Two Strike, Charger. Crazy Horse (Oglala) is not here; he was murdered by federal troops in 1877. Neither is Red Cloud, the great war chief and negotiator of the Oglala. Their Powder River victories are nearly forgotten, overrun by congressional legislation. When this photo was taken Spotted Tail, the charismatic Sicangu chief, had been dead for six years at the hand of a political opponent. Sitting Bull, the Hunkpapa, who has two years to live before he is assassinated at Grand River, stands to the left, a major and powerful opponent to what the tall white officials who stand in the front row are proposing.

It is said in tribal lore that Sitting Bull angrily left this meeting for his home on the Grand River, and when he got there he immediately saddled his horse and traveled to all the reservation enclaves, urging his tribesmen to work against the Allotment Act. Many of them who had thought about the consequences of such land loss agreed with him. The doling out of small parcels of treaty land to individual Indians was a corruption of tribal law as well as treaty law. Sitting Bull had to be killed by the U.S. powers because he stood in the way of building a nation utilizing Indian lands. He had to be killed because he was a powerful man with a great following among all of the bands of the Sioux Nation, even though subsequent histories have made an effort to diminish his reputation.

The Allotment Act and subsequent laws were based in a "vanishing American" theory, an assimilationist policy that, when passed the following year, robbed the tribes of two-thirds of their treaty-protected lands, further reducing them as a people. Sitting Bull was shot to death by federal police in early December 1890, and nearly three hundred starving Minneconjous were massacred at Wounded Knee two weeks later, martyrs to the resistance. These were the consequences of the deliberate and aggressive acts that achieved statehood for North Dakota and South Dakota one year after the Allotment Act was passed, a mean history ironically glorified even today in a region drenched in the blood of Indians.

Genocide, the intentional ruin of a people, we are told by those who study these things, "never just happens. It is a systematic religious, ethnic, or racial destruction of an entire society for the purpose of ridding the perpetrators of an unwanted or hated or unassimilable group."[3] Theorists of colonization admit that forms of colonial power and genocide differ radically from each other, which means that the reason to look carefully at the history this photo images is to understand that the crimes of colonization (theft, killing, oppression, paternalism, forceful submission, proselytizing) are always understood at the local level. Postcoloniality, which is the subject of this collection of essays, requires that *political applications of colonialism* be the major part of the discourse. In Indian history, addressing the true intention of the political has rarely if ever been examined freely because there has been little investment on the part of American policymakers or historians to call colonization a crime. The word is not given great concern in one of the best texts on federal Indian law, *American Indian Law in a Nutshell* by William C. Canby, Jr., which is used in most courses on Indian historical subjects.[4] It is a work of incalculable value to scholars but, unfortunately, says little about the canons of colonial law that are at the heart of the subject matter. Colonialist criticism is not the function of American law scholars, apparently, and is hardly on the tongues of even the American Indian lawyers who have made it through twentieth-century law study centers to occupy tribal places.

The protection of the universality of the law in the United States seems to escape the pressure from non-European and non-American societies like Africa and India, or the work on orientalism done by Edward Said, which means that the value of the scant postcolonial discourse in the United States and Indian Country does not provide a methodology necessary for us to educate ourselves. Nonetheless impediments to understanding the nature of colonial law in the United States can be overcome only if the law is viewed from subject positions of the local, which makes this case study a beginning strategy for examining an occupying power's cultural and political influence.

Political Applications of Colonialism in the Sioux Case

The 1888 photo is not the only evidence of political considerations between the American colonizer and the Sioux, but it is a place to begin. Real events and historical U.S. governmental and court action are at the core of the brutal colonization reflected here. Nineteen years earlier than the posing of this photo, just after the Treaty of Fort Laramie was signed by the Sioux, the Arapahoe, and the Cheyennes, so-called peace commissions were sent to Indian Country to persuade Sioux tribal leaders to "sell" the treaty-protected Black Hills, the place the Sioux consider the sacred place of their origins. This land was never for sale, but at this fragile stage, when the failure of the U.S. military was obvious, some misguided and misinformed bureaucrats and politicians indicated that persuasion could, perhaps, become the name of this newest game. It is a tactic that has moved the case into the present time, unsatisfactorily monitored again.

In 2010 a tribal coalition gathered at regional meetings in the Midwest under the auspices of the Sioux Nation Treaty Councils and the Tribal Chairman's Association to continue the discussion of the "stolen lands" claims. They recalled the threat to the survival of the tribe perpetrated by the "persuasion" technique was rejected in the 1880s, even though the "sell or starve" theme of the commission was heard loud and clear. The "peace" initiatives failed, and a few years later, the U.S. Army, led by Lt. Col. George A. Custer with a thousand men, invaded the treaty boundaries in violation of the most important command of the treaty, Article II, which stated that *white men were not allowed on treaty lands without tribal nation permission.* These are the facts of such tribal gatherings in the modern context.

Custer was killed in 1876 by the strongest Native alliance ever seen in the Northern Plains, made up of the Sioux, Arapahoe, and Cheyenne military. In spite of his resounding defeat, within the next decade he became a national hero, albeit a controversial one. American policymakers, believing their own press accounts, wisely moved away from military solutions and, under the mask of defensive political action, patriotic rhetoric, and congratulatory nationalistic piety, initiated the legal agenda for the destruction of a people through intense colonization and aggressive genocidal tactics, laws best described as unconstitutional.

Within the next year, the U.S. Congress passed the Black Hills Act of 1877 in a fit of political revenge, claiming title to over seven million acres of Sioux lands. In 1980, a hundred years later, the U.S. Supreme Court described this act by Congress thus: "A more ripe and rank case of dishonorable dealings will never, in all probability, be found in our history."[5] The Court made it clear that the Act must be called a "theft" in legal terms, not a "taking," as it had been described in previous decades. This case hangs over all contemporary mechanisms for justice because, though it finally described the confiscation of these lands as a crime, no lands have ever been returned.

The Oglala war leader Crazy Horse was killed by U.S. Army troops at Fort Robinson, Nebraska, the same year that the Black Hills were stolen. Some Native historians have deemed his death a political assassination. The U.S. government had to get him off the warpath so that settlers could move in and democracy could proceed. From that time until the middle of the twentieth century, the Sioux, fleeing into Canada and dispersed on reservations, had no access to the democratic law of the United States to defend themselves from ongoing land thefts. With the buffalo gone, they starved and died of disease by the thousands as white settlers moved into their homelands in a flood of fraudulent migration. It was not only a time of "dishonor," as Helen Hunt Jackson has called it. It was a time of genocide.

Interestingly, *the political applications of colonialism*, that is, assassinations and the passage of unjust laws, were disguised as democratic ideals of freedom and Christianity, but it seems in retrospect that it was always the congressional intent to replace tribal nation law practiced by these indigenous peoples for thousands of years with new and developing federal law not yet two hundred years old. The most significant step toward control by any colonial aggressor is to destroy the self-governance of the people under the guise of protection and democratic ideals.

A mere five years after the theft of the sacred Black Hills another theft occurred, the theft of any hope for tribal self-governance. It has been called the Major Crimes Act of 1883. This law is still at the core of much conflict on Indian lands in the twenty-first century, and is perhaps the most important example of cultural genocide when one talks of repressing justice. Hope for the defense of the sovereign rights of indigenous peoples was dashed by the fervor of a broader constituency. This is the scenario: In 1883, when an Oglala religious figure named Crow Dog shot the important Sicangu political leader Spotted Tail on a lonely road on the reservation as the result of a political disagreement, the idea took root in U.S. government circles that tribal law in these matters, which had existed for generations, would not, should not, and could not be sustained. At first Crow Dog was sentenced to death for murder in the First District Court of South Dakota, even though South Dakota (still a territory) had no jurisdiction in the matter and had not yet even achieved statehood.

The case went to the U.S. Supreme Court, which, in a rare moment of clarity, said that federal and state jurisdiction did not apply. It released Crow Dog, allowing him to go back to his homelands and be punished for his crime according to the law of his people. But the recognition of tribal sovereignty which this case put before the Americans was short-lived. Two years later, Congress acted. It passed the Major Crimes Act, which would claim federal power for seven crimes on Indian treaty lands: murder, manslaughter, rape, assault with the intent to kill, arson, burglary, and larceny. It still holds that power and has since added several more specific crimes. Federal jurisdiction on Indian lands has been the reality ever since. Major crimes are handled by the federal courts on the reservation lands; FBI agents have free access and often conduct raids, especially in the war on drugs, with very little public knowledge or scrutiny. Tribal courts, often staffed by unlicensed law advocates, handle traffic violations, domestic disturbances, drunks, and wife beaters. Non-Indian violators cannot be tried in tribal courts.

The Major Crimes Act was perhaps the most significant and destructive colonial act of genocide outside of the continual land seizures of the 1800s. This legislation didn't just marginalize or control Indians. It wasn't just discursive oppression. Along with the religious policy of subsequent laws passed to force Christianity upon non-Christian peoples, the Act destroyed tribalism and has occupied a conceptual genocidal category in law ever since for discerning scholars of Indian affairs. Until the *Crow Dog* case, there was little federal interference with the law on treaty lands, even though the tyranny of colonial rule was always a top priority of the U.S. Congress.

Along parallel lines, the advance of Christianity often encouraged the idea that forcing moral universality on Native peoples was essential, even if Christian moralists and their compatriots had to act outside of the U.S. Constitution, and they often did. It was the law of the land to force children away from their families for Christian teaching at boarding schools, at first in the eastern United States, and later throughout the West. The man responsible for that outrage is in the front row of the 1888 photo: Captain R. H. Pratt, founder of the notorious Carlisle School for Indians in Pennsylvania. Many of the children of the tribal leaders in the photo were at that moment attending these schools across the country. It was Pratt's pride to claim the children of the famous Sioux chieftains for his enterprise, and, as a former military man disguised as an educator, he never suffered a moment's hesitation.

The recognition of tribal sovereignty was further eroded within a span of less than two decades, and was quickly trampled when the Wounded Knee killings occurred in 1890, a massacre called in historical renderings a "battle," though few of the Indians there, who were mostly women and children, were armed. Land thefts and colonial grabs for power continued until an effort in 1934, with the passage of the Indian Reorganization Act, set up tribal governments as we know them today in accordance with federal regulations. Bureaucrats wrote fraudulent "constitutions" with no legislative function (often called "token" governments by Native critics), which would be regulated by the feds, proposed free elections every four years as a function of "democracy," and promulgated principles of bureaucratic organization based on the bureaucracies of Washington's pattern of colonial law.

This development has proven to be another doctrine of isolation, closing off a reservation to appropriate development to be utilized as a "colony" of the United States, with "absolute territorial rights," "the plenary power of Congress," "title," "trust," and "rights of discovery" held intact by the colonizers even today. Reservations continue to be pockets of poverty, struggling for a banking system and a taxation system, fighting off the economic and political dependency inherent in a colonial vise. Ironically, some call this condition "postcoloniality."

It is the history of the colonist to say "We understand our Indians," or "We will always do right by our Indians," or "We must protect our

Indians." The implication of the colonist's gaze is that understanding the Indian and controlling the Indian go hand in hand, so it all amounts to a self-defeating exercise for Indians if the aim is to throw off the shackles of a colonial past. Academics often use the term "postcoloniality" to imply a series of linkages and articulations that appear to be complicit with yet an opposition to the imperial enterprise. Postcoloniality as a real period of change becomes a useful and wicked device that requires the indigene to deform himself in accordance with various sites of discrimination and domination, particularly in the context of the controlling law and policy that confront Native enclaves.

Colonization is a costly effort for the perpetrator unless resources like water, coal, timber, and gold, along with other natural resources, can catch up with expenditures. Nothing makes this more obvious than the twentieth-century state jurisdiction and termination laws and policies that followed on the heels of the massive land thefts of the previous generations. House Concurrent Resolution 108 (the Termination Policy) was enacted in 1950, at the same time the federal government was initiating a massive Missouri River power project, flooding 550 square miles of Sioux treaty lands for hydropower, again displacing thousands, devastating the environment, and causing endemic poverty and homelessness among the people. These acts were the prime movers of colonial intention at the time.

Public Law 280 (a federal law called in the vernacular "state jurisdiction") was passed at the same time to relieve the insufferable Bureau of Indian Affairs of costly treaty obligations and to reinforce South Dakota jurisdiction over select Indian properties as well as law and order systems on Indian lands. This amounted to the liquidation of the tribal entity almost entirely, causing further devastation through relocation policies and laws that were promulgated to send thousands of, by now, landless Indians to the major cities in the United States on "relocation." It allowed the "trustee" of Indian properties and the congressional power enclaves to gain unconstitutional ascendancy.

This engendered so much anxiety in the halls of justice in Washington, D.C., that an American Indian Policy Review Commission was set up to investigate misdeeds of various kinds. But by 1976 the issue of whether or not Indians' control over their own lives was now becoming dangerous to the lives of white folks was the focus of lawmakers. The *Oliphant* decisions were among the results, decisions from a couple of cases emerging from the Suquamish Tribe in western Washington, whose tribal police attempted to arrest a drunken white man on their lands during Seattle Festival Days. This twentieth-century set of decisions made into law and policy dismantled what was left of the right of all tribes to punish non-Indian offenders on their treaty lands. This came out of the Rehnquist Court, the most implacable anti-Indian court of recent memory.

The twentieth-century legal discussion against the sovereign rights of Indian nations has been persistent ever since, astonishing lawyers across the country who know something about history. This erosion of tribalism indicates that the subsequent rise of the militant American Indian Movement, probably the most important defensive movement since Sitting Bull's time, was something more than mere desperation. It was a declaration of war by a people who felt they had no other recourse.[6]

Though Indian studies scholars continue to try to displace the dominant apologetic historical discourse of the academy with something more critically realistic, they may have to come to the realization that the driving forces of U.S. colonization of indigenous peoples, based in moral superiority and material profit, cannot be undone in this capitalist colonial democracy called the United States without a massive revolution in the law.

It is knowledge of corrupt and corrosive law that is reflected in the eyes of the Natives in the 1888 photo. They recognize that laws stripped them of their own centuries-old ways of tribalism. Their legal traditions were to be replaced, first, by no law at all for decades and, finally, by a vacillating, ever changing mode of colonial control, starvation, and endemic poverty. These are cases of political genocide from which the First Nations are still recovering.

One of the mistakes colonists have made throughout history has been to believe that oppressed people will forever be content with destruction, poverty, and discrimination.

Case Study 2

The Dismissal of a People from the Dakota Prairie: A Case of Literary Genocide (1920–1930)

Photograph by and courtesy of Victoria Linden Wicks.

Pentimento: an artistic work in which "a trace of an earlier composition . . . becomes visible in the present moment after the passage of time."

Midway through the Dust Bowl times and the Franklin D. Roosevelt era, the story and image of a little house on the prairie emerged. It recalled the period from the turn of the nineteenth century until the middle of the twentieth. No Indians appeared in this story, even though thousands of Indians lived in the neighborhood at the time the story was written, having barely survived what is now called in Indian studies "the years of attrition." This story, sometimes called a "memoir" by the more

discerning scholars among us, resembles today a faded painting, a pentimento, a morality tale by those who want to believe.[1] It is used as faux history, as poignant memory, as tragic loss, and it is one of the most popular
books about the Northern Plains ever written for children as well as for
adults.

Literary scholars admit that memoirs are notoriously dishonest. Artists
know that pentimenti are notoriously unreliable. There are few exceptions
to those admissions, and this story is not one of them.

The work spoken of here is *Little House on the Prairie*, a memoir written by
Laura Ingalls Wilder.[2] For some it is a study in midwestern values, for others a pentimento resembling a worn and weathered painting of a hundred
years ago, a self-congratulatory image, compelling fantasy, and a literary
challenge to reality.

Artists might use the term "pentimento" to describe this phenomenon,
something that might have been painted on a canvas but, with the passage of time, has almost disappeared and is now distorted and crumbling
with age. It is an apt metaphor for a biased settler-colonial story of white
folks in the middle lands and, in the throes of time passing, forces us to
ask puzzling questions: What does this story mean in terms of the politics
of white settlers coming into a foreign land and settling comfortably in
sovereign Indian Country at the beginning of the twentieth century? Are
the adventures of a little white girl who lived on an empty prairie with her
farming family espousing Christian values in a harsh but lush environment
a captivating, romantic tale of challenge and survival? Or is it something
much more distorted?

From the publication of *Little House on the Prairie* in 1923, to its phenomenon as an enormously popular television series in 1971, this story
has been successful in imaging, as if from a faded oil painting, what is
often called "the core beliefs" of Americana: the father figure as disci-
plinarian, the mother as pious homemaker, conservative white Americans as stalwart, self-sustaining, and rugged antigovernment individuals
dependent only on family and close-knit Christian fundamentalist community. Most essential of all is the image of the prairie as an empty
and unoccupied place to be snatched up by the righteous. The irony is
that the federal government (from whom the Ingalls family desperately
wanted to be free) made cheap land available to white settlers during
many homesteading decades by breaking treaties with Indians.

The story says little or nothing about the criminal settlement of the midwestern states in terms of treaty agreements with the indigenous peoples, or outright land theft from those who had lived in this prairie country for thousands of years, now being killed in wars, displaced and oppressed by capitalism, confined to small reservations in a new settler-colonial regime. Indeed one of the most significant and long-running Indian land cases in American history, the Black Hills land case, arose in this period, eventually being described as a "theft" by the U.S. Supreme Court a hundred years later. In spite of ongoing conflict and theft, the settler period as revealed in this fiction has been honored in midwestern history as a shining example of progressive democracy.

Today's conservatives, Sarah Palin and Ronald Reagan and others on the contemporary political scene, have loved this series of stories, which means, perhaps, that politics matters in literary studies, and children's books in particular, but, for strategic reasons, readers and authors must make no claim to that rationale, for if they did, it would be called propaganda rather than artistry or history.

Few academics, especially those engaged in the study of the humanities, argue against the power of literature to persuade. Anticolonial scholars such as Ania Loomba of India, who has examined England's historical narrative concerning her country and the struggle for independence, suggest that colonization would not have achieved the massive power it did without the literature and popular storytelling that supported it. We're told by the novelist Tom Wolfe in recent lit. crit. writings that President Abraham Lincoln believed Harriet Beecher Stowe had "struck a match" to the fuse of the antislavery movement with her *Uncle Tom's Cabin* (1852), and that the Civil War would not have occurred without her story.[3]

Thus, the question of whether or not the political implications of literature and the story about the little house are important to today's world is worth examining. This pentimento-like work, this "trace of an earlier composition," played itself out recently as television screens filled with distraught white U.S. citizens from the Midwest cursed the federal government in 2009 for its intrusions into their lives, wept as they confronted weary politicians, screamed and yelled such heartfelt agonies as "This is not the country I grew up in" or "I want my country back!" Women sob on camera, "The country we knew as children is turning toward Big Government, which means [gasp] socialism." White men, middle-aged and overweight, shove and claw at each other, pointing fingers and hollering angrily in each other's faces, "Let's get back to what the founding fathers wanted." They carry guns on their hips, having fought successfully for no-holds-barred gun licensing throughout the states.

In other words, these folks desperately want to get back to what the *Little House on the Prairie* so poignantly and imaginatively represents: dutiful Christianity, freedom on the open prairie, patriotism, community militia to protect the womenfolk, an imperialistic attitude to the world outside (we win, they lose), and, especially, a return to a world in which the white settler is the only title holder to the land.

These unhappy folks, the television spokespersons covering these events explained, were opposing the 2009 health-reform policies of the democratically elected president because they were perceived as being socially inclusive and a government takeover. Barack Obama, a newly risen black U.S. president, was attempting to call upon the country to revise what was being called a "broken" health care system in favor of a "public" option. He told the country that "health care and insurance coverage for everyone" is a universal right, not just an entitlement for the wealthy. He was vilified as a communist or a socialist or both.

On the surface, the idea of health care for all may have seemed like a democratic idealization of government addressing the needs of vast numbers of people, a forward movement to be sought in the new century of progress and technology, urbanization, and global reach. This, however, was a too-liberal agenda that conservatives said invalidated the history of every American's historical right to individualism, the "little house" history of self-sufficiency.

Those who accept the stories of Ingalls Wilder and other early writers as history say they know the real history of the Midwest, having lived through it as heirs of early settlers, and it is not what they see today in the political arena. The life of the pioneer woman Laura Ingalls Wilder and her famous manuscript were acted out in front of television sets across the country to say this new America is not the old America remembered from Grandma's days.

According to the imagination of a woman of Depression-era politics and experience, as well as those she has influenced, the family in the little house on the prairie is today's icon for American self-sufficiency and freedom. A new fervor from pious conservative republicanism, religious fundamentalism, antigovernment libertarianism, and the core belief system of a midwestern Depression era, described by some as political rather than literary, was on the rise.

The 2009 political scenario reflected the themes in the old manuscript. Turned into a series of books, it caught the American imagination early on, and when it became a television series (still available as reruns) it helped to establish what is often called the "core beliefs of Americans" across the country. Like many colonial fictions, it is often used as an explanation for the long-term stability of the United States even in the face of chaos, constant war and strife, invasion and occupation, subtle racism and entitlement issues of the twentieth century. Some historians and teachers, especially in the middle and elementary school grades, have regarded *Little House* almost as a primary source of good history, especially for children.

The woman who wrote the manuscript was an early conservative who espoused what came to be called nonliberal politics, or right-wing idealism. She was against social security because it would weaken the American notion of self-sufficiency, and she openly expressed the hope that President Franklin D. Roosevelt, who was pressing for humanitarian reforms such as social security for the aged, would be killed. Today she would probably be against a national health care plan. She is the fictive voice channeling the contemporary thoughts of western folks from places like Missouri, who wore holsters and loaded guns to midwestern television "town hall" events in 2009. Their presence and hers suggested by the signs they carried in demonstrations that President Obama might be in imminent danger from the citizens of the country, just as Roosevelt might have been in danger from the citizens of his era. Some critics have become fearful of this faux history. They believe the Ingalls vision is an exaggeration of the notion of freedom derived from a false exemplification of what the prairie embodies. They say that freedom is a thing to be protected, but that history has many interpreters, and they argue that government, contrary to the outcry, does have a meaningful role to play in ordinary lives.

In the early twentieth century, Laura Ingalls Wilder, as expected of a country wife, raised a family, among them a daughter who is largely responsible for the renewed interest in the original manuscript and who herself wrote a novel called *Free Land*. She is largely uncritical of a time when the federal government was taking Indian treaty land and giving it to "settlers" for three cents an acre or mere occupation. Pioneerism and "the poor will always be with us" and "doing good works" was a cover for the deaths and starvation of the Native peoples who were said to be "vanishing" but who were not. Indian neighbors of the Ingalls family were instead pushing for land reform and sovereign indigenous treaty rights to be recognized. Native activism of the early 1900s was ongoing, including a groundbreaking lawsuit initiated by the Sioux tribes for the return of the Black Hills, agitation for the development of tribal governments, criticism of missionary and military schools isolating the young from their tribal communities, refusal to sign land sessions.

The Ingalls family invaded not only the Dakotas and Nebraska for free (and stolen) land, but also the Osage land in Kansas, where they first built a home. This was clearly an illegal enterprise, and the family claimed to be astonished and aggrieved, pouring out antigovernment protestations, when federal troops came to evict them in accordance with the law that protected Indian treaty lands from such invasion. In fiction and in real life, according to the family story, the United States cheered them on even in their futile lament because they were known to embody the values of the white settler Christian population in the middle lands, as others were not.

This "prairie house" country, imagined to be free and unencumbered by the complexities of today's world, is the place today's mainstream American populations and its media tell us "we knew as children." Self-flattering images are produced of the past settler folks, believing themselves to be civilized and thrifty and prudent investors in America's future. These imaginations had few fans among the Natives. Sioux television watchers, in particular, found them to be the subject of ridicule, just as the Tonto stories of early movies were thought to be a joke.

Nonetheless such imaginings made up 1950s and 1960s television fare. Ronald Reagan, the oldest president ever to hold the office, talked often of the United States as "the shining city on a hill," and we are told that Little House was his favorite television program. The former president no doubt would have relished the scene when the Ingalls grandfather meets the threat of federal troops coming to evict him from Indian land by getting out his fiddle and singing, "We'll rally round the flag, boys," the battle cry of freedom.

These scenes helped to develop today's mantra against taxes and big government by so-called values voters in places like modern South Dakota, Nebraska, and the Midwest in general. The legislators from these areas have cut budgets for schools and decent housing and passed an "English-only" law as well as one that not only permits the carrying of concealed weapons anywhere in the country, but even gives ten-year-olds a license to carry a gun.

Values voters in today's democracy believe that these "rights" are American "rights of freedom," and many of them suggest that government is the enemy of the people. All of this echoes the songs of the old grandfather of the Ingalls clan, just as the oldest president of the United States, Ronald Reagan, told us in the 1980s that "government is the problem, not the solution." The fantasy has come back to haunt Americans, who now must live in the global, technological world of today.

Many Americans in the Midwest, sitting in their darkened living rooms with their children and grandchildren watching the small screen, have taken this faded painting into their hearts, even in the face of evidence that it is horribly inaccurate, incomplete, and self-serving. They cling to such depictions because it is simply more pleasant to believe they are entitled to resources and land and America's largesse because they are white and righteous in colonizing and Christianizing "others" who are neither. These stories, seductive and mythic and real, justify their seizing of assets belonging to others, stories that are true for the people who need them to be true. It is what the settler public in the United States has needed, both pragmatic and moral.

If *Little House on the Prairie* is analyzed as colonial settler literature for white children, however, and moves into a broader field for study, it can be asked, How might postcoloniality proceed without serious revision? The answer is, It cannot.

If scholars can agree that literature and literary study in the academy have been among the crucial sites of political and cultural influence, the faux-historical record is perhaps as dangerous, racist, noninclusive, and antidemocratic as any representation in storytelling and history played out through the decades. To call for a revision of academic goals may be a way to address a dishonest history. Recently, America's need to idealize its history and its innate goodness in the settler-pentimento manner has led it to transport intrusive colonialism throughout the globe. Several colonial wars in Asia and the Middle East have been initiated by the U.S. government in the twentieth century, and some critics have accused such stories as *Little House on the Prairie* of being among the instruments used to tell Americans that they don't have to examine past aggressive behaviors concerning the invasion and occupation of other peoples' lands because of the righteous development of this country. Such critics suggest that these uncritical and congratulatory narratives have played into the far-reaching results that have helped shape our political and military power into an industrial complex feared by the entire world.

America's stories, especially those written for children, rarely examine the colonial settler dark side of our concomitant histories. Driven by the notion that all Americanisms are good and that Americans are being discriminated against in a new world that has become critical of its colonial and aggressive past, these stories make it difficult to interact to new circumstances brought about by the passage of time. Just as an old painting cannot be altered entirely by the passage of time, neither can the inevitable introduction of a new image make the old one disappear; thus the fantasy of the little house becomes visible as an icon of uncritical entitlement for white settlers in the name of freedom on an empty prairie. It becomes the colonist's dream and invader's alteration of reality as morality tale in contrast to the clear analysis of America's colonial crimes against others. The awfulness of this dilemma is that it is sustained as real history and classic literature in academia and the media. This means that the intellectual foundation of the United States is warped, and therefore we can learn nothing from our nationalistic historical experiences. Learning nothing condemns us to making the same errors of domination and plunder over and over again.

Being critical of a colonial past does not suggest that all is wrong in the United States. Saying that the *Little House* story is not history does not mean that it isn't a good story, but it may mean that to use the story as something other than fantasy at any educational level is propagandizing in favor of a colonist's right to occupy and steal. Since it is a story without Indians, taking place in a prairie setting where there are thousands of Indians present, might even be called racist. Without going that far, we can say that this story must be understood and examined as essentially a memoir. We must say too that memoirs, though often engaging, are notoriously dishonest.

On a more hopeful note, what readers of this work need to admit is that to cling to a fraudulent colonial past makes it that much more difficult to interact with new circumstances brought about by the passage of time. It solidifies a perspective that will not accommodate a global community in the twenty-first century. Just as an old painting cannot be seen in all its clarity after the passage of time, the inevitable introduction of a new image cannot make the old one disappear. One paints over it, but the oil paints of the original will have to be acknowledged by the viewer as the legacy of time traces its own origins and aftermath.

This fantasy of the "little house" becomes visible as a pattern of entitlement for intruding white settlers in the name of freedom on a supposedly empty prairie. If the colonists' dream and invader's alteration of reality as morality tale becomes visible as a composition telling of righteousness and systemic justice for aggressive invaders and foreign settlers, there will be no opportunity for a nation that is becoming more imperialistic every day to discipline itself as a world power.

At the moment of the prairie occupation told so poignantly by the Ingalls Wilder narrator, Indians were being driven from their homes by brutal federal and state laws, their children were taken by the legal system and put unwillingly into Christian and military schools thousands of miles away from their people, their economic systems were being destroyed, and they were dying of starvation by the thousands in their own land. It wasn't just a way of life that was being altered by the settlement of whites; it was the destruction of a people who had lived successfully on this same prairie for thousands of years.

While it may be true that fictional stories can carry whatever weight a reader might be willing to bear, the notion that the memoir cannot be anything but a commemoration of personal experience and opinion has to be acknowledged. The capacity of Middle America to resist the story of the "little house" is the challenge of our time because, even though it is narrow-minded, unreal, and dishonest, it touches the heart of the white immigrant class and their offspring, which is a vast audience. Indigenous peoples like the Lakota/Dakota Oyate, who often play no roles in the story of their own country in works like the Ingalls Wilder oeuvre, have always claimed the primordial nature of the universe and their place in it. But in doing so, they have been different enough to be excluded from what some may call the imposed and settler midwestern voice. Others simply chalk it up to the ever present "vanishing American" theory.

What the Natives knew about the midwestern country was plowed under by self-aggrandizing fantasy keepers turned historians and memoirists, just as the prairie grasses were killed for the next crop of milo or wheat, and the trees chopped down for another "little house" to shelter another burgeoning wave of settlers, mostly white immigrants from Europe. The old grandfather of the Ingalls Wilder story continues to tell us, *There were no people on the prairie, just Indians.* Thus he plunks down his house illegally on lands belonging to others without a second thought. This dilemma is sustained as history and literature, while the intellectual foundation of the United States is implicated in a founding myth that sustains cultural conflict and, ultimately, the experience of genocide of indigenous peoples.

The midwestern voice is often thought to suggest an exploration of a specific geography and its people in the middle lands of a place known for its infinite diversity, not in personal or racial terms, but diversity in the environment. Perhaps that is what makes *Little House on the Prairie* so compelling to those who desperately want to believe in the innocence of place, rejecting an ugly history of aggressive war, Indian-white conflict, colonization, and dispossession.

Today the Midwest is a place of settler populations as well as indigenous peoples, both of whom often describe themselves as bare survivors: settlers who have barely survived the hot summers and awful winters, droughts and cyclones; Indians who have barely survived the white man's invasion. Because of the implantation of a New World theory of being and governance brought by Europeans in direct opposition to an Old World theory of indigenousness, conflict has been inevitable, which means that the struggle for unity and diversity is ongoing.

The Midwest is a place related in spirit as well as history to the rivers and the hills, and it is the story of the struggles of all comers who have tried to live together in an incomparable landscape. But the deception that goes with all nationalistic narratives like *Little House on the Prairie* gives an unfair advantage to those colonists who want to model history instead of examine it. Just as the Lewis and Clark diaries are idealized as benign history instead of records of invasions of sovereign lands, so does the *Little House* as master narrative create a cleansing of U.S. aggression.

Today there is some faint recognition that the Midwest is not a place of entitlement for invaders and conquerors, nor a place made for the white colonists' dreams, and the story Ingalls Wilder promotes is sometimes examined as an excuse for economic theft of resources, lands, and colonization. Like many of the Christian-oriented stories of colonization, it has stoked the fires of imperialism and rigid fundamentalism. At the heart of the "I want my country back" lament of the year 2009 and later is the continued dismissal of Indian history. This dismissal raises important questions concerning competing visions and rival histories in the American story and impacts America's global influence in a monstrous act of self-deception. To recognize this story as a *colonial* story in which the invasion and occupation of a place possessed for millennia by Native peoples as the basis of how Americans find success is one of the ironies of this nationalistic story as it seeks a broader audience across many geographies. Such historical lies and deceptions cannot and should not be sustained as historical truth. The Ingallses were not just innocent bystanders to a racist history; they were participants.

To use the narrative of *Little House as history* at any level of educational experience, be it elementary, high school, or college literature courses, is an outrageous assault on the traditional authority of indigenousness in any country and a literary act of genocide in the United States. The dismissal of the presence of indigenous peoples in an area they have claimed for generations as places of origin should be rejected as the substance for any meaningful curricular development in our schools.

Perhaps the story should be replaced by Helen Hunt Jackson's *Century of Dishonor* if Americans are ever to grasp the enormity of their self-deception.[4]

Part IV

Postcoloniality
A Mask of Civilization

Is Now the Moment?

There are stories in the oral traditions of every tribe that tell of how the people *moved on* in the universe from their mystic beginnings, and how they *migrated* across the abyss into Humanity. The stories say that there was only water and sky when the first Dakotas (the Ikce Wicasta) appeared. Tradition, expressed in the stories, ceremonies, and rituals, tells the Oyate that when they behaved on the earth in stellar ways, they were mimicking the holy persons, who told them they had obligations to free themselves from when they would acquire human flaws and had obligations to pay attention to the power of the sun when it would appear, and all of the Tunkashinas (grandfathers) as they became known to them. This continuous process, embedded in language, went on for thousands of years and continues even in modern times. All of this signifies the relation to power in the universe that has always been acknowledged by every living thing in the Dakota/Lakota world.

Realizing that the power indigenous peoples face in modern times is revived in a different world, we still ask: Is now the moment to reclaim our origins? The theoreticians in Indian law and literature whose works are consulted by historians and writers everywhere in this country are the newest destiny and are of necessity varied and eclectic. It is no exaggeration to say that many law scholars and essential historians, perhaps thousands of thinkers and writers, have found opportunities to enter the seemingly irresistible story of how it is that an indigenous nation survives an aggressive capitalist democracy in the modern world. Often they are people who know little or nothing of the esoteric and mystifying ways of the ancients, yet they have been forced to recognize the presence of the "un-vanished American."

A body of modern work, Indian law, emerges as a code of modern ideas from the substantial investigations of such scholars as the Harvard Professor Felix Cohen. A good reference volume that contextualizes the influence of Cohen in modern indigenous affairs is *The Indian Reorganization Act: Congresses and Bills*, edited by Vine Deloria, Jr., which makes available the documents of the premier years of reform in federal Indian policy, along with the influential testimony and writings by Cohen.[1]

Specialists theorize that the tone and themes of legal wranglings between whites and Indians across the country, but particularly in the Northern Plains, have changed since Cohen's time. Those disputes have now culminated in a watershed moment, which is ripe, we are told, for remediation and reconstruction and even reconciliation. Unfortunately, the past twenty years have also seen the rise of state power over tribal nation principles to an alarming extent, something that Cohen would have found objectionable and surprising since he laid down the substance of Native sovereignty as a modern concept. Evidence includes the flooding of tribal lands, initiated by state officials and federal mandate in the 1950s and 1960s over the objections of the Missouri River tribes, and the *Oliphant* case, emerging from state interests in Washington State a decade later, which took away the right of tribal nations to punish nontribal residents for their transgressions on Indian lands. Both of these events, and much legislation in between, indicate a weakening of the tribal nation sovereignty of tradition as well as what a few select early theorists in law tried to articulate.

Both of these outrages in law may have been seeded as the so-called termination laws of the 1950s gained agency in the Department of the Interior. This was at the time when John Collier's tenure as the commissioner of Indian affairs (1933–45) was coming to a close. In 1953 several states passed Public Law 280, giving state governments their first real hold on Indian affairs.

Vine Deloria, Jr., one of the foremost Native scholars in Indian law, complained about both Cohen and Collier.[2] Cohen, who had been hired in 1933 to write legislation for the 1934 reorganization of tribes and setting up tribal governments, followed Collier's lead. Deloria accused them of advocating structures that were rooted in Western ideologies rather than Native traditionalism. It is a complaint that continues today in Indian Country.

Some say the rise of oppositional power from the state structures calls for a constitutional amendment as the only defense. They insist that badly abused Indian law principles must be modernized and corrected to fend off state and federal interests. And they believe the U.S. Constitution should be amended to recognize the status of Native peoples in the United States. While that vague "recognize the status" is not defined in proposed amendment drafts recently made available, it is assumed that the status is a sovereign status, not a continuous colonial paradigm, both phrases subject to historical interpretation and that awful bugaboo in modern law, empiricism.

The Canadian example, which is suggested as a pattern for such recognition, reads, "The Constitution of Canada expressly provides that the existing aboriginal and treaty rights of the aboriginal people of Canada are hereby recognized and affirmed." Thus there is precedence for such a drastic move, even though there are no studies describing the outcomes of the Canadian First Nations principle.[3] Other countries that have recognized the status of their indigenous populations are Nicaragua, Argentina, Brazil, Honduras, Colombia, Mexico, and Russia. These are often called decolonization "reforms."

What is missing from all of this discourse is the fact that many of the movers and shakers of Indian law who set down the early principles had scant notion of indigenous history as it concerned political systems and governing constitutions of the past. Not too many scholars or politicians paid much attention to the fact that dozens of tribes, perhaps as many as sixty, had constitutions that predated anything that the Department of the Interior envisioned. Some say that tribal constitutions go back to the Great Binding Law of the Iroquois Confederacy, even to the fifteenth century. Indeed David E. Wilkins references this history in *Documents of Native American Political Development*.[4] If it is the case that these ancient structures of tribal organization were not encouraged in the thrust for self-rule, a serious omission has occurred. Ignoring or omitting the organizing principles of the indigenous nations in the early years of the United States probably has brought about much conflict and contradictory results as the 1934 governmental enclaves were (and are) put in place for modern times.

It is not only Deloria and Wilkins who found the Cohen and Collier work wanting. Frank Pommersheim has criticized two of the three Cohen principles that Deloria described as faulty. First, according to Pommersheim, Cohen claimed that because the tribes were "conquered," they were subject to federal legislative power that effectively terminated their external sovereignty but sustained their internal authority. This, says Pommersheim and many other legal scholars, is an argument used to sustain the "plenary power" of the Congress, yet many tribes were never "conquered," and many of them never went to war against the Americans. Therefore, Pommersheim suggests, this seems to be a specious argument. Second, Pommersheim notes that Cohen wrote that tribal powers had been justifiably qualified by federal laws and treaty provisions, but that any powers not expressly modified remained vested in the tribe and its governing bodies.[5] Indian law scholars criticize Cohen in this matter for vesting far too much power in the U.S. Congress.

Others who read these works, including this author, worry that the emphasis on these constitutions has delayed and continues to delay the study of court systems on Indian lands. Cohen himself, while sure that court systems were at least obligatory, believed that to call for separation of powers and the legislative powers of the tribal entity was of secondary importance, and suggested that the tribal court systems were unnecessary and troublesome. This explains why few tribes today incorporate the principle of a separation of powers; anyone who has worked for the tribes and tribal enclaves knows this deficiency to be a monstrous source of inefficiency, corruption, and conflict.

Without efficient indigenous court systems and without reliable tribal nation legislative functions, no democracy can exist, and no postcolonial structures will be developed for the First Nations concept. Explored in today's reality, the early semisovereignty couched in European doctrines of discovery and the rule of law, which is supposedly grounded in the "natural justice" proclaimed by a democracy called the United States of America, remains a detriment to Native Americans. Very little has been done by law to rectify the absurd notion that Indian lands and properties can be appropriated simply in the name of Christianity and democracy.

Any analysis of what is wrong or what is right in Indian Country would be incomplete if it did not talk about the newest developments in the third world. There is no question that what might be described as an amendment to the constitution law theory, suggested by many of the scholars in the field of Indian law, provides an avenue for an exchange of views. The precapitalist Native groups of North and South America, now urbanized and half-absorbed into the social pluralism that is called modernity, are experiencing a feeling of hope and power. The ravages of colonial wars, the conflicts between imperialists and Nativist movements, the humiliations and bitter disappointments nourished by decades of despair and anger are past, perhaps, and the struggling semi-independent enclaves believe that Western-educated Native engineers, doctors, lawyers, and scholars can improve the lot of their own people. They, along with the scholars of Indian law throughout the United States, have learned how to critique the principles of discovery that, five hundred years after the fact, keep indigenous peoples subjugated, poverty-stricken, and a U.S. congressional stroke of the pen away from extinction. These new working-class Native intellectuals and Native mentors, like those familiar to me—Mario Gonzalez, John Echohawk, Billy Frank, Jr., Jim Wilson, David Wilkins, Lionel Bordeaux, Elouise Cobell, Jim Riding In, and hundreds of others rising from their tribal homelands—know it is vital that they look toward an intellectual revision of the history of what is called "the rule of law," embedded as it is in European provinciality, if not criminality. Not all of them agree with the latest solution offered by some scholars to lessen Indian-white conflict, a constitutional amendment making American Indian tribes more like states, and many are looking at the Canadian example with skepticism, since there is little evidence of actual positive movement in defense of First Nationhood and land restoration even in that country.

The colonial themes embedded in constitutional law have yet to be tried successfully in court; thus it appears that with few formal charges of fraud and inhumane conditions on Indian reservations (even in the *Cobell* matter), such themes seem to be ex post facto legalized. The current state of affairs allows the outright thefts of indigenous powers. The allotment legislation in spite of Lone Wolf's objection comes to mind. The *Oliphant* usurpation of tribal defense, taking away the tribe's right to its own law and order over nontribal members, the *Crow Dog* case in 1884, and countless others offer little hope of true restitution, if left to stand. All of these practices and events are well-known and have not been challenged successfully in accordance with tribal thinking, which means that the U.S. judiciary engages in various technicalities for the purpose of presenting a façade of legality to indigenousness to obscure its original notion that tribal nations were (and are) a separate country. These are hard concepts to grasp, since tribal nations are located within U.S. borders and are surrounded by state governmental powers.

In the writing of the U.S. Constitution, tribal nations were recognized as sovereigns outside and on the margins of the new republic and its law. That is what is at the heart of the ongoing conflict, suppression, and colonization. What makes anyone think that revising the U.S. Constitution to ward off state power will assure tribal nation sovereignty, even if the tribes were willing to erase hundreds of years of their own history and autonomy? Who are the lawyers who will defend the original purpose of the Constitution's stance toward indigenous nations in the face of this state power?

Even more troubling is the ambiguity of the amendment proposed in, among other writings, a text by an eminent law professor at the University of South Dakota, Frank Pommersheim, which may turn out to be a substantial pattern for other law scholars to take seriously. It should be said that this proposal, while nothing new in substance, is in a draft stage and without clear support from either academic or tribal enclaves at this point. At other points in history this state-tribal analogy has been given some recognition in the discussion stage. Two of the most salient points are as follows:

1. The inherent sovereignty of Indian tribes within the United States shall not be infringed, *except* by powers expressly delegated to the U.S. by the constitution, and
2. The Congress shall have the power to enforce, *by appropriate legislation*, the provisions of this Article.[6]

Would such a proposal, with its exceptions, have changed the outcome of *Lone Wolf* in 1901, as just one example of the flaw in this thinking? Probably not, since the appeals court in this matter found that "reservation Indians with assigned lands had no vested rights but only the right to occupy 'at the will of the government,'" and the court system, as usual, protected the interpretation that the Constitution can delegate to the Congress and the courts its inferences.

The suggestion that the amendment (with its fanciful and useful "exceptions") will protect native nation autonomy may be criticized as an ideological mechanism for further oppressing Indian people and imposing further injustice, and, most important, for the self-serving rationale to protect the sanctity of the U.S. Constitution. What might make this workable, lawyers tell us, is actual cases brought before the courts by inventive thinkers who want to see it work. But this will take years, even decades, to accomplish. However, so as not to sound too pessimistic, one can say it is true that anything can happen when a change of philosophy about the function of the law prevails.

Concerning the issue of how to go forward, there are risks. Many constitutional law scholars masquerading as Indian law scholars have embedded an analysis in favor of an amendment in the defense of the U.S. Constitution, placing the blame for failures in justice squarely with the U.S. Supreme Court and the U.S. Congress, which have both "departed from the Constitution to inhabit plenary realms of unbounded federal authority." In making this statement, Pommersheim refers to the 1903 assumption of plenary power by Congress in *Lone Wolf v. Hitchcock* (187 U.S. 553).[7] He also cites *Oliphant v. Suquamish* (1978) and *Montana v. U.S.* (1981), all reflections of what has been called modernity in indigenous law. He points out that in the beginning of a treaty relationship (nation to nation), the United States, the Congress, and even the courts recognized the sovereign status of Indian tribes through the Commerce Clause (Art. II, sec. 2, cl. 2), and his analysis cites an erosion of those principles through subsequent years of attrition. These are the reasons, he says, an amendment is necessary. They are perfectly reasonable assumptions embedded in an imperial legacy by all of us who are unable to perceive of any alternative arrangements. But issues of land restoration and the correction of past legislative abominations are left untouched in this reasoning.

While all of this may assist practitioners in their lawyerly craft, and while it is a strategy to bring indigeneity closer into the colonial realm so pervasive in the theories of origin concerning the United States, little of it provides an adequate rationale for the separatism that is required for indigenous life and law and geography to have the power that comes with autonomy. The "discovery" of land on this continent embodies a doctrine of colonial law that remains the most entrenched legal doctrine at the base of all law concerning the indigenes on this continent. There is the denial that this idea is basic to colonization, yet there is no question that it has been used to justify genocide and elimination of indigenous populations. It is also justification for social practices that are a detriment to indigenous peoples, such as in child custody cases on the reservation, and heavy-handed law-and-order strategies concerning domestic relations. It is noted in a 2010 newsletter from the Indian Law Resource Center, under the headline "Native Lands Were Not Lost by 'Discovery.'" The newsletter encourages legal scholars to revisit the matter of the discovery doctrine, suggesting that corrupt law practices are to blame for land loss, not the doctrine itself.

This seems to argue with the position of David Wilkins, Vine Delo-ria, and countless others who have said that the discovery principle "gives the discovering European explorers absolute legal title and ownership of American soil, reducing Indian nations to being mere tenants."[8] This may be considered a political interpretation, yet one borne out by a couple of hundred years of experience. Speakers for the law persist in their own myopic view of themselves as defenders of the law and the Constitution. Recently the mother of all law scholars in Indian Country, Robert T. Coulter of the Indian Law Resource Center, said in the same newsletter, "It is disturbing to see statements by some Indian advocates saying that the 'doctrine of discovery' actually took away or denied land rights as a matter of law. Fortunately, the 'doctrine of discovery' did not, as a matter of law, actually take away Indian land, and we should not say that it did."[9] While Coulter's criticism may not just be a matter of semantics to those not trained in constitutional law, he seems at the very least to be chastising willing critics of the theory of discovery for not making clear their distinctions between doctrine and law. There is no question that everyone who treads in these legal waters, and especially those who teach, must be more precise in their commentaries.

Coulter, like many others, defends Chief Justice John Marshall, who, he says, understood and stated in 1831 and 1832 that ownership of Native lands were guaranteed and land rights were recognized (not granted) by treaties. In typical law-speak, Coulter writes, "The supreme court has accepted and reaffirmed such a body of law in modern cases." Nonetheless, he says, the doctrine is racist and unjust, and we can attack it for being racist and unjust.

Most scholars who are not trained in the law, including the writer of this text, do not defend the matter of discovery as it is applied in the law for a host of reasons. But these scholars still believe that discovery allows the law to assume that the land of the United States has had no prior human jurisdiction, a false assumption registered by every discipline known to scholars. One may say that the law has assured this assumption in its practice throughout the years. This might mean that one cannot say that such a doctrine is not a function of the philosophy of constitutional objectives.

If such a doctrine is embedded in the philosophy of law, how does a tribal constitutional amendment integrating indigeneity into a colonial structure (to make tribes more like states in a continuing federalism) assure a separate sovereignty, which is what tribal nations seek? To put tribes in the same category as states is still in defense of colonial America in its efforts to announce the end of indigeneity. Relationships between nations as advised in the treaty process (cut short in 1871, a mere forty years after and probably a direct result of the Marshall rulings) must be defended at the heart of the constitutional revision, and it cannot be if the "exceptions" still exist in the amendment.

The events chronicled briefly in this book examine some of the stunning differences between indigenous theory and colonial theory in evaluating not only what the law means, but what the historical events brought about by the law have come to mean. Generally, in the case of colonial America's founding and continuing myths of the wars against its indigenous populations, along with the subsequent genocide of hundreds of thousands of humans, the law is merely lip service given by scholars to the idea that invasion can be described as "encounter," genocide as "convergence." The notion that making tribal nations into enclaves to be treated like states in the context of federalism will bring about "equality" needs further analysis. Changing the history of the indigenes may be an answer to ending certain outstanding conflicts, but past efforts to do so have ended in the same question: Is this "justice"? What does it do about the land thefts, which have been more or less swept under the rug of judicial reasoning? Does it do anything to further the solution of returning lands to rightful owners? It is probably a fact that without the return of substantial land bases, no Indian nation will be able to continue its commitment to its people.

Constitutional federalism being sought in the law could, perhaps, curtail oppressive state law if the appropriate cases were taken to litigation, but it does little to defend the reality of world populations, not just tribal nations in the United States, that claim indigeneity. Bringing the First Nations in America closer to statehood, still under the controlling thumb of the U.S. Constitution, is hardly the condition sought by separate nations. The relentless exploitation of Native populations, resources, and geographies and the unanswered criminal charge of theft of a continent from the indigenes must be acknowledged in our concomitant histories if the United States is not to be found out as an unstable force in the world.

The truth is, these differences between colonial theory and indigenous theory have been evident for five hundred years or more, and for the most part they have been ignored by mainstream American thinking. One significant difference is that the colonial trait of success in acquiring territory and resources, feeding as it does into the hand of capitalist democratizers claiming success and worldwide leadership, also feeds into the second difference held by these intruders: the fantastic image of benign and deserved "dispossession," conquest, defeat, and inevitable death to the indigenes. Both differences are misleading because they create subjugated communities in a democracy that, in its defense of itself, claims that Native Americans, if they are to survive, should be preserved through colonization from mass slaughter, if for no other reason, as a moral undertaking.

This dilemma continues to be at the heart of problem solving in the real world, if not the law. The colonization that results from that defense requires that the "winners" and the "losers" create pacts following certain brands of political correctness. Somewhere, sometime in decades past, I read Edward Said's question about European colonization of the third world, though I can no longer remember in which of his many texts I read it. The question haunts my particular effort to write about this tribal nation scholarship which has been the thrust of my work of recent years. Said speaks in the voice of the European, adopting the unquestioned assumption that it is the destiny of Western nations to rule and lead the world. Is it not, he asks, "our errand into the wilderness"?[10]

"Our errand into the wilderness" is the phrase that I cannot forget because it is the essential thought of the colonist. These are the plenary words of a man of two worlds, which requires of colonized peoples that they become a part of their own colonization. "Our errand into the wilderness" is a phrase that rings in the ears with great loathing and fear of any indigenous person, yet colors the assumptions about how to live our lives in a colonized, modern world.

The failure to see Said's almost forgotten statement as a critique of the broad face of colonialism throughout the world is a failure to acknowledge the forgotten sentiment at the heart of the Indian-white (indigenous-settler) conflict in the United States. That sentiment is the reason that postcoloniality continues to be a word to "dazzle the minds" of settler thinking and immigrant theorists who make up much of the academic knowledge base. When Said spoke of the great colonizer, the United States, he questioned the poignant need of the colonizer and the colonies to come to terms. He was among those academics who articulated the reality that this is the continuing dilemma of great imperialist powers in our time. Going along with his occasional benignity, this dilemma may not be so much about the resistance to the simple cohabitation of settlers and indigenous peoples. After all, indigenous peoples and immigrant peoples have occupied the same earth for centuries. Instead, as this book has claimed from its first pages, it may be that what matters is the aggressiveness of colonization for the purpose of constructing the conditions for plunder. That implicates capitalism as a economic system that, for American Indians, has meant the use of the law by the United States to place a façade of legitimacy on unfair deals. The war of "discovery" and "conquest," then, is a political condition, not a battlefield, nor a moral choice. The thing is, it concludes by making half the world live in endemic and killing poverty.

Cohabitation is not the same as colonization. The remarkable reality of the differences in the United States concerning the origins of cohabitation does not account for the implacable persistence of indigeneity and its resistance to political pacts instead of treaties as solutions, constitutional amendments instead of land restoration. The record of history has proven that state-tribal pacts, embedded as they are in a colonial mentality, have not been successful in rescuing the poor and disenfranchised.

Dam building on Indian lands without the consent of the indigenous peoples who live there and over their strenuous objections, as well as casino development on Indian lands, a brainstorm engineered by politicos far from the scene of the crimes, have seemed to enrich only the manipulators of the colonial system, not the recipients of it. Such activities have brought about revisions, dislocations, and configurations that, on the one hand, rationalize the recognition of the human interdependence that remains the backdrop for hope for the future, yet, on the other hand, seem to bring more grief to an economically helpless population unable to run its own affairs.

What does account for the resistance is the reminder that treaties were signed between equal nations (separate countries) in the beginning of this relationship, an equality that has never been realized. Since the beginning, and particularly since *Lone Wolf v. Hitchcock*, the so-called nation-to-nation substance of an equal relationship in the law has been severely curtailed. Thus "pacts" between colonizers and the colonized, a major move toward colonization brought about by the failure of legislation, are by their very nature corrupt, a metaphor for the institutionalization of colonial power. They are agreements between imperial and nonimperial powers acting as instruments for further economic bureaucratization instead of freedom, a reality that results in continued colonization.

It's not that prior to the nineteenth century, the fervor of aggressive genocidal tactics of such legislation as *Hitchcock* did not occur. It's not that law and policy that challenged the rise of corrupt legal thinking toward indigenous peoples in the twentieth century did not have substance. It's that some of the genocidal tactics pointing to international intentions were initiated in an era of worldwide imperialism by European nations. The consequences of this era of economic boom were mostly unthought of, unpredicted, or ignored, all in the name of financial power and politics. Indigenous peoples have become the victims of these tactics throughout the world.

In any case, U.S.-tribal treaties were pushed aside in the formulation of political interventions, while what was seen as the uselessness of defending these engagements that might have warded off the ravages of alienation and domination were not taken seriously by lawmakers and legislators. At the base of this has always been the "vanishing American" theory and the rise to power of such democratizers as Teddy Roosevelt, who promoted Americanism as "big stick" foreign policy. In 1877, the year that Roosevelt was elected, Congress adopted legislation that would become the most famous and long-lasting land theft case of two centuries, the Black Hills Act, which confiscated 7.7 million acres of treaty-protected land from the Sioux Nation. The reality is that a nation of settler-developers of capitalism cannot steal land and resources from a Native people and then wonder why the Native people are poor.

Presently 371 of these active treaties with Indian nations, signed and delivered by the inchoate United States, are available in defense of sovereignty and indigenousness and as an intervention to the ravages of colonial law, even land thefts. In terms of the law, this means that the "reserved rights doctrine," emanating from the treaty process and ignored by white supremacists, colonists, and imperialists since the beginning of this nation, should be utilized to prevent the legal dispossession of indigenous peoples' rights and resources without their consent. The reserved rights doctrine, embedded as it is in treaty and given agency, if not strictly upheld even in the Marshall discussion, means that Indian tribal nations, the landlords of this hemisphere, are sovereign nations that may grant rights to the United States, not the other way around. That treatise is essential to the theory of indigeneity and to the defense of lands. It may not be too late to rejuvenate some of the principles of that doctrine, and that may be what Marshall hoped for.[11]

Some theorists say that the federal government of the United States does not grant, has never granted, and cannot grant rights to Indians, though two hundred years of contradiction and conflict and deliberate omission in the law has unfortunately amounted to more than empty posturing or academic theorizing of this reality. It has resulted in criminal behavior on the part of the U.S. government and its courts, which supposedly represent one of the most important democracies of any age.

The theory of indigeneity has long been choked off by the self-serving lawyers and politicians and leading intellectuals of the United States, who want to assert imperialistic machinations into this vast history and culture, as well as by complicit Native leadership that has, for survival reasons, one assumes, adopted an "accommodation" stance. Native nations will eventually assert themselves as a separate country for several reasons. The most obvious rationale for the assertion of self-rule is the connection to specific geographies where the holy presence of indigenous creators can be found. This is called the indigenous "primordial attachment" to the land.

The treaty process means to Native peoples more than merely an end to conflict or self-determination or whatever convenient term is used to describe justice; it means that any relationship a people has with the universe starts in the land and the holy persons who have inhabited it since the beginning. It starts in the primordial influences that have accompanied them in their emergence. That is why the Sioux people in the historical 1888 photo of the first case study in this text carry their sacred religious object, the red-stone pipe, to the negotiations into which they are being forced.

Economically and culturally speaking, on Indian lands today there are huge deposits of uranium, gold, silver, cadmium, molybdenum, platinum, manganese, timber, natural gas, oil, copper, zinc, and thirty percent of all the coal reserves in the country. Most important of all, on Indian lands there is essential evidence of the presence of ancestors who are still believed to be in charge of a spiritual and magical world that affects the fate of the living. In Indian Country the water that helped the stars give substance to geographical and primordial primacy is being fought over in courts throughout the country with little regard for indigenous survival needs.

A major solution to colonial-indigenous conflict in the United States, and perhaps throughout the world, begins with honoring treaties and returning stolen and otherwise confiscated indigenous lands. This is one of the only avenues to mending the criminal "errand into the wilderness" by white Europeans and their inheritors, the Americans, spoken of by Edward

Said. He is a major decolonization theorist who has said about his own legacy in the Arab world that Israel must return land to the Palestinians. It is the only avenue of accommodation between the imperialist and the imperialized which is so deeply embedded in many imperialist histories and in our own American history. The resistance by colonists to the idea of the return of confiscated lands of the indigene allows such a solution to go unexamined.

In addition to the return of lands, organizational work on Native enclaves must be continued, with Native leadership directing its talents toward efficient economic development of what they own, that is, land and resources, not casinos and tourism. Experiential theory tells us that American colonization of the Indian world began with acquiring the land, expanding, administrating, investing, and setting up the structures of privilege, schools, hospitals, and financial institutions, necessary for nation building. The present hostility between whites and Indians to such development makes it clear that efforts at restoration must now be taken over by the Native people themselves.

Today Native engineers, physicians, scientists, attorneys, writers, and all manner of professionals are moving out of the academic centers of the country into the broader United States as the result of affirmative action and other programs. Where are they? Too often they are serving the needs of American colonial systems rather than their own national interests. They are running museums for the edification of American tourists and historical interests, writing 638 grants for the Bureau of Indian Affairs, getting elected as overseers of colonial governments on Indian lands, and seeking MBAs in order to run gambling casinos on Indian lands. Indian leadership really has to look at what has happened to our intellectual class as a very serious cultural, political, legal, and moral crisis, not just a need for better housing financed by the feds on the reservation, or a stimulus package to create jobs for husbands, fathers, and heads of households. It's not just a question of money on the table. It is instead a steady crippling of nationalism that derives from various theories of failed liberation as well as a willingness on the part of intellectuals to repeat the imperial colonial experience simply because it is easier.

That's why, perhaps, "mutual consent" in the field of Indian law (since 1934) has become a dubious force rather than a joke that can be laughed off as a meaningless bureaucratic requirement. In the context of Indian leadership (whether political or legal), integration is too often revealed to be a coercive, half-hearted measure or even a paper-pushing task rather than full participation and agreement, especially when tribal protests should be taken into account. It may mean that in this contemporary universe of how to get things done, indigenous theory is on a collision course with colonial tradition that cannot be avoided or fantasized away. It may mean that Indians are in for a long, continuing fight, and postcoloniality or autonomy or self-rule is still a long way off.

In the struggle to make "postcoloniality" a meaningful term rather than just a mask of civilization or a term to "dazzle the minds" of academics, these political, legal, and moral issues probably cannot be dealt with by critics who are unwilling to accept the sensibilities of others. They probably cannot be dealt with if the actual experiences that are alien to them are ignored or omitted from the discussion.

State Governmental Power versus
Tribal Nation Autonomy

There is no question that the issue of state power embedded in the law of the past several decades must be revisited, as the review of works by Pommersheim, Deloria, Wilkins, Holm, Gonzalez, and countless others assert in the previous pages. Most legal scholars believe that the writers of this contemporary reality are on the mark when they say that the most important issue today in terms of justice for the indigenous peoples of the West and the Northern Plains is the usurpation of tribal autonomy by state law. This is the thrust of scholarly analyses in recent books by both Pommersheim and Biolsi.

In the West, and the Northern Plains (specifically in what used to be called the Dakota Territory), state governments did not become legal entities until years after the tribal nations had signed treaties with the U.S. government. This historical fact signaled, in the law, their sovereign condition. In the Great Plains, for example, the state of South Dakota and the state of North Dakota (formerly Dakota Territory) did not sign any substantial agreement of statehood with the federal government until 1889, decades *later* than the tribal agreements with the federal government, called treaties, were signed and sealed. According to the Indian law expert Felix Cohen and others, this set up a principle of the primacy of tribal nation sovereignty in Indian law. This primacy needs to be acknowledged by legal experts in the region in discussions of the U.S. Constitution, its possible interpretation, and its proposed amendment. Where there is such a thing as primacy in Indian law, the possibility of forcing tribal nations into mimicking state enclaves is an expansion of state power that promotes an anatomy of further plunder, all the while erasing thousands of years of indigenous knowledge and theory. Such mimicking of state enclaves required of tribal governments proposes a relationship that is a violation of treaty agreements, to say nothing of how requiring tribes to disavow the legacy of indigenousness and thousands of years of occupancy can be called equality.

Several well-known scholars, particularly the legal scholars mentioned earlier, have provided insights into central and enduring features of the colonial relationship between state, federal, and tribal governments in the United States. Most of this scholarship points out an unfortunate trait in legal thinking attending most of the legislation concerning the Sioux Nation, a major example used throughout this text: the constant need to dismiss for generations what it is that the Sioux nationalists have said about their condition, and the fear that Indian thinking on these matters is too aggressive, or in conflict with what the majority of state citizens needs, or evidence of unscholarly thought, or, very simply, un-American in its outlook. Dismissing Indian nationalism as a power to meet state needs, as is being suggested in some academic discourses, may be a step to alleviate particular conflicts, making the lives of lawyers and politicians less complicated, but it could also be a step into oblivion. The "vanishing" of Indian nationhood would surely become a reality if such reorganization in the law were to occur.

It is evidenced in every discipline rising from Euro-American thought that there is a constant need for the Indian to be deprived of his own ambitions. This makes him mimic and hesitate and makes the guise of postcoloniality confirm and subvert a real solution to conflict. When the 1903 *Lone Wolf* matter was said to be settled and the Indian had no access to the courts, his only reaction was to go into the mode of "reorganization." By 1934, in order to prevent the mass starvation of the surviving Native populations, and deprived again of his own ambitions, the Native's only recourse was acceptance of the colonial bureaucratization called the Reorganization Act. Getting ready for regimentation and co-optation and the setting up of further colonial structures prevented the rallying cries of those who objected from being heard. Many of the objecting leaders remembered that Sitting Bull and Crazy Horse had been assassinated by federal troops for their tribal "ambitions," and they knew that leadership from the tribes was under constant watch and revision.

This most recent proposed postcolonial solution—amending the Constitution, requiring tribes to behave like states—seems to be rising from the legal profession, not from historians or theologians, nor from the tribal enclaves themselves. Failure might again prevail because of the lack of attention paid to the indigenous voice. In many instances, law professors have now taken over the development of Indian studies as an academic discipline, suggesting that law and society courses must prevail in an academic world struggling to access what Indian studies might really mean to its constituents. Even though it has taken a very long time for bright white lawyers to finally admit to the illegality of the very law and theories of the law they have espoused for generations, the colonized and the colonizer still find themselves on separate pages struggling for consensus.

Clear examples of that divide appear in the works of several white lawyers who for decades have claimed the right to make genuine proposals and suggestions for alleviating poverty and injustice on reserved lands. Seldom do the proposals come from indigenous voices on reserved lands. Whether these Native voices have any better solutions than their lawyers is open to debate, but ignoring them has not been particularly effective in lessening intragovernmental stress. Describing the reality of endemic poverty and dissatisfaction on the part of the governed is of significant concern to those in charge of the law, yet a critique of coloniality itself is rarely part of the dialogue.

Anyone who has followed the writings about the Sioux (Lakota/ Dakota/Nakota) could not help but be attracted to Frank Pommersheim's book *Broken Landscape,* yet it is clear that looking at this vast history for the purpose of defending the U.S. Constitution rather than defending tribal nationhood, which seems to be the thrust of the solutions offered, may be another example of the separate intentions that have led us to this moment.

In the final analysis of American coloniality and postcoloniality as it applies to the Indian experience, tiptoeing around the issue of what happens if a law becomes illegal cannot be the final solution to decades of a policy by which a nation maintains or extends its control over colonies or foreign dependencies. Looking at the question of whether or not there is a mistake in the foundation of the law and the U.S. Constitution, relying as it does on "the doctrine of discovery," is a horror most Western thinkers cannot contemplate. Rather than tiptoeing away, they should assure themselves that such an eventuality as understanding and admitting to a colossal error without end must not necessarily be a revision of those documents, but a condemnation of them vis-à-vis tribal nationhood and a clearing of the way to a new path.

What must occur is the recognition that the First Nations of America are indeed a separate country as a whole, yet a collection of foreign dependencies seeking in the new century full autonomy with longtime interests in making nation-to-nation friends throughout the world. That is a huge and fearful undertaking, but one that must be taken on if internecine conflict and poverty are to end.

To merely amend the Constitution so that tribal enclaves can inhabit a different subservient condition called "tribal statehood" is an oxymoron and absurd and will never be accepted by the tribes unless they are forced to do so. Congress may rectify its actions, and that would be helpful, but the challenge to its own colonial history will not come easily.

Failing to disavow the mistakes of historical and legal experience and failure to return lands for the basis of economic development on Indian lands feeds into the continuation of colonial thinking. The need for the disavowal of the discovery doctrine cannot be ignored if the hope is for Indian nations to move toward genuine postcoloniality. Some worry that casting out the power of discovery, in which some scholars insist the "trust" responsibility is anchored, might forever sever an important protective relationship between First Nations and the powerful United States. These are the people who believe that the "trust" mechanism of the federal government is a guarantee of protection. Others are sure that the treaty process itself must be invigorated as the most powerful weapon the western tribes have in the struggle toward autonomy and true postcoloniality.

Conclusions

Coloniality and Postcoloniality: Academic Myths and Masks of Civilization

Contemporary leaders of the Sioux Nation and other large land-based indigenous peoples agree that the plunder of Native lands and resources and rights by the United States of the past five hundred years, sanctioned by federal colonial law in cooperation with the rise of aggressive state law, must stop, not only because conflicts must end but because endemic poverty and discrimination against Natives in the wealthiest nation on earth is a crime against humanity.[1]

There is general agreement that it is time to say that in a colonial relationship such as that which has existed between the indigenous peoples of America and the U.S. government since the beginning, a pattern of subjugation of a weaker population by a stronger one has been the life blood of the rationale for America's success as a nation. Models of exploitation that have nothing to do with its claim to being a democracy said to be the envy of the world have developed in the United States. Endemic poverty, oppression, domination, and death have been the result for Native peoples. The shame of this reality and the destruction of a precious environment inhabited for thousands of years by Indians is now of national importance.

Thus Native leaders have begun, again, to take on in new ways the curtailment of what they see as the continuous land theft and plunder referenced in many recent works such as this one. The tribes intend to have their traditional hunting and religious lands returned. They call for the defense of treaties and tribal nationhood (i.e., sovereignty), the lessening of which has never been agreed to except under duress by any tribal governing system. They call for the end of congressional plenary power over them. Perhaps these objectives are the same, because they challenge a system of domination and expand the possibility of freedom from constant theft and endemic poverty by the more powerful governing entity.

The continuing effort to defend themselves against a capitalist democracy sometimes works for Indian nations and sometimes does not. That is the nature, perhaps, of being caught in the web of colonialism and what is often referred to as federal Indian policy. Until that web is penetrated and destroyed, postcoloniality will continue to be a word to "dazzle the minds" of those who have no stake in tribal nation autonomy.

The crushing dependency brought about by the use of colonial power is the cause for the Alice-in-Wonderland nature of how the United States talks to its colonies in the modern world and keeps them subdued. To give a heads-up concerning what is to come, a brief look at a couple of recent issues is revealing. One of the tacit reminders of the devastating nature of colonization is the seldom examined issue of taxation, the foundation of any democratic ideal. Constitutionally and historically, Indian tribal status in the United States has protected tribes from taxation, a development of early and continuous Native autonomy and, some say, dependency.

The Internal Revenue Service, which is one bureaucracy that supposedly has no relationship to tribal nation lands because the phrase "Indians, not taxed" in the Constitution is a reminder of what can and should take place, recently astonished the Indian world by auctioning off 7,100 acres of treaty-protected tribal land in South Dakota for the supposed payment of a federal tax debt. This was land owned by the Crow Creek Sioux Farm, a corporation under the aegis of the Crow Creek Sioux Tribe, Ft. Thompson, South Dakota. The IRS sold the land to pay for federal employment taxes unpaid by the tribe, even though the tribal officials had been informed by an official of the Bureau of Indian Affairs that they did not have to pay taxes because the tribe was a federally recognized sovereign nation.[2]

Ignorance and confusion is no excuse, but the fact is, to make Indians landless has always been a strategy of the federal government as a function of its "vanishing American" theory toward Indians. It is obvious now that federal taxation has become the most recent tactic to be used to achieve that landlessness. In addition, state governments, by denying any legitimacy concerning the status of indigenous peoples in this country, have complained for decades that the Natives in their midst do not share the tax burden of ordinary citizens. Any manipulation of the law and the Constitution, therefore, to rid themselves of these historical realities embedded in the earliest agreements (treaties) will be acceptable to the general white population of Middle America. Thus there has been no public outcry concerning this offense of land seizure committed by the Internal Revenue Service, and little defense mounted by lawyers. "Settlements" are often the tactics used in these troubling matters, when in fact a rigorous plan to develop economies requires not only the return of lands, but an appropriate method of making those lands an integral part of tribal strength.

Bad and inaccurate advice notwithstanding, the land was confiscated from the poorest tribe, which has the reputation of having the most inefficient and corrupt tribal leadership among tribes in the region. Prayer ceremonies were scheduled by officials on the reservation, and contact was made with the South Dakota Tribal Chairman's Association in Rapid City. Emails were sent out asking for assistance from various bureaucracies, but neither the auction nor the legal decision was stopped. Lawyers were contacted, but they had few answers, and there was little defense. A Santee Sioux lawyer and professor of law in Idaho, Angelique Eaglewoman, published an op-ed piece that probably expressed the Crow Creek Sioux tribal opinion, suggesting that a long court battle could ensue. She wrote, "Tribal lands are not subject to seizure in this manner under the Non-Intercourse Act, 25 U.S.C. ~177, *without congressional consent.* The 7,100 acres the IRS has attempted to snatch from a sovereign tribal government cannot be so easily taken, particularly under the guise of an illegitimate imposition of federal taxes in the first place."[3]

"Congressional consent," as indicated in the law, is a defense that probably could have held up justice in the case for years. A "settlement" was undertaken instead of a vigorous defense. Little information from the local press and regional politicians was forthcoming at the time of the land seizure. Surely, though, the relationship one nation has with another nation, not always a smooth path to be sure, should be of interest to everyone in the region. The reality is, though, that the colonization of Native enclaves has been accepted for a very long time, which means that such illegal acts occur and treaties are allowed to be put aside. The lawyers simply "settled," money was borrowed from a neighboring casino tribe, and the debt was paid. To this date, little has been done to protect this tribal nation, nor any other, from the IRS of the federal government.

Corrective action in many land cases may be reaching its breaking point, and this particular land seizure may be among the cases that could have brought about a complete examination of the actions of federal agencies. The Sioux Nation may desire to take seriously into the twenty-first century the resurrection of its treaty responsibilities, expecting that such renewal of treaty status could be the force of the future. But there is an astounding change in the laws of colonization that must occur for that reality to come about.

The notorious *Cobell* case, another federal governmental theft concerning land and payments to land owners on the reservation, which was fought out in the courts over many decades, closed in 2009 after thirteen years of litigation.[4] This is another human rights violation and crime of "trust" that should be of interest to all justice-minded Americans, but like others, it has little meaning to non-Indians except to be taken as evidence, again, that Indians are troublesome and a drag on the average American who believes his or her precious taxes and rights are eroded by Native claims. To bring an end to this case in 2009, a fragile settlement was agreed to, which was deemed unsatisfactory to the Indian claimants. It seems to reveal a losing effort but a challenging and heroic one in which Natives are expected to accept $3.4 billion for the centuries of theft, euphemistically called the "mismanagement of funds," by the colonial governmental bureaucracies that hold such lands "in trust." No one on the tribal homelands knows if checks and balances have been put in place in these Washington-based bureaucracies that handle trust land matters, and it remains to be seen what "set-asides" for things like land consolidation and college scholarships, stated as principles of the case decision, might mean to tribal nations. Since it is a class action suit, not one brought by tribal governments, it will be some time before the meaning of this case can be fully realized. One thing seems unchanged by this effort of Native peoples to get justice: the reality that law firms throughout the land "made out like bandits," a comment by a tribal member at an open meeting in South Dakota.

These two unaccountable and casual examples, culled from the hundreds of such U.S. governmental actions toward its "colonials" in the new century, seem to be unthought of, unpredicted, and out of the hands of mere Indian mortals, yet they are bold blasts of modern imperial behavior indicating that such a term as "postcoloniality" is a staggering fraud. Paying off Indians for land thefts and federal government malfeasance does nothing to renew a land base and assure economic development. This means that to talk of postcoloniality is a fraud. It may be perpetrated by writers, researchers, governments, academic institutions, and historians of all stations simply because to do anything seems to be an enormous task requiring research and legislative action. Until the history of the beginnings of U.S. development of its laws toward the indigenes is rewritten, postcoloniality may be thought of as a ridiculous ruse of academe.

Beyond Doctrine: An Embassy Mission to a Foreign Government

Plunder and constitutional amendments and historical revisions aside, some say a new political era may be in the making. Leaders of the Congress of American Indians are putting in place mechanisms that they believe will provide for the eventual autonomy of Indian nations and the final throwing off of colonial rule.

Then again, maybe not.

In order for hope not to go extinct, consider this. In a strategic move to do good and perhaps to put themselves closer to the arena of power where they will no longer be invisible and vanished, more than three hundred surviving Indian nations, who make up the lobbying Indian Congress, celebrated the festive opening in 2009 of an International Embassy of Tribal Nations at 1514 P St., N.W., in the heart of the U.S. capital city, Washington, D.C. This may be seen as the first useful move toward helping America understand that indigenous America is a separate country—not a colony, not a vanishing entity, not a new world of land and resources that a more powerful nation can continue to plunder. This move is the culmination of years of planning by the National Congress of American Indians, a longtime lobbying institution organized in the 1940s, to enhance the presence of tribal sovereign nations in Washington, where much of the legislative action takes place.

The newly purchased embassy includes three office buildings, three carriage houses, and parking space for twenty-two vehicles. One of the buildings now houses the D.C. arm of the Native American Rights Fund, long housed in Boulder. W. Ron Allen, an NCAI board member, Ernie Stevens, Jr., chairman of the National Indian Gaming Institution and citizen of the Oneida Nation of Wisconsin, John Echohawk, the Pawnee director of NARF, and dozens of other tribal leaders hailed this event as a significant move toward strengthening and defending tribal autonomy. So did Senator Tom Udall, a Democrat from New Mexico who has been a tribal advocate for most of his professional life.

As further evidence that the indigenous tribal nations in the United States are going to push the U.S. government to honor centuries-old treaties, a hope that still lives in the hearts of the Indian people, is their effort to buy back land and put it into "federal trust." This, surely, is a shot in the dark, yet also a clear indication that the promise of cohabitation between nations is more than a fantasy. These land purchases, it has been said, will protect Native cultures and preserve the tribal way of life as well as protect the burial grounds of their ancestors and where sacred rituals are held.

More significantly, these purchases provide a land base for continued economic restructuring to some of the poorest people in the country, even though there is great opposition from local governing agencies, who say that their tax base is diminished even as they pay for service for the tribal populations in their midst. With a land base and an economic future secured, it is believed that a new relationship with other nations, including the United States, can ensue.

In the final analysis, it seems there is not a corner of life in Indian enclaves and territories, perhaps on the entire globe, that has not been touched and influenced by the empire building and aggressive colonialism so deeply embedded in the American experience. The controversial and extraordinary reach of Western imperialism continues its relentless colonization. How culture and politics have produced a system of domination of Native peoples and lands is a matter worth examination. Native writers, intellectuals, and politicians continue to produce the oppositional stance so necessary to exposing the criminality of the law, the rugged, brutal, and racist policies that stem from the law, as well as the everyday practices of discrimination.

If the phrase "our errand into the wilderness," Edward Said's poignant description of U.S. colonization, imperialism, and nation building, seems a rather academic assessment of the strategy of plunder, others are not so sure that this benign description of colonization bodes a secure future for autonomous indigenous nationhood. Contrarily, there are some political activists who see the phenomenon of freedom toward autonomy going off-course. Lyrically capturing this "errand into the wilderness," Said, a longtime observer of U.S. and international war and conflict, tries to help Americans direct their action toward a benign capitalism and democratic ideal that will be loved by the whole world. But for the American Indian, there is another side to the story.

Such a heartwarming phrase as "our errand into the wilderness," when used to describe the theft of an entire continent, is rejected by Bill Means, a leader of the Lakota American Indian Movement now residing in Minnesota, where he is at the hub of Native activism. He offers striking clarity to the matter and definition of colonization that is not quite so poetic. "With all due respect," he tells reporters from the *Minneapolis Star Tribune*, "I think the United States is continuing a policy of 'Indians are not humans.'"[5] A citizen of the Great Sioux Nation and a consistent leader of the American Indian Movement as well as director of the International Indian Treaty Council, Means is known to work every day for the return of the sacred Black Hills to his people. He believes in the hope of people like the now deceased Royal Bull Bear (former Oglala chairman of the Grey Eagle Society), who said, "I believe the government will return the Black Hills. For over a hundred years we've fought for our Treaty Rights."[6]

Because Means continues the tribal protest against theft and discrimination, and because he continues to share the hope for justice in the Black Hills case, his name comes up whenever there is an awakening on the part of the media and the American public. He is part of the legacy of the American Indian Movement, which both Means and Bull Bear believed in the 1970s had a chance to change the Indian world. Years later, Means now says with the flashing sarcasm that is his own, and with the final conviction of those still on the front lines, "Only in America if you steal something and hold on long enough does it become yours."[7]

His cynical words, said in objection to that corrupt but unfortunately demonstrable idea, ring in the ears of every scholar at home and abroad. They suggest with clarity that Americans may sooner or later be forced to confront the corrupt laws of their own past behaviors toward indigenous peoples. Whether they can proceed to becoming more than mere observers who will rise to the occasion and be responsible for their own history is as yet unresolved.

Much of what is now rendered in the American story gives the impression that the colonization of American Indians, like the enslavement of African Americans during the expansionist era, has just gone the way of bad ideas everywhere: no conflict, no wars, no aggression, no protest, no fingerprints, no crime. This ugly history somehow vanishes into the forgetful mist of years. This means that one cannot expect a civil war on the part of Americans to protect the indigenes.

To those who pay attention, though, the claim that colonization has just ebbed away and is no longer a feature of modern Indian life, or that colonizing structures and attitudes have just faded away, is the final insult.

To write that Indians are now postcolonial, as some writers are wont to do, is to announce the end of Indians. Anyone who lives on or near an Indian reservation in the United States knows that it is not possible to just dismiss with a wave of words the colonial structures that keep Indians in poverty and that, while American Indians are among the most implacable survivors of a bad history, their condition as colonized peoples is intolerable. Hard work to achieve the overhaul of colonial structures is demanded.

To believe that endemic poverty and the loss of human rights of Native peoples are just a function of an unfortunate history or unintended circumstances of ongoing events is surely the most effective way to write Indians out of American history forever. The art of writing the history and politics of how we are governed and the analysis of structural victimization are important business if real solutions are to be sought. This is not just a call to conscience. Nor is it just a way to squelch revolutionary movements. It is the crucial means by which we can come to understand how constitutional law and Indian law and international law are shaped.

This struggle for indigenous rights matters to the United States for all the reasons representative writers, from Sinclair Lewis to Thoreau to Felix Cohen to Thomas Nast and Vine Deloria, have said it matters. We are all responsible to history.

Most of all, the continuing struggle is a way to say that the Age of Colonization for American Indians and all other colonized peoples throughout the world must come to an end. While this text has centered its discussion mostly on the issue of colonization of the Great Plains area, where western U.S. treaty tribes reside, there are broader national and international analyses of the condition of Native peoples available in the work done by the United Nations in New York and Switzerland. Indeed the United Nations work focuses on the rights of Native peoples throughout the globe. The passage of the Declaration on the Rights of Indigenous Peoples by the United Nations Human Rights Council on June 29, 2006, at the Palais des Nations in Geneva, Switzerland, may be the most encouraging worldwide postcolonial move by scholars and activists to date, even though it is still a work in progress. What is called a "working document" is available from the General Assembly of the United Nations. The Teton Sioux Nation Treaty Council, along with other indigenous groups throughout the world, has been involved in the development of the Declaration beginning in 1984, when the UN Working Group on Indigenous Populations, in the context of many years of deliberation with indigenous peoples throughout the world, recognized the need.

Some people believe the Declaration, which was initially rejected by the United States, Canada, New Zealand, and Australia, provides the legal mechanisms to resolve issues of long-standing criminal behavior toward indigenes by colonizers. Others believe that further analyses of these documents are necessary to show the limits and dangers endemic in the text approved by the UN General Assembly. They say that the Declaration is limited in two ways. First, its primary emphasis is on the rights of individuals, minorities, and people rather than on indigenous nations, although the word "collective" in the document is meant to imply "nations." But implication, say those who have been on the front lines of this project for decades, is not enough. Second, many rights are stated as directives to nation-states, but there is no enforcement mechanism available. The Declaration says that domestic remedies are to be used, yet history has told indigenous nations that powerful antagonists at the domestic level cannot be overcome without international intervention. Critics say that because the Declaration fails to provide an enforcement mechanism for the treaty nations in North America, the status quo will prevail, no land will be returned, and plunder will continue. The Declaration promises to protect the land and the political, educational, and religious rights of the indigenes that colonizing nations have trampled on, but without providing the victims mechanisms to protect themselves. Over the decades, many antagonists and critics emerged, but the broader international focus is a welcome sign that help may be on the way.

Charmaine White Face (Zumila Wobaga), a member of the Oglala Sioux Tribe of Pine Ridge Indian Reservation in South Dakota, has been a delegate to the UN and a spokesperson for the Tetuwan Treaty Council for ten years. She is the founder of a Native environmental organization called the Defenders of the Black Hills, based in Rapid City, South Dakota, and has worked with the Tetuwan Treaty Council on land issues since the death of the Oglala Treaty Council leader, Anthony Black Feather, in the past decade.

The Sioux Nation developed its treaty council format for modern leadership shortly after the death in December 1890 of their revered war leader, Sitting Bull, and have been active since 1893 in the defense of their lands and indigenous rights. They have not always been happy with the bias of political agendas in the region. White Face has said that while the treaty councils have been stubborn and effective in stating their goals, the UN Declaration itself is limited because there are no enforcement mechanisms and no penalties; thus, she says, "the directives or laws have no teeth." Her position is that the Declaration should not just be a statement prohibiting discrimination against indigenous population and groups, but must also show the necessary intent to defend national legacies, for example, the treaty tribal nations of North America. "Who will help us defend our treaties," she says, is the major task ahead for the United Nations to grapple with. Her view is that the Declaration is still a long way from being a solution mechanism for that question, because the United States and other English-speaking states, the major colonizers of the modern world, find it difficult to come to a consensus. (A draft of the Declaration and a brief analysis is available through the United Nations Human Rights Council.)

In the final analysis, treaties signed between the U.S. government and the First Nations seem to hold the solution to age-old conflicts. To return to these documents, then, is to begin to understand how Native peoples organized themselves politically and culturally from the 1500s to the 1930s. It was in the 1930s that the U.S. government began its "reorganization" to put in place colonizing strategies for governing the indigenous population. Resistance to these strategies has been ongoing. The shape of postcolonialism begins in the essays and histories written by the indigenes. A new volume by David Wilkins will become the foundation for postcolonial studies in Indian territory.[8]

What makes the indigenous people of the United States unique is that they continue to practice a form of self-government that is at once accommodating yet in direct opposition to the colonial oppression inherent within their relationship to the United States.

Appendix

The Ongoing Struggle for Recognition of Tribal Nation Citizenship Rights

I sent the following letter, dated May 12, 2007, to the editors of the *New York Review of Books* in response to the "Open Letter Calling on the U of C to Reverse Its Recommendation to Dismiss Professor Ward Churchill," published April 12, 2007, an advertisement from Defend Critical Thinking.org. The letter was never printed, and no letter on this subject from an indigenous scholar was ever printed in the *New York Times*.

The future of Indian Country is in the land, yet blood, race, and sovereignty provide the most controversial and heated debates these days. Speakers at Federal Bar Association meetings don't talk so much about land theft (which is ongoing) as they talk about identity issues and gaming. If that seems unfair, just ask the Seminoles, or the Cherokees of Oklahoma. A couple of anonymous comments from the latest FBA meeting illustrate the banality of what passes for law theory: "I really hope tribes can get away from this notion of blood as the essence of Indian identity," and "There might be some kind of long-term benefit for Indian Country if we can adopt some expansive notion of Indian identity," and "We need other blood in our cultures." Taku? Taku?

This discussion will *not* take up the specific questions and comments referenced above except to say that the ongoing struggle for what can be claimed as tribal nation citizenship rights seems to provide a never-ending battleground for ignorance, self-centeredness, individualism, and fraud. A case in point is the example of the so-called Churchill case. In the case for dismissal from his university position in 2005 and 2006, Ward Churchill provides a case in point. Churchill had falsely claimed to be an Indian for decades. He got a professorship in the Ethnic Studies Department at the University of Colorado in 1973, probably using that self-proclaimed and pretend credential, perpetrating a "fraud" through that claim, got away with it for years, and is still getting away with it. After he made his now famous "Little Eichmann" remarks, the university has been trying to fire him for inadequate research credentials, but *not* because his claim to Indian identity was unsubstantiated. In the subsequent investigations Churchill was not charged with identity fraud by the University of Colorado in their effort to dislodge him from his university position, yet that is what a major critic, John P. LaVelle, professor of law at New Mexico School of Law, as well as countless other Native Scholars throughout the United States, contend it was. This failure on the part of UC reveals how little is understood of American Indian citizenship protocols, and how without sympathy such protocols are held by those in academia and elsewhere. Substantial investigations have shown that Churchill has no citizenship in any Indian nation and possesses no blood quantum nor a blood relative to tie him culturally, politically, or legally to a tribal legacy. Yet the charges against him ignore that aspect of his case.

One of the reasons for the failure to sustain the charge of fraud against Churchill is that fraud, we are told, has not only to be based in deception but also *it has to cause harm,* and there must be documentation showing to whom it is harmful. There is no doubt that Churchill's claim was based in deception (many researchers say he duped the university into giving him a professorship through his unsubstantiated claim to Indian legacy, in spite of his inability to produce citizenship papers from any officially documented tribe in the United States), but *that deception was a matter of indifference to the University of Colorado.* One clear reason for this indifference is because the university did not want to bring about more scrutiny to its own possible flaws in hiring practices. The truth is, because tribal citizenship is a matter of indifference and denial to much of the United States, there is now an entire cottage industry of people who claim to be Indians but are not; it is a cottage industry of frauds since recent times when so-called tribal claimants found that through that claim they could be eligible to receive any number of benefits.

Tribal citizenship has been recognized by the tribes since time immemorial, but since 1934 formalized ways to identify tribal citizens have been based in codified tribal law. Think what you want about the system, it exists and awards a political standard to those who qualify. It is possible that the university may not have even asked for credentials at all in this matter, but only those who have read the indictments would know whether that is true or not. The fact is, the university has not called Churchill's actions fraudulent in this case, in spite of the reality that this university (and others like it) has had forty years upon which to rely in order to identify an applicant as a tribal citizen. The academic dilemma brought about by the Churchill case has underscored the fact that universities have been lending their supposed credibility to such fraudulent behaviors in violation of the law.

In the process of understanding that fraud, in the legal sense, must cause harm, we ask: *Who is harmed?* Even though the university may not have asked this question, their action in dropping the fraud charge suggests that they answered their own question by saying, *No one is harmed.* The university did not take into account that Indian nations are the victims in this case and that there is substantial harm to the sovereign rights of the heritages of Indian nations through this diminishment. Indian nations are harmed because these frauds take away from them the right to define their own citizenship protocols. Such frauds allow any person on the street to qualify as a tribal citizen based on his or her own eligibility requirements, without kinship rules (blood), without recognition by the tribe (sovereignty), without making any contribution to a tribal legacy through gratuitous self-serving declarations.

The university officials also dismissed the possibility that their students could be harmed as they would recognize such imitation and falsity as outright lying by university officials. Isn't institutional lying harmful to a university's constituencies? There is very little research on this question, which means that in the university's dismissal or ignorance of tribal nation citizenship (or enrollment) requirements, there was apparently no legal concept that they would cite publicly. Even if university officials failed to know that Native citizenship is a condition of historical reality and significance, common sense should have told them that had Churchill claimed French citizenship without documentation in order to ingratiate himself into the Modern Language Department, or Italian or German or Syrian citizenship, the institution surely would have charged him with fraud and dismissed him forthrightly. Surely, it would follow that students of such a professor would have felt humiliated and cheated.

After the dismissal of the charge of fraud, the university did charge

Churchill with plagiarism, that is, "unacknowledged copying," or "creative imitation" (irony abounds), or "literary theft," but even that charge has been weakened in the subsequent discussions. For most of us, it would seem reasonable to say that plagiarism, while it may not always be a stable thing in the law, is a failure of originality. It would seem reasonable that this failure of originality is enough to stifle the notion that universities have the obligation to truthfulness to their clients. Revealing that there is a dreadful lack of understanding of the contested issues in Native affairs, and even underscoring the notion that truthfulness to clients is not necessarily a university ideal that can be pursued in all respects, a full-page advertisement appeared in April 2007 in the *New York Review of Books*. It deplored the dismissal of Professor Ward Churchill as an attack on his academic freedom to have an unpopular opinion, which it indicated is "the oxygen of the life of the mind." It was signed by such notables as Noam Chomsky, Massachusetts Institute of Technology; Derrick Bell, visiting professor of law, NYU School of Law; Howard Zinn, professor emeritus of Boston University; and even Rashid Khalidi, Edward Said Professor of Arab Studies at Columbia, among many others. These folks, in their "defense of critical thinking," may be on the wrong track if they fail to examine the bitter misfortune of this country's intellectuals to defend the rights of America's First Nations. There is no excuse for this coterie of U.S. scholars to trample on the larger issue of Native rights in defense of a man who does not deserve their amicable or shallow or radical dispositions. What motivated a few scattered Native scholars to defend him is an even more inexplicable act of injustice.

Copyright in scholarly work is something else, vis-à-vis the charge of plagiarism, and it may be that this case will live or die on whatever evidence can be bolstered by lawyers of one side or the other. The charge of copyright invasion is still hanging in ambiguous limbo in this case, since the university is now simply bogged down in a discussion of academic freedom, that is, the freedom to have a controversial or offensive opinion, which is, by anyone's measure, not an academic crime. *Copyright is a legal concept,* and there are protocols concerning those charges that can be defended in courts of law. Without question, *citizenship is a legal concept* too, and it cannot be simply ignored in the case of American Indian nations and their people, who have possessed dual citizenship in this country for many decades. The question of why it is not a significant charge against this fraudulent claimant underscores the failure of the examination of racism and politics in academia and should not be allowed to stand.

This may be the perfect moment for Indian studies scholars through-out the country to mount a demand that American universities stand by the side of the indigenous populations of this country in defense of First Nation citizenship. *The defense of citizenship is, after all, one of the most important functions of any sovereign nation.* It may be time for university structures to become real democratic institutions and stop perpetuating authoritarian and colonial rule as it concerns Native populations. The growing hostility toward the naïve, destructive rhetoric of non-Native scholars and institutions underpinning Western policies has been at the forefront of the development of Indian studies as an academic discipline since its inception. But make no mistake. If we choose to defend tribal nation citizenship rights at American universities, we will have a fight on our hands. The truth is, there is a powerful stream of thought in our soci-ety which persists in believing that American Indians are just some kind of romantic and savage and doomed race condemned to vanish without citizenship rights, neither American nor tribal, without land and Native legacy. This thinking has been at the heart of the Churchill dilemma, and Churchill himself, while claiming a position of advocacy historian to Na-tives, has been blindly influential in shaping this absurd notion.

In the final analysis, the struggle for tribal nation citizenship rights has never been thought of as a valuable democratic ideal in the United States, the supposed icon of democratic ideals throughout the world. To know of that denial is to understand how important a tribal model of Indian stud-ies as an academic discipline has become in the First Nations' comeback from the cultural near-death of the past two centuries. The continuing encroachment of a global civilization is causing the death or near-death of cultures throughout the world, many of them the Native cultures of this continent, and while most of us are going about stamping out the brush fires of unified capitalism, endemic poverty, casino wealth, domestic vio-lence, and educational genocide, we are not always successful in looking at the cause that is related to the history of the diminishment of sovereign rights facing Indian tribes from the beginning. It must be said that to make global society work, the first thing an aggressor nation must do is to take away the sovereign right of a weaker nation to say who its citizens are. This is the first step toward domination and despair, and it has been going on for a very long time.

The Churchill case should offer insights into this ongoing threat, and we must come to some agreement about what we expect of the academies of learning in this country. That is what Indian studies is all about, and we have much to gain from the careful study of this particular moment. It is not about "right-wing pressures." It is not about the "relentless pursuit of and punitive approach" toward a man who made unacceptable statements regarding the World Trade Tower disaster. It is not about speaking out on controversial issues. We all do that.

It is about whether or not tribal citizens in the United States stand as members of the nations-within-a-nation against fraud and aggression. There are few rules for these kinds of influential offenses against us, but the lack of precedent does not mean that we cannot find meaning in this case. When indigenous citizenship rights in the United States are threatened, as they often are, we are all harmed. Change could, miraculously, come out of this fiasco, but only if we stand on the principles that defend tribal nation citizenship.

Notes

Preface

1. Godfrey Hodgson, *The Myth of American Exceptionalism* (New Haven, Conn.: Yale University Press, 2009).

2. Henry Louis Gates, "Critical Fanonism," *Critical Inquiry* 17, no. 3 (1991): 457–70; Edward Said, "Permission to Narrate," *Journal of Palestine Studies* 13, no. 3 (1984): 27–48; Homi Bhabha, "The Post-Colonial and the Post-Modern," in The Cultural Studies Reader, ed. Simon During (New York: Routledge, 1993), 189–208. These scholars warn of the consequences of the ascendancy of the colonial paradigm. The so-called Western academic institution, they say, refuses to become more tolerant toward anticolonialist methodology and debate.

3. Frederick Jackson Turner, "The Significance of the Frontier in American History," in American Historical Association, *Annual Report for 1893* (Washington, D.C.: American Historical Association, 1894), 199–227.

4. Daniel Jonah Goldhagen, *Worse Than War: Genocide, Eliminationism, and the Ongoing Assault on Humanity* (New York: Public Affairs, 2009).

Introduction

1. Russell Jacoby, "Marginal Returns: The Trouble with Post-Colonial Theory," *Lingua Franca,* September–October 1995, 30–37. Because I am consistent in seeing things from the perspective of my own tribe, some commentators have accused me of engaging in "beneficent ethnocentrism." That, perhaps, is the kindest thing said of my ubiquitous tribal perspective.

2. Mario Gonzalez, Robert J. Miller, James Riding In, Susan Miller, Tom Holm, David Wilkins, Vine Deloria, William Thornton, Jack Forbes, Ed Valandra, and Steven Crum are some of the names that appear in analytical Indian studies texts with great frequency. They are Native scholars who have critiqued the American Indian

political systems in law and politics and are named in most bibliographies on the Native scholarly scene.

3. David Vine, *Island of Shame: The Secret History of the U.S. Military Base on Diego Garcia* (Princeton, N.J.: Princeton University Press, 2009).

4. Mario Gonzalez, an Oglala attorney now in private practice in Rapid City, is perhaps the foremost critic of this "removal" period on the Pine Ridge Reservation in South Dakota as it concerns this event. Much of the background information can be read in Mario Gonzalez and Elizabeth Cook-Lynn, *The Politics of Hallowed Ground: Wounded Knee and the Struggle for Indian Sovereignty* (Champaign: University of Illinois Press, 1999), 337–83.

Chapter 1

1. Gerald Vizenor, *Fugitive Poses: Native American Indian Scenes of Absence and Presence* (Lincoln: University of Nebraska Press, 1998), 15.

2. Linda Tuhiwai Smith, *Decolonizing Methodologies: Research and Indigenous Peoples* (New York: Zed Books, 1999); Taiaiake Alfred, *Peace, Power, Righteousness: An Indigenous Manifesto* (New York: Oxford University Press, 1999); Waziyatawin Angela Wilson, ed., *In the Footsteps of Our Ancestors: The Dakota Commemorative Marches of the 21st Century* (St. Paul, Minn.: Living Justice Press, 2006). Such writers as mentioned here are at the forefront of the Native scholars most critical of the master narrative of colonialism. Their works are part of a growing indigenous movement to reclaim the tribal past on this continent.

3. David Wilkins, *American Indian Sovereignty and the U.S. Supreme Court: The Masking of Justice* (Austin: University of Texas Press, 1997), 309.

4. United Nations Committee on the Elimination of Racial Discrimination, *Report of the United Nations Committee on the Elimination of Racial Discrimination* (New York: United Nations, 2008).

5. An excellent contemporary review of this history can be found in Robert J. Miller, *Native America Discovered and Conquered: Thomas Jefferson, Lewis and Clark, and Manifest Destiny* (Westport, Conn.: Praeger, 2006).

6. Northwest Ordinance of 1787, Art. III, 1 Stat. 50-52 1989, in *Of Utmost Good Faith,* compiled by Vine Deloria (San Francisco: Straight Arrow Books, 1971) is a good reference here.

7. Kimberly Tallbear, comment on "red nation consulting," http://naisa.org/blog/517, posted August 29, 2008.

Chapter 2

1. Vine Deloria, *We Talk, You Listen: New Tribes, New Turf* (New York: Macmillan, 1970).

2. Dee Brown, *Bury My Heart at Wounded Knee: An Indian History of the American West* (New York: Holt, Reinhardt, & Winston, 1970).

3. Paul Chaat Smith and Robert Warrior, *Like a Hurricane: The Indian Movement from Alcatraz to Wounded Knee* (New York: New Press, 1996).

4. These theorists came much later than Brown, but such works as Bhabha's "The Other Question: Homi K. Bhabha Reconsiders the Stereotype and Colonial Discourse," *Screen* 24, no. 6 (1983): 18–36, and even the literary criticism on Salmon Rushdie show the dominant trajectory of so-called colonial thought in telling history. The contradiction and resistance that is missing from Brown's work can be studied through the readings of Bhabha, and one can see how far removed that scholarship is from the Brown work.

5. Duane Champagne, "American Indian Studies Is for Everyone," in *Natives and Academics: Researching and Writing about American Indians,* ed. Devon A. Mehesuah (Lincoln: University of Nebraska Press, 1998), 184.

6. Ibid.

7. Peter Schmidt, "New Association Takes 'Big Tent' Approach to Studying Native Peoples," *Chronicle of Higher Education*, May 22, 2009, A8, http://chronicle.com/faculty.

8. Ibid. Riding In has collaborated with the Seminole historian Susan Miller in editing a collection called *Native Historians Write Back*, available from Texas Tech University Press in 2011.

9. Elvira Pulitano, *Toward a Native American Critical Theory* (Lincoln: University of Nebraska Press, 2003), 37. Pulitano's work would probably not have been noticed by Native American studies in any disciplinary way if it had not appeared in the work of literary scholars Jace Weaver, Craig Womack, and Robert Warrior of the collective examining humanities and literary theories. Native studies scholarship and theory has focused more fully recently on law and political science and history, though literary theory continues to be extremely influential in the foci of many university curricular enclaves.

10. This conference centered on the use of indigeneity as a category of research analysis, a weapon to be used to diminish the influence of colonial thinking in scholarship. See www.ais.illinois.edu/news/features/indigeneity/.

11. Norman Finkelstein, *This Time We Went Too Far: Truth and Consequences about the Gaza Invasion* (New York: OR Books, 2010). Finkelstein has written extensively about the misuse of history in the Middle East wars and has accused the Jews of exploiting the Holocaust. In 2008 he revised his work *Beyond Chutzpah: On the Misuse of Anti-Semitism and the Abuse of History* (Berkeley: University of California Press, 2005).

12. Churchill is probably best known for his *Fantasies of the Master Race: Literature, Cinema, and the Colonization of American Indians* (San Francisco: City Lights, 1998), but also because of the essay he wrote after the Twin Towers were destroyed in 2001.

13. Students for Academic Freedom was an organization on many college campuses during the Bush era thought to have a right-wing influence.

14. Michael Medved, townhall.com, September 9, 2007.

15. Colin Powell, with Joseph E. Persico, *My American Journey* (New York: Random House, 2002).

16. Daniel Jonah Goldhagen, *Worse Than War: Genocide, Eliminationism, and the Ongoing Assault on Humanity* (New York: Public Affairs, 2009).

17. Lawrence M. Freidman, *A History of American Law*, 3rd ed. (New York: Simon & Schuster, 2005), 386.

18. Donald L. Fixico, *Relocation and Termination: Federal Indian Policy, 1945–1960* (Albuquerque: University of New Mexico Press, 1986) is perhaps the best summary of the consequences of these 1950s laws.

19. Documents from UNESCO are a good source for this history.

20. Angela Cavender Wilson (Waziyatawin), *What Does Justice Look Like? The Struggle for Liberation in the Dakota Homeland* (St. Paul, Minn.: Living Justice Press, 2008). Among her other publications is *Remember This: Dakota Decolonization and the Eli Taylor Narrative* (Lincoln: University of Nebraska Press, 2005). She is the coauthor of *For Indigenous Eyes Only: A Decolonization Handbook* (Santa Fe, N.M.: School for Advanced Research Press, 2005).

21. Elizabeth Cook-Lynn, review of *What Does Justice Look Like? The Struggle for Liberation in the Dakota Homeland*, by Angela Cavender Wilson, *Wicazo Sa Review: A Journal of Native American Studies* 24, no. 2 (2009): 190–93.

22. Wilkins, *American Indian Sovereignty and the U.S., Supreme Court*, 309–20.

23. *Jourdain v. Commr.*, 617 F. 2nd, 507 8th Circuit, 1980. References to this case can be found in David E. Wilkins and K. Tsianina Lomawaima, *Uneven Ground: American Indian Sovereignty and Federal Law* (Norman: University of Oklahoma Press, 2001) and Miller, *Native America Discovered and Conquered*, which is a good source for a summary of this thinking.

24. Ania Loomba, *Colonialism/Postcolonialism* (New York: Routledge, 1998), 17.

25. Taiaiake Alfred, *Peace, Power, and Righteousness: An Indigenous Manifesto* (Don Mills, Canada: Ontario University Press, 1999); Tuhiwai Smith, *Decolonizing Methodologies*.

Chapter 3

1. Robert M. Utley, *The Last Days of the Sioux Nation* (New Haven, Conn.: Yale University Press, 1963) gives the most comprehensive summary of accounts written by early historians such as James Mooney, whose reports appeared as early as October 1891 in a manuscript called "Ghost Dance" available to history and anthropology professors across the country, who quickly accepted and promoted the story. The Utley work also includes military reports, which allow him and others to conclude that the

Sioux have been "conquered" through a pseudo-military event, the law allowing the plunder of land, theft, and massacre of unarmed people. For this drama to be played out in this way, religion had to play a huge part in the story told by these writers, and it still does.

2. Homi Bhabha, "Postcolonial Authority and Postmodern Guilt," in *Cultural Studies,* ed. Lawrence Grossberg, Cary Nelson, and Paula A. Treichler, eds. (New York: Routledge, 1992), 56.

3. Alfonso Ortiz, *Being and Becoming in a Tewa World* (Chicago: University of Chicago Press, 1968), 4.

4. Gregory E. Smoak, *Ghost Dances and Identity: Prophetic Religion and American Indian Ethnogenesis in the Nineteenth Century* (Berkeley: University of California Press, 2006). This is an example of a work in what is called the "new historicism" concerning the Plains tribes and can be used to interpret Lakota/Dakota ceremonial life. Though Smoak does not take up the issues of the Sioux in Dakota Territory specifically, his work is significant concerning the similarities of Native participants according to culture. He is a professor and researcher at Colorado State University who has examined the Ghost Dance of the Shoshone/Bannock, which may be used as a model for other Plains groups. There are many similarities.

5. Ibid., 14.

6. Edward Said, *The Politics of Dispossession: The Struggle for Palestinian Self-Determination, 1969–1994* (New York: Pantheon, 1994), 33–55 has had an influence on every Native American writer, including Elizabeth Cook-Lynn and Mario Gonzalez, who wrote *The Politics of Hallowed Ground* during the early era of Indian studies. Said's work is a significant contribution to all postcolonial research.

Chapter 4

1. Goldhagen, *Worse Than War,* 198.

2. Ibid. In addition, several works are good reference reading, including Asa Briggs, *Victorian People: A Reassessment of Persons and Themes, 1851–1867* (Chicago: University of Chicago Press, 1955), which gives insight into the struggle of finding and answering the social questions of eliminating peoples under a blanket of morality. Clearly there is a longtime European historical notion that outside thinking and radicalism was and is a threat to the permanent stability sought by nondiverse groups after the aristocracies fell.

3. Helen Hunt Jackson, *A Century of Dishonor* (New York: Harper & Brothers, 1881), especially 3–32, 137–44.

4. Ibid., chapter 4; Andrew F. Rolle, introduction to Helen Hunt Jackson, *A Century of Dishonor,* textbook ed. (New York: Occidental College, 1965).

Chapter 5

1. Robert F. Berkhofer, Jr., *The White Man's Indian: Images of the American Indian from Columbus to the Present* (New York: Vintage Books, 1978). This is a survey of more than five hundred years of colonial history and probably should be on every shelf in Indian studies enclaves. The preface and part 1 ("Invention and Perpetuation") are particularly helpful in understanding the formal debate that went on in 1550 at Valladolid, when Juan Gines de Sepulveda sought to justify colonization and eliminationism.

2. Felix Cohen, "The Erosion of Indian Rights, 1950–1953: A Case Study in Bureaucracy," *Yale Law Journal* 62, no. 3 (1953).

3. Elizabeth Cook-Lynn, *New Indians, Old Wars* (Urbana: University of Illinois Press, 2007), xi.

4. Gore Vidal, *Lincoln* (New York: Vintage, 2000).

5. Hannah Arendt, *The Origins of Totalitarianism* (New York: Harcourt, Brace, Jovanovich, 1973). Arendt's study was first made available as three essays in 1950 and housed in the Library of Congress.

6. Roy Basler, ed., *Collected Works of Abraham Lincoln* (New Brunswick, N.J.: Rutgers University Press, 1953).

7. Jackson, *A Century of Dishonor*, 163.

8. Brown, *Bury My Heart at Wounded Knee*, 65.

9. *Ikce Wicasta: The Common People Journal* is now out of print.

Chapter 6

1. Thomas Biolsi, *Deadliest Enemies: Law and the Making of Race Relations on and off the Rosebud Reservation* (Berkeley: University of California Press, 2001). A thorough review by Circe Sturm appears in *Ethnohistory* 51 (Summer 2004): 673–74. Edward Charles Valandra, *Not without Our Consent: Lakota Resistance to Termination, 1950–1959* (Champaign: University of Illinois Press, 2006) is also a suggested reading on these subjects.

2. U.S. Senate, Miscellaneous Document 1, 40th Congress, 2nd session, 1868, 1319.

3. Richard Wright, *Native Son* (New York: Harper, 1940); Tom Wolfe, *The Bonfire of the Vanities* (New York: Bantam Books, 1987); and Elizabeth Cook-Lynn, *From the River's Edge.* (New York: Arcade, 1991) are postcolonial fictions that pointedly discuss the responsibilities of modern superpowers toward the powerless.

4. Elizabeth Cook-Lynn, *Anti-Indianism in Modern America: A Voice from Tatekeya's Earth* (Champaign: University of Illinois Press, 2007), 162.

5. This is best explained in the concluding chapter of Wilkins and Lomawaima, *Uneven Ground.* See also Vine Deloria, Jr., and David E. Wilkins, *Tribes, Treaties, and Constitutional Tribulations* (Austin: University of Texas Press, 1999).

6. David E. Wilkins, *American Indian Sovereignty and the Supreme Court* (Austin: University of Texas Press, 1997), 309.

7. Peter d'Errico, "Perspectives," *Indian Country Today*, July 1, 2009, 5.

8. To read further on these matters, consult Steve Newcomb, *Pagans in the Promised Land: Decoding the Doctrine of Christian Discovery* (Golden, Colo.: Fulcrum, 2008), another text advocating changes in federal law. Recent cases such as *Carcieri v. Salazar* and *Vasquez v. Hittery* are useful readings indicating it is time to overrule precedents in federal Indian law.

Chapter 7

1. Elizabeth Cook-Lynn, *Then Badger Said This* (Fairfield, Wash.: Ye Galleon Press, 1983). This book is now out of print.

2. Albert Camus, *"The Myth of Sisyphus" and Other Essays* (New York: Knopf, 1955).

Chapter 8

1. This piece was originally published in *Native Sun*, a newspaper owned and edited by the longtime Lakota newsman Tim Giago, in Rapid City, South Dakota. I sent it to him with a note: "Hey, Tim, this is *supposed* to be funny. Do you think it is?" A man who gets irony and the absurdity of Indian life wrote back, "I think it is hilarious!," and printed it in the following issue.

Chapter 9

1. Robert H. Keller, Jr., and Michael F. Turek, *American Indians and National Parks* (Tucson: University of Arizona Press, 1998); Alfred Runte, *National Parks: The American Experience* (Champaign: University of Illinois Press, 1987).

2. Gonzalez and Cook- Lynn, *The Politics of Hallowed Ground*, 38.

Chapter 10

1. There is considerable interest in American Indian studies about what is envisioned in Middle Eastern studies as comparable violent colonization theory. Not enough has been done in these comparison studies, though Rashid Khalidi has taught and lectured at Columbia University for many years and is director of the Center for Middle Eastern Studies and editor of the *Journal of Palestine Studies*. There seems to be a major disconnect between feminist studies, American Indian studies, and Middle Eastern studies at American universities. Indeed it was Jewish feminist scholars at Columbia who started an inquiry into the Middle Eastern studies regime at the university, claiming "discrimination." Khalidi has published such works as *Under Siege:*

PLO Decision Making During the 1982 War (New York: Columbia University Press, 1986) and *Sowing Crisis: The Cold War and American Dominance in the Middle East* (Boston: Beacon Press, 2009), among many other titles.

Chapter 11

1. Joseph H. Trimbach and John M. Trimbach published *American Indian Mafia: An FBI Agent's True Story about Wounded Knee, Leonard Peltier, and the American Indian Movement (AIM)* (Parker, Colo.: Outskirts Press, 2007), now available as an ebook and in a Kindle edition on Amazon. It is a 652-page diatribe by a former FBI agent who says he was there, an eyewitness to the protest period. It is, according to the blurbs, a "true history of the American Indian Movement." In reality, it provides legitimacy for the actions of the federal government which was attempting to carry on its two hundred years of foreign hegemony on this poverty-stricken reservation of the Oglala Sioux despite the humiliating conditions under which the people live. There are many legal thinkers and generations of economists and professors who find this book useful to legitimize the eighteenth-century colonial genocide in the United States, and the Trimbach book is widely circulated for that reason. It relies entirely on FBI documents.

2. Patricia Albers and Beatrice Medicine, *The Hidden Half: Studies of Plains Indian Women* (Lanham, Md.: University Press of America, 1983).

Chapter 13

1. *Chronicle of Higher Education*, May 31, 2009, section C.
2. *Chronicle of Higher Education*, August 29, 2008.

Chapter 14

1. Philip Deloria, *Playing Indian* (New Haven, Conn.: Yale University Press, 1998).

2. Bill Ashcroft, Gareth Griffiths, and Helen Tiffin, eds., *The Post Colonial Studies Reader* (New York: Routledge, 1995), 9.

3. © Bruce Arnold Casion analytics/casino.com.au. December 2008.

4. Private email exchange.

Chapter 15

1. Goldhagen, *Worse Than War*; also see Cook-Lynn, *Anti-Indianism in Modern America*, 210–16 for an assessment of "hate crimes" as a feature of genocide.

2. Ugo Mattei and Laura Nader, *Plunder: When the Rule of Law Is Illegal* (Malden, Mass.: Blackwell, 2008), 13. This is an important postcolonial assessment of the devastation inherent in colonization throughout the world.

3. Ibid; Cook-Lynn, *Anti-Indianism in Modern America*, 185–195. For additional reading, see Ashcroft, Griffiths, and Tiffin, *The Post-Colonial Reader*, 119.

4. William C. Canby, Jr., *American Indian Law in a Nutshell* (Eagan, Minn.: Thomson/West, 1981).

5. Quoted in Wilkins, *American Indian Sovereignty and the Supreme Court*, 233.

6. Vine Deloria, Jr., *Behind the Trail of Broken Treaties: An Indian Declaration of Independence* (Austin: University of Texas Press, 1985). This book, originally published in 1974, reviews much of this record and forces Congress to review its own actions.

Chapter 16

1. I am indebted for this metaphor, "pentimento," to a scholar from Rice University's History Department, Patricia Seed, who published a book called *American Pentimento* (Minneapolis: University of Minnesota Press, 2001). She outlined how it is that all colonials in the United States want to create a morality tale of entitlements, subtitling her book *The Invention of Indians and the Pursuit of Riches*. The use of the metaphor in a text on postcoloniality, however, serves to remind readers that much of the Ingalls memoir can be discredited because of its unspoken association with taking over the land and omitting the experience of the collective. Can such an individual narrative be squeezed into a single formal pattern without being called propaganda?

2. Laura Ingalls Wilder, *Little House on the Prairie* (New York: Harper Brothers, 1935). The series of eight *Little House* books was first published between 1932 and 1943 as children's books; four more books were added in 1962, 1971, 1974, and 2006. It is essentially a memoir given over to history. The Ingalls family lived in DeSmet, South Dakota, homesteading there, but also lived in Missouri, Kansas, Minnesota, and Iowa, midwestern states that have taken up the work of history of the region. This literary project can be used as a perfect model to understand how the elite immigrant population in the middle Plains of America by design or accident provided the aesthetic and ideological grounding of white Americans to create an independent, decolonized American society and culture without indigenous presence or intrusion. That is one of the reasons it is taught in all midwestern classrooms and why it eventually made its way into the historical literary works of white supremacy. It cannot be considered postcolonial in any sense, because white settlers were the agents of colonial rule. No matter how difficult their lives were in the early part of the settlement (poverty, chaos, blizzards, crop failures), they were not subject, as Indians of the region were, to genocide, economic exploitation, cultural decimation, political exclusion, and federal policy and law toward Indians. Yet their stories set the pace for prairie identities without challenge.

3. Tom Wolfe, "Faking West, Going East," *New York Times*, April 25, 2010.

4. The colonist power in literature is particularly true of the literatures of South

America. For example, Eduardo Galeano in *Open Veins of Latin America: Five Centuries of Pillage of a Continent* (New York: Monthly Review Press, 1973) deals with the fear emerging democracies have of the power of the imperialist United States.

Chapter 17

1. Vine Deloria, Jr., ed., *The Indian Reorganization Act: Congresses and Bills* (Norman: University of Oklahoma Press, 2002).

2. Ibid.; Vine Deloria, Jr., "Reserving to Themselves: Treaties and the Powers of Indian Tribes," *Arizona Law Review* 38 (Fall 1996): 966.

3. Frank Pommersheim, *Broken Landscape: Indians, Indian Tribes, and the Constitution* (New York: Oxford University Press, 2009), 312; Constitution of Canada (1982).

4. David E. Wilkins, *Documents of Native American Political Development, 1500's to 1933* (Oxford: Oxford University Press, 2009).

5. Pommersheim, *Broken Landscape*, xix.

6. Ibid., 307.

7. Lone Wolf, a Kiowa, supported by the Indian Rights Association, filed suit in the Supreme Court in 1901 to defend the Kiowas' treaty rights and to prevent the United States from designating such lands as "surplus" and available to whites.

8. Wilkins, *American Indian Sovereignty and the Supreme Court.* Wilkins has been a steadfast scholar in the defense of sovereignty at all levels and has recognized the ubiquitous antagonists even in less academic circles. For example, he responded with a letter to the sports editor of the Sunday *New York Times* (July 25, 2010) under the heading "When Native Sovereignty Doesn't Go Very Far." A passport dispute kept the Iroquois men's lacrosse team from going to the 2010 world championship, and Wilkins's comment was brief: "When the United Nations adopted the Declaration on the Rights of Indigenous Peoples in 2007, native peoples throughout the world felt a palpable and long-overdue sense of relief. . . . But the diplomatic brouhaha that has engulfed the Haudenosaunee lacrosse team, derailing their travel plans to Europe to play the sport they invented, is a harsh reminder to native nations that their inherent sovereignty will be acknowledged only when it comports with the forms and protocols of states. In other words, if natives don't play by the rules adopted by states—use state-issued passports, not indigenous documents—they will not be allowed to play. It's ironic that the British appear to have forgotten that it was the Haudenosaunee, or most of them, who allied with their British treaty partners and not the Americans during the Revolutionary War. That memory should count for something."

9. Indian Law Center, newsletter, no. 2 (2010), available at mt@indianlaw.org.

10. See, for instance, Edward Said, *Culture and Imperialism* (New York: Knopf, 1993).

11. The "reserved rights doctrine" is a consequence of treaty making and should

be taken seriously, but instead it has been diminished by U.S. courts and political arrangements, just as Pommersheim has noted. David Wilkins's texts on the Supreme Court are among the few examples of research that devote much time and space to the articulation of these reserved powers. His analysis of how the courts and states' rights folks have handled this principle of law as it concerns the fifteen modern cases he takes up is compelling. Wilkins is a scholar who disturbs like no other law scholar the risks one sees to democratic ideals when these omissions occur.

Chapter 19

1. When a university reader of this text noted that my conclusion begins with the phrase "Contemporary leaders of the Sioux Nation," he wrote in red pencil, "Explain the use of Sioux Nation. Who are these? There is no contemporary polity by that name." After reading these 250 pages, a scholar notable for his work in Indian history still resists the idea that the "Sioux Nation" as a political reality exists. He probably speaks for the mainstream of American citizens from Florida to Toronto who don't know we are in their midst. This term is written in treaties, it is said in all Lakota/Dakota prayers, it is in government documents from the earliest times, yet we still must be confronted with the "vanishing American" theory and asked to explain "Who are these? There is no contemporary polity by that name." I am at a loss to explain the absence of the Sioux Nation as a national polity according to this scholar, when there are clearly indications that *the indigenous nation* in America is a condition known historically and politically. Today there are seven bands described in English in all federal documents (Oglala, Sicangu, Santee, Yankton, Sihasapa, Minneconjou, and Hunkpapa), and they make up the citizenry of the Sioux Nation.

2. Newspapers throughout the area took up the story in January and February 2009, but then, like all the crimes perpetrated against Indians by the bureaucracies of the United States, the outrage fell into almost complete silence.

3. Angelique Eaglewoman, op-ed, *Native Sun Weekly* (Rapid City, S.D.), December 20, 2009.

4. In the U.S. District Court for the District of Columbia, *Elouise Pepion Cobell, et. al., Plaintiff, vs. Ken Salazar, Secretary of the Interior, et. al., Defendants*, 1; 96CV01285-JR., class action settlement agreement.

5. Bill Means, "Counterpoint," *Minneapolis Star Tribune*, December 15, 2009, A13. *Indian Country Today* in Canastota, New York, ran a series of letters to the editor and articles on this subject in the same week. Means, among others, is still a target of federal agents, who have a major presence on every Indian reservation in the country. AIM trials that go back to 1974 are still being held in federal courthouses throughout the region. A 2010 case ended with the release of a Pine Ridge man; two other trials connected with the killing of Anna Mae Aquash ended in 2011 with guilty verdicts for Arlo Looking Cloud and John Boy Graham, who were charged with her murder.

6. Quoted in Don Doll, *Vision Quest: Men, Women and Sacred Sites of the Sioux Nation* (New York: Crown, 1994). The statement by Taninyan Opi (Royal Bull Bear) is on p. 50. Some good news concerning land issues in Indian Country: 840,000 acres of land has been put in trust in Indian Country. The Winnebago tribe has put more than 700 acres in eastern Nebraska into federal trust (over state government objections) in the past five years. Three tribes have bought land around Bear Butte, a sacred place in the Black Hills of South Dakota, to keep it from further development in Meade County by land-hungry motorcyclist organizations who hold a convention called "the Sturgis Rally." This is not done without controversy, a continuous condition in the historical debate about these matters because, as Rodney Bordeaux, a powerful president of the Rosebud Sioux Trib e (Sicangu) believes, the tribes should not have to buy back stolen and illegally confiscated treaty lands. President Obama's administration has proposed to spend $2 billion to buy back and consolidate fractured lands to be put into tribal control (title?) for economic development. Further information can be found at the Federal Bureau of Indian Affairs website, www.bia.gov; White Earth Recovery Project, http://nativeharvest.com/; Indian Land Tenure Foundation, www.indianlandtenure.org/; Citizen's Equal Rights Alliance, www.citizenssalliance.org/.

7. Means, "Counterpoint."

8. David E. Wilkins, ed., *Documents of Native American Political Development, 1500s to 1933* (New York: Oxford University Press, 2009).

Index